A COMPLETE GUIDE TO
ANIMALS AND THEIR HABITATS

WILD LIFE ATLAS

John Farndon

A New Burlington Book
Conceived, edited, and designed by Marshall Editions
The Old Brewery
6 Blundell Street
London N7 9BH, UK
www.marshalleditions.com

First edition copyright © 2002 Marshall Editions
Revised edition copyright © 2010 Marshall Editions
Text copyright © Barnsbury Books

For Marshall Editions
Art Director Ivo Marloh
Managing Editor Paul Docherty
Editor Liz Lambert
Layout Jon Wainright
Production Nikki Ingrams

US Edition
ISBN 10: 1-84566-338-1
ISBN 13: 978-1-84566-338-4

UK Edition
ISBN 10: 1-84566-337-3
ISBN 13: 978-1-84566-337-7

Originated in Hong Kong by Modern Age.
Printed and bound in Singapore by
Star Standard Industries (Pte) Ltd.

1 3 5 7 9 10 8 6 4 2

Contents

Introduction

Perhaps uniquely in the universe, our planet teems with life. As human exploration penetrates to the darkest corners of the Earth, we are finding life in every nook and cranny, in every environment no matter how extreme. Strange fish lurk in the pitch black of the very deepest oceans. Birds are found nesting atop some of the world's highest mountains.

But what is most astounding, perhaps, is the sheer variety of life—swimming in the vast oceans, flying through the air, and slithering, crawling, or running over the world's land surfaces. More than 1.5 million species of animals have been named so far, and most zoologists believe there may be many, many more as yet undiscovered. There are over 4,000 known species of mammals, 6,800 species of reptiles, 4,780 amphibians, 9,000 species of birds, 24,000 fish, 1 million insects, and perhaps 400,000 other tiny creatures that go by the general name "invertebrates," including 60,000 kinds of spider.

We owe this rich diversity of life to hundreds of millions of years of evolution, hundreds of millions of years of subtle changes, generation by generation, as some creatures survived to pass on their quirks to their offspring and as others with their own quirks died out. Of course, those creatures best equipped for the prevailing conditions survived; those poorly equipped passed into the oblivion of extinction.

Conditions change, of course, and over time many creatures have found themselves in the same position as the dinosaurs—initially well adapted to their environment, but then ill-equipped to survive the changes occurring in the world around them. But conditions do not only vary over time; they vary across the face of the planet, too.

Every region on Earth has its own unique conditions, and during the long roll of evolution, a unique range of creatures has developed to suit each particular place. An endless sequence of chance changes has created the host of different animal species that inhabit the Earth today, each particularly adapted to survive in its own special place, each occupying its own niche in the environment.

Every species has its home and every home has its species. Just as the gentle deciduous woodlands of Northeast America provide a habitat for sawflies, raccoons, and black bears, so the wide open savanna of Africa is home to elephants, baboons, and lions. Climate, plant life, terrain, the availability of food and shelter, and many other factors have given every region its own distinctive range of creatures.

This book provides an overview of where the world's animals live and why they live there. The book travels the world, habitat by habitat, from the scorched grasslands of the tropics to the frozen wastes of the Arctic and Antarctic. Each chapter focuses on a particular habitat and

introduces, continent by continent, the range of creatures that make this habitat their home—the predators, the grazing mammals, the birds of the air, the insects, the reptiles, and all the rest. Within each chapter special feature pages explore the nature of the habitat and the complex web of inter-relationships between all the animals that live there. Vivid wildlife panoramas peer into each habitat and capture a living moment in African rain forests, Asian temperate woodlands, or North American taiga and tundra.

Yet it is a sad fact that by the time you read this book, some of the animals in it may have vanished forever. Today we are witnessing what may be one of the greatest waves of animal extinctions ever, as more and more species fall victim to rampaging human activity. There are now over 5,000 species in the high risk category, and many more under threat. Experts predict that

a fifth of all the world's animal species may be lost in the next 20 years.

Many factors are to blame for this impending tragedy. The loss of habitats as forest is cleared by farmers and loggers. The relentless spread of cities. The poisoning of the land by pollutants and pesticides. The deadly gun of the hunter. The more we know and understand the reasons for this massacre, the better equipped we will be to prevent it—so this book identifies some of the key species that are in danger in each habitat and the factors that are putting their existence at risk.

Despite this, the world is still blessed by an astonishing wealth of wildlife, and it is this that the *Wildlife Atlas* celebrates in presenting a unique view of the animal and plant life of our planet.

JOHN FARNDON

Animal homes

There are many ways of dividing the world into natural regions. Zoologists divide it into five regions. Climatologists divide it by climate. Botanists divide it by plant type. There is a close relationship between climate and vegetation type, and both play a key role in determining

Grassland food web

where each kind of animal lives. So in this book, the world is divided into broad "habitats"—regions where a particular environment for animals is created by the climate and plant life—such as tropical rain forests and deserts.

Sumatran rain forest

Animal groups

The animal world is divided into animals that have backbones, called vertebrates, and those that have none, called invertebrates. Invertebrates are mostly small creatures, such as insects and mollusks—although giant squids grow up to 60 ft (about 18 m) long. The main groups of vertebrates are: fish, birds, amphibians, reptiles, and mammals. In this book, birds and mammals are further grouped according to where they spend most of their time (birds of the air and ground birds) or how they find their food (birds of prey, predatory mammals, browsers, foragers, and grazing mammals). The groups vary from habitat to habitat, because some kinds of creatures are rare or absent, while others are much more common.

Tropical grasslands

More than one-third of the world's land surface is covered in grass. Much of the grassland was created by farmers who cleared forests for their livestock to graze on. But there is still a great deal of grassland that is entirely natural, especially in the tropics.

•

Tropical grasslands occur where there is rain for only half the year and the rest is too dry for trees to grow. Apart from a few isolated thorn and palm trees, grass here stretches as far as the eye can see under wide-open skies. In the wet season, the grass is green and lush. But in the dry season, the land is parched and the grass turns yellow.

•

Even so, grasslands are incredibly productive habitats. Every square yard (0.8 sq m) of African grassland grows over four pounds (1.8 kg) of plant matter a year—half as much as pine forest produces—from just a thin covering of grass. So tropical grasslands can support a huge amount of wildlife and are home to some of the world's most spectacular creatures.

Where are tropical grasslands?

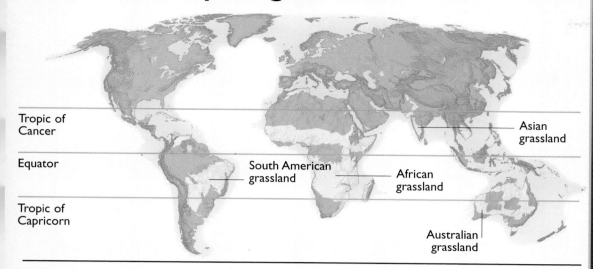

Tropic of Cancer

Equator

Tropic of Capricorn

South American grassland

African grassland

Asian grassland

Australian grassland

Comparing tropical grasslands

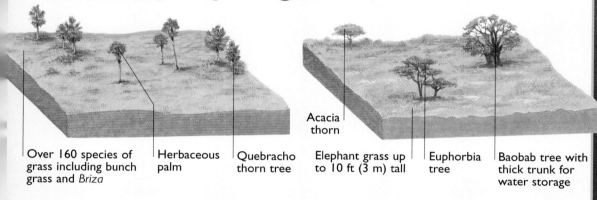

Over 160 species of grass including bunch grass and *Briza*

Herbaceous palm

Quebracho thorn tree

Acacia thorn

Elephant grass up to 10 ft (3 m) tall

Euphorbia tree

Baobab tree with thick trunk for water storage

South America
South American grasslands are often parklike landscapes of clustered trees and shrubs dotted with tall palm trees. Here and there is espinal, a dry forest of spiny, thorny shrubs and low trees. The thorny quebracho tree shoots up almost everywhere in the South American grasslands and in places forms dense thickets that rise like islands amid the sea of grasses. There are over 160 species of grass, some growing as high as a person on horseback.

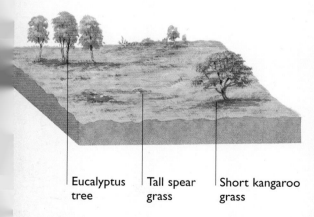

Eucalyptus tree

Tall spear grass

Short kangaroo grass

Africa
The savanna is the tropical grassland covering much of central Africa, especially in the east. The savanna varies with the length of the dry season. Stretching along the dry southern edge of the Sahara Desert is the Sahel—a vast area of thorn savanna that is dry, sparse grassland scattered with thin trees. Dry thorny grassland also covers a large area of southern Africa at the fringes of the Kalahari Desert. There are places that are relatively moist, where small forests of broad-leaved trees, such as euphorbias, grow quite densely.

Australia
In Australia, the tropical grass of the bush covers a huge arc round the north of the continent from east to west. In the northeast, in Queensland, the dry Mitchell grassland is distinctive. In the moister areas, tall spear grass and shorter kangaroo grass grow. Most Australian grassland trees are evergreens, such as eucalyptus, acacia, and bauhinia. Their waxy leaves reduce water loss, which helps them to survive the dry season. In the northwest, the most common trees are baobabs.

Tropical grassland environments

Tropical grasslands are warm—typically averaging over 80°F (27°C) during the day. In the dry season temperatures can soar to 130°F (54°C). Most get 20–60 in (500–1,500 mm) of rain a year, but most of this comes in a five- to eight-month wet season. The rest of the year is almost bone-dry. Even in the wet season, water evaporates quickly in the warm air.

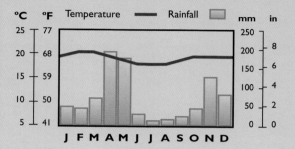

°C   °F   Temperature — Rainfall   mm   in

25 ┬ 77   250
20 ┼ 68   200   8
15 ┼ 59   150   6
10 ┼ 50   100   4
5 ┴ 41   50   2
                                     0   0
     J F M A M J J A S O N D

Sun and rain
This graph shows rainfall month by month, and the average monthly temperature for Nairobi in the African savanna. The wettest months are from November to May. The dry season begins in June and also lasts five months, until the rains come again in November.

Thunderstorms
When it does rain on tropical grasslands, it rains in torrents. Typically, huge gray thunderclouds build up in the heat of the morning, then the storm begins in mid-afternoon. Isolated trees are often struck by lightning, starting fires in the dry grass.

New grass
In the hot dry season, the grass can turn to straw and may even be burned away by bush fires. It looks dead, but even though the grass is burned, its roots are safe under the soil. The grass soon sprouts new shoots when the rains finally come.

South American tropical grasslands

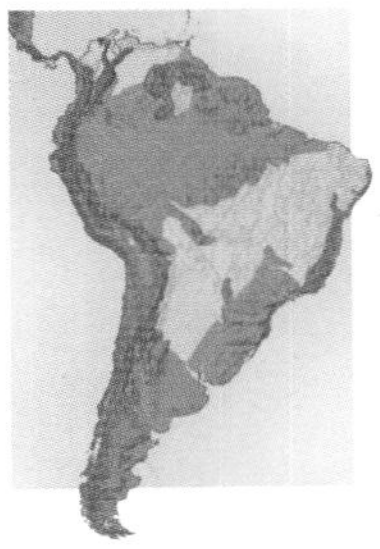

The tropical grasslands of South America are very different from those of Africa. African savannas are huge expanses of grass, where vast herds of large grazing animals can thrive. But South America's grasslands are much more varied, with bogs and dense scrub in many places. So, instead of grazers, the dominant animals are large rodents, such as capybaras and agoutis, and foragers, such as tapirs and peccaries, as well as many birds.

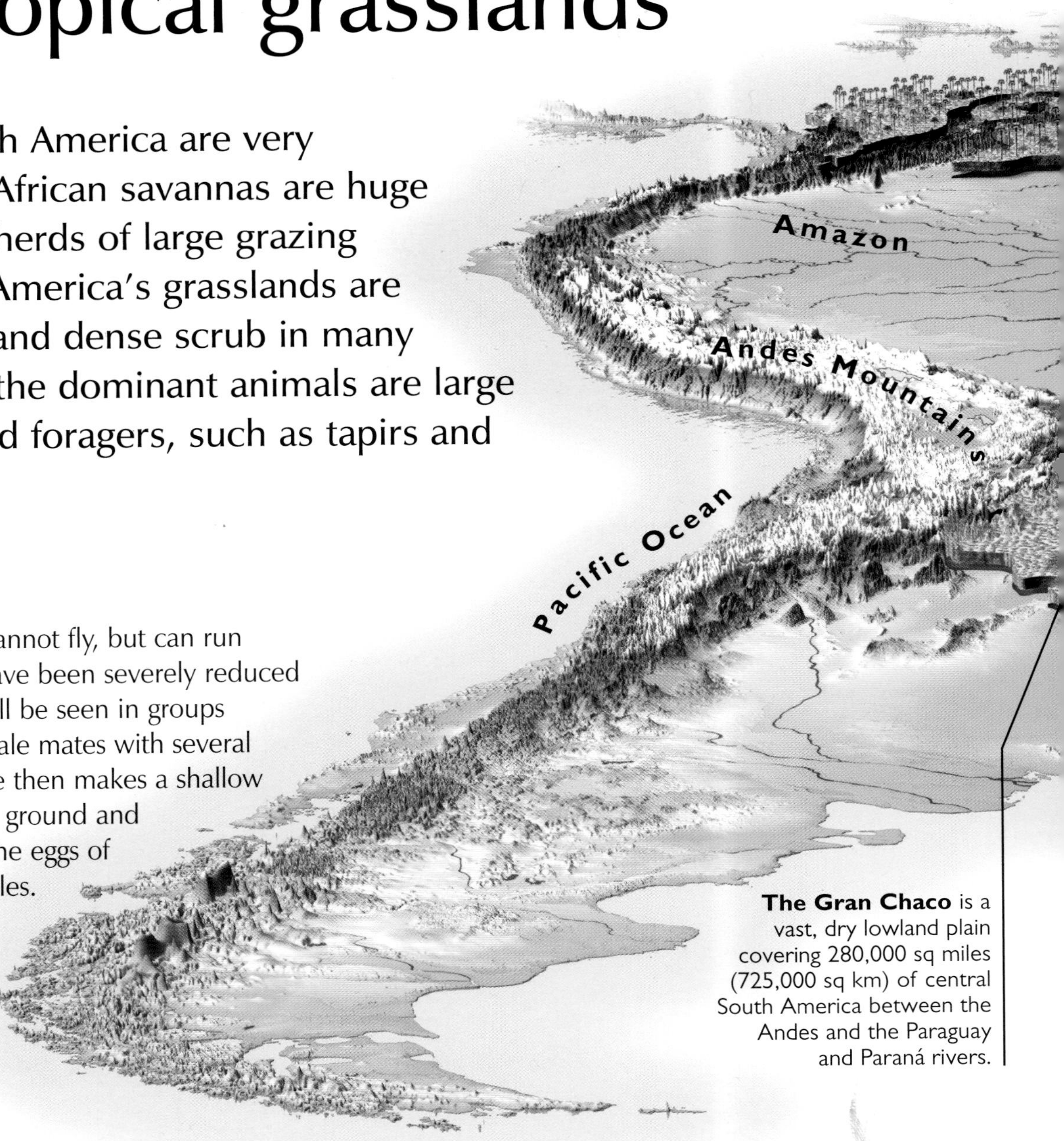

Amazon

Andes Mountains

Pacific Ocean

The Gran Chaco is a vast, dry lowland plain covering 280,000 sq miles (725,000 sq km) of central South America between the Andes and the Paraguay and Paraná rivers.

The greater rhea

Greater rheas are huge birds that cannot fly, but can run very fast. Although rhea numbers have been severely reduced by hunting and farming, they can still be seen in groups of about 30. At breeding time, the male mates with several females. He then makes a shallow nest on the ground and incubates the eggs of all his females.

Ground birds
The scarcity of trees means that many species of bird of the South American grasslands are ground-dwellers. Besides the rhea, tinamous, nothura, rhynchotus, quails, and others strut through the grass, and various finches forage for seeds.

Capybara
Capybaras are the largest of all living rodents, growing to 4 ft (1.25 m) long and weighing over 120 lb (55 kg). They are quite shy and live in groups along riverbanks—diving in quickly if predators, such as jaguars, appear. They browse on leaves, but, in farming areas, they may occasionally steal melons and grain.

Rodents
The grassland swamps are a good habitat for large rodents. Besides the capybara, agoutis, and coatis, various cavies and taco-taco scrabble through the reeds. Many small rodents live here, too, such as alcodons and various mice. There is also a giant otter, which is much bigger than European otters.

King vulture
King vultures have wings spanning nearly 6 ft (1.8 m). They feed mostly on carrion—animals that are already dead. They are strong fliers, spending hours soaring high up, scanning the ground for corpses. Vultures have sharp eyes and a good sense of smell, too, which is unusual for birds.

Reptiles and amphibians
Swamps and rivers provide ample habitats for many reptiles and amphibians. Besides snakes, such as boas and pit vipers, there are other reptiles, such as crocodile-like caimans, river turtles, iguanas, and lizards, such as the teyou. Poisonous tree frogs and toads, such as *Bufo rufus*, are often seen here.

Boa constrictor
Boas are a family of large constrictor snakes that kill their prey by squeezing it. They swallow their victims whole, then spend days digesting them. Special jaws allow their mouths to open very wide. A large meal, such as a capybara, can be seen as a lump moving gradually down the snake's body as it is digested.

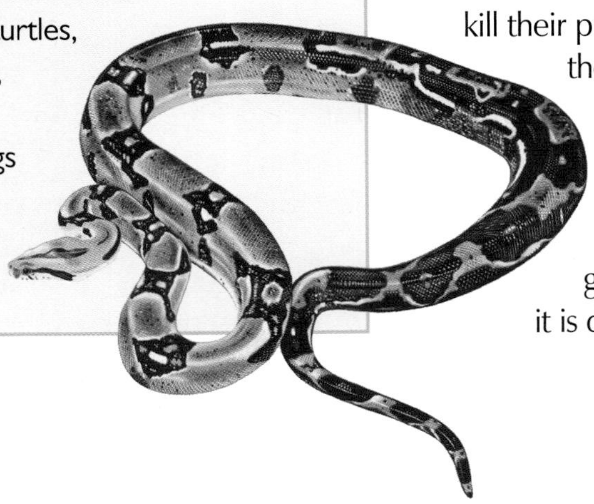

Birds of prey
The birds and small creatures of the South American grasslands make rich pickings for a host of predatory birds, such as hawk-eagles, Swainson's hawk, chimango, caracara, falcons, chacalacas, kites, and nighthawks. Black vultures and king vultures swoop down on carrion.

The Llanos is a vast area of low-lying grass and swampland covering 350,000 sq miles (900,000 sq km) of Venezuela and northeast Colombia.

The Gran Sabana is a high tableland of grass and scrub, bounded by steep cliffs. Its inaccessibility makes it a valuable refuge for many rare species.

Atlantic Ocean

Paraná

The Cerrado is a land of grasses and shrubs south of the Amazon rain forest, covering one quarter of Brazil. It is as big as western Europe and home to five percent of all the world's animal species.

Puma

Also known as mountain lion and cougar, the puma is a graceful cat that roams throughout the Americas. Adults grow up to 10 ft (3 m) long and weigh up to 220 lb (100 kg). Despite its size, it has a voice like a domestic cat, only louder. It is a hunter and feeds on deer and guanaco.

Predatory mammals

Four big cats prowl the grasslands—jaguars, jaguarundis, ocelots, and pumas, plus smaller cats like the gato pajero and gato montes. Two large dogs also hunt here: the rare maned wolf and the rarer bush dog.

Fish

The rivers and swamps of the South American grasslands hold more species of fish than any comparable habitat. There are characins, such as the dorado, the pencil fish, voracious meat-eating piranhas, and their harmless cousins, the pacus.

Grazing mammals

The grasslands support few large grazing animals except llamalike guanaco and deer, such as pampas deer, and gray and little brockets. Herds of these animals have been much reduced as cattle ranches have spread.

Rufous-tailed jacamar

This colorful bird perches on branches, waving its head as it scans the air for insects. When it spots one, it darts off to snap it up in midair, then flies back to its perch. It may bang the insect against the branch to kill it before eating it. The birds lay two to four eggs in a tunnel in the ground, which is dug by the female.

Red piranha

Piranhas are barely 15 in (38 cm) long, but they swim together in such huge shoals that they can strip a large animal to its skeleton in just a few minutes with their razor-sharp teeth. Usually, they are attracted to prey by the scent of blood.

Pampas deer

This tiny deer once roamed down into the pampas (treeless plains) of Argentina. Now farming and hunting have wiped it out from much of its range and it lives only in the Cerrado and the Gran Chaco.

Birds of the air

Many of the birds seen in the air above the South American grasslands are seasonal migrants, such as swifts, orioles, and wrens. Natives include anhingas, woodpeckers, parakeets, hyacinthine and other macaws, doves, and flycatchers. Insect-eaters include ovenbirds, puffbirds, hummingbirds, and tanagers.

Insects

The South American grasslands are home to a huge range of insects, including many flies and beetles and beautiful swallowtail butterflies. However, the dominant species are termites and ants, especially fire ants and army ants.

Giant armadillo

Giant armadillos are stout, short-legged animals that grow up to 40 in (1 m) long. Unusually for grassland animals, they move slowly, but they are protected by a tough armor of horny plates. When attacked they scurry to their burrow or simply curl up. They feed mainly on termites, digging into their nests with strong, curved front claws.

Army ant

Over 150 species of army ant live in tropical South America. They get their name because they march in troops to find prey. Unlike other ants, they do not build nests, but live together in "bivouacs," built with living walls of ants clinging together.

Foraging mammals

Among the foragers are piglike animals, such as the peccary and tapir. Both are related to horses. Ants and termites are so abundant that they provide food for quite large animals, such as the giant anteater and the giant and nine-banded armadillos. Porcupines feed on plant stems and fruit.

Survival in grasslands

For the animals of the South American grasslands, life is a constant battle for survival. The long months of the dry season mean that every creature has to struggle to find food and water, while the lack of hiding places among trees makes life dangerous all year round. For plant-eating animals, survival means eating grass or the roots and tiny fruit of scrubby trees. But these herbivores provide food for a range of large predators, such as jaguars, pumas, and maned wolves.

Who eats what

As in every environment, animals in the South American grasslands depend on each other for survival. Plant-eaters get the food they need from surrounding vegetation. But all other animals need to eat other animals to survive. Jaguars eat animals like rhea and deer, while wolves eat armadillos, and armadillos eat termites. Indeed, all grassland animals are linked together in chains of food dependence, and these food chains are interwoven in a complex, finely balanced web of dependence. A change to even one tiny part of this web—perhaps due to human intervention—can upset the whole balance.

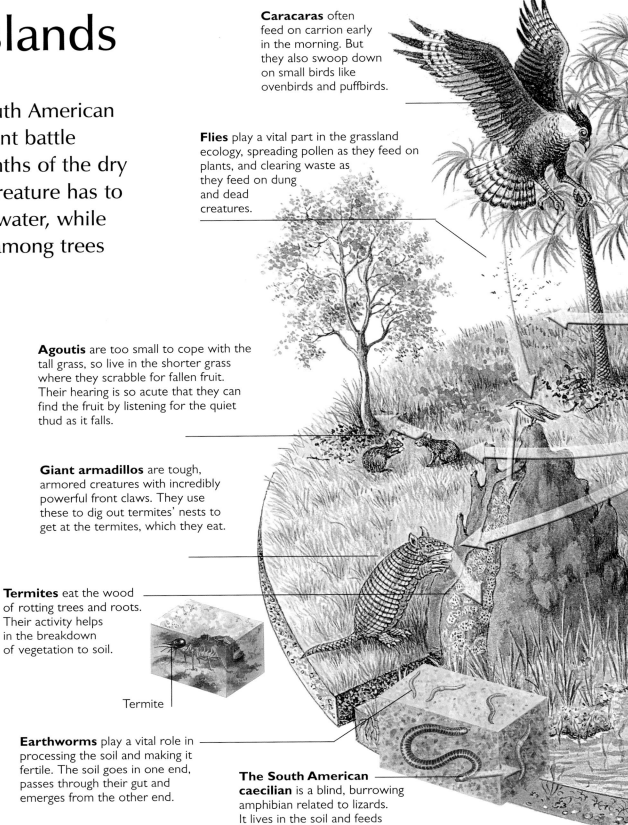

Caracaras often feed on carrion early in the morning. But they also swoop down on small birds like ovenbirds and puffbirds.

Flies play a vital part in the grassland ecology, spreading pollen as they feed on plants, and clearing waste as they feed on dung and dead creatures.

Agoutis are too small to cope with the tall grass, so live in the shorter grass where they scrabble for fallen fruit. Their hearing is so acute that they can find the fruit by listening for the quiet thud as it falls.

Giant armadillos are tough, armored creatures with incredibly powerful front claws. They use these to dig out termites' nests to get at the termites, which they eat.

Termites eat the wood of rotting trees and roots. Their activity helps in the breakdown of vegetation to soil.

Termite

Earthworms play a vital role in processing the soil and making it fertile. The soil goes in one end, passes through their gut and emerges from the other end.

The South American caecilian is a blind, burrowing amphibian related to lizards. It lives in the soil and feeds on earthworms.

Grassland adaptations: Long legs

With nowhere to hide, many creatures rely on speed to escape predators. Indeed, many grassland animals are among the world's fastest runners. Thomson's gazelles in Africa reach 50 mph (80 km/h). The rhea's African cousin, the ostrich, can tear along at 40 mph (65 km/h). To achieve these speeds, grazing animals like gray brockets and rheas have developed long, slender legs. Some predators, such as cheetahs, can run just as fast to catch them.

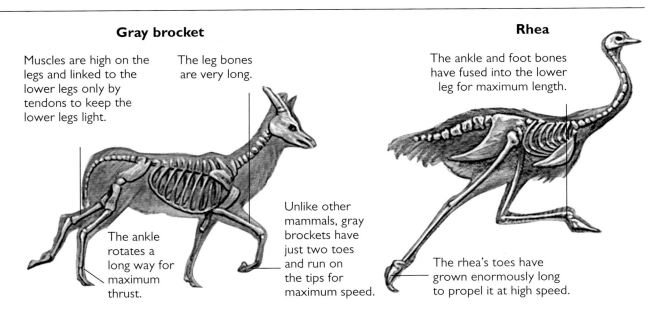

Gray brocket

Muscles are high on the legs and linked to the lower legs only by tendons to keep the lower legs light.

The leg bones are very long.

The ankle rotates a long way for maximum thrust.

Unlike other mammals, gray brockets have just two toes and run on the tips for maximum speed.

Rhea

The ankle and foot bones have fused into the lower leg for maximum length.

The rhea's toes have grown enormously long to propel it at high speed.

Puffbirds sally out from perches on branches to catch large insects in flight. Sometimes, they drop to the ground to forage for ants.

Maned wolves prey on armadillos and agoutis, as well as cuis (wild guinea pigs), rabbits, and viscachas (burrowing rodents). They also eat insects and birds as well as fruit and sugarcane.

Ovenbirds are small warblers that forage on the ground, poking through the grass and scrub for ants, termites, and spiders.

Gray brockets are small deer that live only in tall grass where they can hide. They feed on the tops of grass stalks and fruit from caesalpina and zizyphur trees.

Greater rheas live in the tall grass and feed on the grass tops—often feeding with deer herds. They also eat fruit and insects.

Jaguars prey on the larger grassland animals— brockets, rheas, and capybaras. They also attack peccaries, but the peccaries can often fight them off.

Capybaras feed on the short grasses by the waterside, and so avoid competing with deer (and farmers' cattle).

Jaguar

The jaguar has a bulky build, but, like many predators, in grass it is very quick and graceful. It can reach high speeds over short distances, climb trees, and even swim well. It relies on getting in close to its prey unnoticed, or lying silently in wait to make a kill. When it catches prey, its strong jaws can pulverize skulls.

Wildlife at risk!

Maned wolf

Fewer than 2,200 maned wolves now survive— mainly because their natural habitat has been destroyed as Bolivian and Paraguayan ranchers convert grassland to soybean farms. Many have been shot, too, by farmers angered by the wolves' fondness for chickens.

Guanaco

Guanacos are South America's largest land mammal, but their population has fallen dramatically. A century ago, there were over 8 million guanaco. Now there are only about 100,000—and numbers are dwindling fast as ranchers fence off grazing land and sheep compete for grass.

The human factor

Huge areas of grassland have been taken over for livestock farming in recent years, especially in the Brazilian Cerrado, but the impact on wildlife has received little attention. Putting cows and sheep to graze and erecting fences is less dramatic than clearing rain forest, but its effect on wildlife can be just as devastating.

African grasslands

The vast savanna grasslands of Africa are among the most spectacular of all wildlife habitats, home to some of the world's largest mammals. Everywhere, there are herds of large grazing animals, such as antelopes and zebras. There are browsers, too, such as elephants and rhinos. Then there are large predators—most famously the big cats, such as lions and cheetahs.

Sahel
The Sahel is where the dry northern bushlands or "Sudan" savanna merge into the Sahara. Rare oryx, damas, dorcas, and red-fronted gazelles live here.

Browsers and foragers
Savanna trees provide food for browsers, such as elephants, giraffes, black and white rhinos, warthogs, and various antelopes—eland, kudu, gerenuk, steenbok, and Kirk's dik-dik. Yet, as more savanna is used for farming, trees are becoming less abundant as a food source.

African elephant
African elephants are the largest land animals. Bulls (adult males) stand 11 ft (3.4 m) high and weigh more than 5 tons. Elephants eat for 16 hours a day, feeding mainly on leaves, and often knock down trees to get at high branches. They also dig up roots and shrubs with their tusks. Family groups of females and young are led by the oldest female. Adult males roam alone.

Bushveld
In the south, the dry savanna fringes are called bushveld. Large herds of tsessebe, kudu, springbok, and hartebeest live here, as well as small groups of dik-dik.

Primates
Baboons and vervet monkeys sleep in trees to avoid predators, and vervet monkeys often forage in the trees, too. Greater and lesser bush babies spend their lives entirely in the trees and leap agilely from branch to branch.

Impala
Impala are among the most graceful antelopes, known for their agile running and jumping. To escape predators, such as lions and hunting dogs, they can travel 33 ft (10 m) in a single leap and race along at 50 mph (80 km/h). The strongest males lead herds of females and young.

Birds of prey
Many birds of prey find rich pickings here, including bateleur snake eagles, gabar goshawks, augur buzzards, marabou storks, and vultures, such as Ruppell's Griffon. These feed on the carcasses of large animals killed by lions and dogs.

Olive baboon
Baboons are big monkeys with strong jaws. They live on the ground in troops, which contain females and males of all ages. There is a strict hierarchy, but they do form friendships with one another.

Grazing mammals
Savanna grasses provide food for huge herds of grazers—zebras, waterbucks, and buffaloes; many antelope species, including sables and roans; wildebeests and hartebeests; and many kinds of gazelles, such as Thomson's and Grant's.

Secretary bird
Secretary birds are nearly 6 ft (1.8 m) tall. They get their name from their long head feathers, which look like the quill pens clerks once stuck behind their ears. They are famed for their ability to pin down and kill snakes with their feet.

Reptiles and amphibians

The lack of moisture means few amphibians live in the savanna, but there are many reptiles, including numerous chameleons, such as Jackson's and Meller's, barking geckos, lizards, leopard tortoises, and snakes.

Boomslang snake

The boomslang snake lies in wait on tree branches for chameleons and birds, with its front end hanging motionless in the air. If provoked, it will inflate its neck, then strike. Although less than 2 ft (60 cm) long, it is very dangerous to humans, with a poisonous bite that causes internal bleeding and death.

Nile

Lake Victoria

Serengeti

East Africa is the heartland of the grass savanna. The Serengeti in Tanzania is home to over half a million buffaloes, wildebeests, zebras, and gazelles, as well as elephants, giraffes, rhinos, lions, and cheetahs, plus 450 species of birds.

Insects

Under the savanna are vast nests of harvester termites that send out workers to forage for grass to feed the young. Flesh flies and carrion beetles feed on rotting carcasses left by vultures. Occasionally, vast swarms of locusts appear and may devastate crops.

Praying mantis

Praying mantises get their name because they hold their front legs together as if praying. They are the most fearsome predators of the insect world. They can even seize and eat small frogs. Typically, they make a kill with a swift bite to the neck. Female mantises will often bite the male's head off while mating.

Ground birds

With scant cover in the open savanna, there are fewer ground birds here than in some habitats. The flightless ostrich relies on running fast on its long legs to escape from predators. Other ground birds include yellow-billed and ground hornbills, kori bustards, and helmeted guinea fowls.

Rock hyrax

On rock outcrops in the savanna live rabbit-sized creatures called hyraxes. They look like guinea pigs, but are related to elephants. In fact, the hyrax has a brain like an elephant's, a stomach like a horse's, and a skeleton like a rhino's.

Small mammals

The savanna is famed for its large animals, but many small mammals scurry among the grasses, including elephant shrews, striped mice, and spring hares. Zorillas are skunklike mammals that hunt at night and rest in burrows by day. Like skunks, they spray an odor when alarmed.

Predatory mammals

The herds of hoofed grazers provide prey for big cats, such as lions, cheetahs, and leopards, and for dogs, such as hyenas and jackals. Cheetahs use speed to catch prey, such as gazelles, while hyenas and lions rely on teamwork.

Oxpecker

Oxpeckers ride around on the backs of cattle, zebras, and rhinos, where they feed on ticks, helping to keep these animals free of parasites. One oxpecker can eat 2,000 ticks in a day. Oxpeckers hiss when alarmed, warning their hosts of danger.

Sociable weaver bird

Sociable weavers get their name because they live together in unique nest colonies built of grass and mud in trees. With thatchlike roofs, the nests are up to 13 ft (4 m) high and 26 ft (8 m) long. Inside, there are up to 300 chambers, each home to a pair of birds. The chambers are set in clusters, each with its own entrance tunnel in the "basement." A few birds work all year-round to keep the nest tidy.

Lion

Lions are among the biggest of the big cats. Males, with their great manes, are 10 ft (3 m) long and weigh up to 500 lb (230 kg), but the females do most of the hunting. Lions live in families called prides and usually eat every four days or so, consuming up to 110 lb (50 kg) of meat in a meal. They spend around 20 hours a day resting.

Birds of the air

The savanna air is filled with birds, such as "go-away" birds (turacos), shrikes, flycatchers, starlings, hoopoes, rollers, bee-eaters, and many weaver birds, including vast flocks of quelea.

Grazers and browsers

The alternating wet and dry seasons in East Africa's Serengeti create the world's most amazing animal migrations. Every May, the rains stop, the land dries up, and vast herds of wildebeests begin to move in search of grass and water—snorting, bucking, and kicking up dust. They are joined in their trek by a multitude of zebras and antelopes—and are tailed by hungry lions and dogs. When the rains come again and fresh grass springs up, the herds return to complete a yearly migration cycle, during which they cover more than 1,500 miles (2,400 km).

Grassland adaptations: Browsing levels

Just as each grazer has adapted to make the most of certain grass conditions, so each browsing animal in the savanna has adapted to reach branches at different heights. Many browsers, such as rhinos and dik-diks, can reach lower branches, so competition here is severe; but big animals, such as elephants and giraffes, can reach much higher.

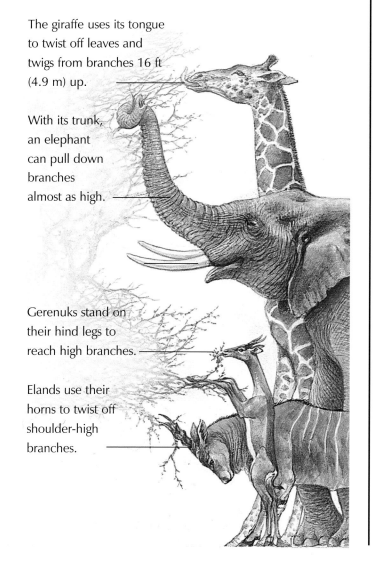

The giraffe uses its tongue to twist off leaves and twigs from branches 16 ft (4.9 m) up.

With its trunk, an elephant can pull down branches almost as high.

Gerenuks stand on their hind legs to reach high branches.

Elands use their horns to twist off shoulder-high branches.

W E T   S E A S O N

1. In the wet season, when the grass is plentiful, herds of zebras, wildebeests, and Thomson's gazelles intermingle on the high southeastern plains. Calves and foals are born in February.

7. Toward the end of October, the skies darken, the rains begin to fall, and the herds begin their journey back to the grassy plains of the southeast.

6. As the drought takes its toll, Griffon vultures that have been trailing the herds swoop down on animals that have died.

The great migration

The great wildebeest migration in the Serengeti has developed over tens of thousands of years, and is minutely attuned to variations in the environment. The herds rarely move at exactly the same time, or along the same route, and the migration changes in response to local variations in grass growth. In some years, a dry spell may set the herds moving from the open plains earlier; fire damage may block the path in others—then attract the animals the following year as fresh growth springs up. The timing of the rut, too, seems to vary to coincide with a full moon.

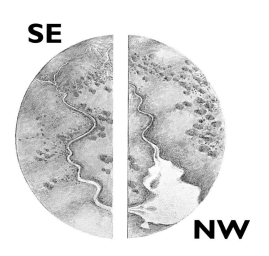

SE

NW

2. Toward the end of the wet season, the herds begin to gather for their migration and males start their ritual mating fights or ruts.

Thomson's gazelles trail behind the wildebeests feeding on the high-protein seeds and young shoots left behind after the wildebeests have eaten down the leafy grass stalks.

3. By the time the trek begins, zebra herds are 200,000 strong, Thomson's gazelle herds are half a million strong, and wildebeests a million and a half strong.

Wildebeests follow the zebras and feed on the lower leafy part of the grass left behind after the zebras have eaten.

Zebras lead the way, eating the coarse top layer of red oat grass. As they push on through the tall grass, they make a path for the small animals to follow.

DRY SEASON

4. As the dry season progresses, the herds move on farther to the northwest into more wooded areas. Many die as they cross crocodile-infested rivers.

5. Toward the end of the dry season, rivers dry up and water holes shrink. The herds, led by zebras, reach the woodlands of the northwest.

Wildlife at risk!

White rhinoceros

The white rhino is one of the most widely studied endangered animals. There are currently 18,000 white rhinos—17,500 of which are of the Southern subspecies. Sadly, the Northern subspecies has been poached so heavily that fewer than 10 exist today.

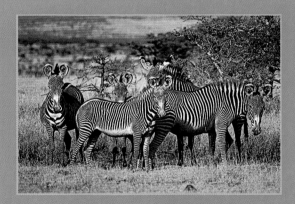

Grevy's zebra

Grevy's is the largest zebra and lives in arid parts of the savanna. In the 1970s, the species was decimated by poaching, because the skins were fashionable. Now the zebras are protected from poachers, but are threatened instead by growing cattle herds taking grazing land.

The growing desert

A drier climate in recent times has reduced the savanna fringes to desert. The problem has been made much worse as remaining areas are overgrazed, both by herds squeezed into a smaller area, and by farmers' livestock.

Hunting cheetah

The cheetah is the world's greatest sprinter. Because cover is sparse on the savanna, a cheetah relies on a burst of speed to catch prey, such as a gazelle, and can reach 60 mph (100 km/h) in five seconds. It leaves the ground twice in its running cycle—first with front and hind legs bunched up (pictured), then with them fully extended. During one of these leaps, the cheetah can travel almost 23 ft (7 m) through the air.

Australian grasslands

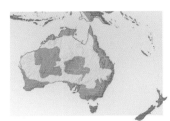

The vast, scrubby, rolling plains and plateaus of Australia's empty interior, or outback, are home to many of the continent's unique range of creatures, from kangaroos and wallabies to bandicoots and marsupial moles. Much of the outback is very arid, and creatures that live here must cope with little water. In lusher areas, wild animals have to compete with sheep and other livestock.

The Great Western Plateau
Covering most of western Australia, the Great Western Plateau is vast. It is 1,000–1,500 ft (300–460 m) high and is mostly covered in mulga and mallee scrub.

Gulf of Carpentaria

Gibson Desert

Great Victoria Desert

Nullarbor Plain

Great Australian Bight

Red kangaroo
Red kangaroos are the biggest kangaroos—the biggest of all marsupials, standing over 6 ft (1.8 m) tall. They can travel at 40 mph (65 km/h) and leap 30 ft (9 m) in a single bound. They get their name from the male's back and chest, which turns red in the breeding season. Females are called "blue fliers" because of their blue-gray fur.

Grazing mammals
Australia has no native hoofed grazers. Instead, it has the kangaroo family with their strong back legs and long feet for hopping. There are 69 species, divided into two families—macropods (kangaroos and wallabies) and the smaller potoroids (potoroos and bettongs).

Wedge-tailed eagle
These eagles are Australia's biggest birds of prey, with 7½ ft- (2.3 m-) wingspans. In groups they can kill a kangaroo. The Tasmanian species is now endangered.

Birds of prey
Since big birds of prey can reach Australia, it has many species that are also found elsewhere, such as Brahminy kites. But there are local varieties, such as the Australian kestrel, the gray goshawk, and Australian hobby.

Insects and spiders
Australia's grasslands are home to many ants and termites, including the magnetic termite which aligns its nest north-south. There are many cicadas, beetles, flies, and spiders, too.

Giant stick insect
Australia has many species of giant stick insect. In 2001, a species thought long extinct was found living on an island off the east coast. It is 6 in (15 cm) long and is said to look like a walking sausage.

Ground birds
With few large predators, ground birds have flourished. Besides the emu, there are ground parrots like the turquoise grass parrot, as well as bowerbirds and "megapods"—large birds, such as mallee fowl and brush-turkey, which lay their eggs in mounds.

Emu
The emu is the world's second largest living bird, growing 6 ft (1.8 m) tall. It has only stubby wings and cannot fly, but can run on its long legs at speeds of up to 30 mph (50 km/h). If cornered, it kicks hard. It feeds mainly on roots, fruits, and leaves.

Frilled lizard

When frightened, the frilled lizard may lie camouflaged like a stick. When spotted, it opens its mouth wide, flings open its frilled ruff, and hisses loudly. However, it is actually quite harmless. It lives mainly in trees, but it also runs on the ground, and can travel up to 30 ft (9 m) in a single leap.

Reptiles and amphibians

In the Australian grasslands lurk many highly venomous snakes of the elapid family, including the deadly brown snake and the taipan. Australia also has about 500 species of lizard, including the gecko, skink, and giant goanna. In the northern rivers, there are smaller cousins of the giant estuarine crocodiles of the coast.

Egg-laying mammals

Australia's long isolation has allowed two unique primitive egg-laying mammals, or "monotremes," to survive—the platypus and echidna.

Echidna

Echidnas, or spiny anteaters, are egg-laying mammals measuring about 20 in (50 cm) long. There are two species, each with short legs and strong claws for digging into the ground to get at ants, a long thin snout, and a long tongue for licking up the ants.

Predatory mammals

Before dingos arrived with seafarers 3,000 years ago, Australia's only large predator was the thylacine, a wolflike marsupial. Dingos drove thylacines to extinction on mainland Australia and are now the only large predators.

Budgerigar

Now kept in cages in homes all around the world, the budgerigar is a parakeet (small parrot) native to the Australian grasslands. Wild budgies are always green and travel in large flocks. They rarely stay in one place for long, moving on constantly in search of food. They feed on seeds, mainly in the morning to avoid the hottest part of the day.

Birds of the air

The Australian grasslands' rich bird life includes many parakeets and cockatoos, best known of which is the colorful galah, known for its raucous call. There are also many nectar-sipping honey-eaters and insect-eating bee-eaters.

Dingo

The dingo is a wild form of the domestic dog thought to have originated in Asia. Before the Europeans arrived, dingos' main prey was kangaroos and wallabies. Nowadays, they also hunt rabbits and sheep, so farmers try to fence them out and poison them.

17

Fish

Australia's interior is dry, but its rivers and billabongs are teeming with fish, including the huge Murray cod, mouth almighties, yellowbellies, boomer bass, rainbowfish, and gudgeons. Little smelts and yabbies (crayfish) are found in hot, muddy pools.

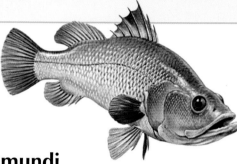

Barramundi

The barramundi is a huge fish, up to 6 ft (1.8 m) long. It spawns in rivers and lakes in northern Australia before swimming to the sea. It starts life as a male and remains so until it reaches the sea. Then after five years, it becomes female to swim back up river to spawn. It is thought the salt water of the sea stimulates the sex change.

Small mammals

The Australian grasslands are home to many small mammals, including small marsupials unique to Australia, such as the marsupial mouse, bandicoot, wombat, and the mouselike phascogale. Many estivate (stay dormant) in summer to cope with the heat.

Hairy-nosed wombat

The rare hairy-nosed, or plains, wombat is one of the world's largest burrowing animals, up to 3½ ft (1.1 m) long. With its shovel-like front paws, it can dig long burrows where it rests in the day. Like other marsupials, it carries its young in a pouch until they are big enough to survive outside.

Pouched mammals

One hundred million years ago, Australia began to drift away from the rest of the world's continents, and a unique range of wildlife developed there in isolation. In particular, there are two kinds of mammal found almost nowhere else—marsupials, which raise their young in pouches, and monotremes, which lay eggs. Remarkably, these creatures have evolved to fill niches similar to those of their counterparts elsewhere.

Marsupial niches

Marsupials first evolved 100 million years ago and once lived all over the world. Placental mammals, whose young are born more fully developed, were thought to have evolved later, and to have driven marsupials into extinction almost everywhere but Australia, where they survived in isolation. Recent finds of 115-million-year-old placental mammal fossils in Australia, and analysis of DNA from both kinds of mammal, suggest that they may have lived alongside each other for millions of years. Whatever the truth, it is clear that the Australian marsupials have evolved to fill roles in the habitat similar to those occupied by their counterparts elsewhere. This is known as convergent evolution.

The small Tasmanian devil is now almost the only marsupial hunter, although there was once a marsupial lion.

Bandicoots and numbats (banded anteaters) are insect eaters, with long snouts and strong digging claws.

The marsupial mole is a blind burrowing animal with strong front paws for tunneling through the ground.

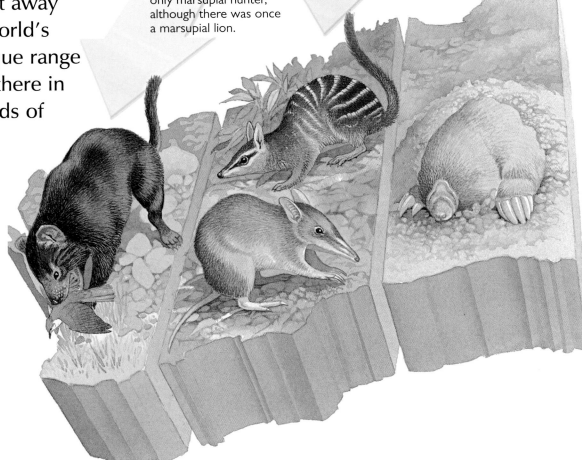

Carnivores

Leopard
Big cats and wild dogs are the large predators of the placental world. They now have no marsupial counterparts.

Insectivores

Giant pangolin
Placental anteaters like giant pangolins and anteaters also have long snouts and strong digging claws.

Burrowers

Giant golden mole
Placental moles are remarkably similar to their marsupial counterparts.

Grassland adaptations: Big feet for hopping

Placental grazing animals run on four thin legs to escape predators, whereas many marsupials hop on strong hind legs and feet (and tails). The hind legs of a red kangaroo are roughly 10 times the size of its front legs. When moving slowly, kangaroos use all four legs, but when they need to move fast, they rise up on their hind legs and hop. It takes a lot of energy to start hopping, but very little energy is needed to hop faster. In contrast, four-legged mammals need more and more energy as they run faster.

The inner toes of the kangaroo family have grown especially large and strong.

Besides marsupials, many rodents hop, including the northern hopping mouse and the U.S.'s kangaroo rat. They also have long inner toes.

Rock wallaby

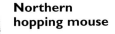

Northern hopping mouse

Wombats fill a similar niche to marmots and badgers but grow larger because there is no competition. Oddly, there are no large marsupial foragers.

Koalas, possums, and cuscuses are tree-dwelling marsupials that feed on vegetation.

The red kangaroo is a big grazing animal like antelope, deer, and buffalo, but is strikingly different. It has few predators to avoid and relies on hopping on its two big feet, rather than running, to escape.

Herbivores

Elephant
Elsewhere in the world, there are not only small foragers like badgers, but also giants like elephants.

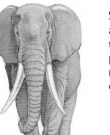

Tree-dwellers

Vervet monkey
Squirrels, marmosets, and monkeys, such as the vervet, are the placental equivalent of marsupial tree-dwellers.

Grazers

African buffalo
In the rest of the world, big grazers like the buffalo have developed long legs and hooves—and safety in numbers—to escape from predators.

Mallee fowl

The mallee fowl is a large ground bird that builds a compost heap to keep its eggs warm. In fall, the male digs a hole (pictured) and fills it with vegetation. When it rains in spring, the vegetation rots and heats up. The female then lays her egg, which is kept warm by heat from the compost. The male keeps testing the temperature, and adds sand to save heat if it is too cold, or opens up the mound to let out heat if it is too hot. This way the mound stays at exactly 91°F (33°C), which is why the mallee is known as "the thermometer bird."

Wildlife at risk!

Bridled nail-tailed wallaby
The bridled nail-tailed wallaby gets its name from the little nail of bone on the end of its tail. Once common, it was hunted as a pest and for its fur so vigorously that by 1960 it was believed to be extinct. A few were rediscovered in 1973 in Queensland, but it is still very rare.

Numbat
Unlike other marsupials, numbats, or banded anteaters, are active during the day. These small creatures consume up to 20,000 termites a day. Many have been killed by foxes introduced from Europe and now survive only in the Wandoo bushland of southwest Australia.

The cassowary
The cassowary is a large flightless bird of Australia's rain forests. It plays a crucial role in distributing the seeds of 150 species of forest plants, but loss of its habitats and road accidents have severely reduced its numbers.

Tropical rain forests

Where there is enough rain in the tropics, forests grow—and the combination of year-round warmth and moisture makes tropical rain forests the lushest, greenest, densest, and most richly varied natural habitats on Earth.

•

Tropical rain forests cover barely six percent of the world's land surface. Yet they contain 50 percent of its plant and animal species. Some scientists think it may be as much as 90 percent. Indeed, more species of amphibian, bird, insect, mammal, and reptile live here than in all the other habitats put together. One study found more species of ant living on a single rain forest stump than in all of the British Isles.

•

Yet rain forests are incredibly fragile environments—partly because the plants and animals depend on each other to an exceptional degree. Here, almost all trees rely on animals to disperse their seeds; elsewhere, dispersal by the wind is the most common method. As more and more rain forest is affected by human activity, the very existence of thousands of animal species is endangered.

Where are tropical rain forests?

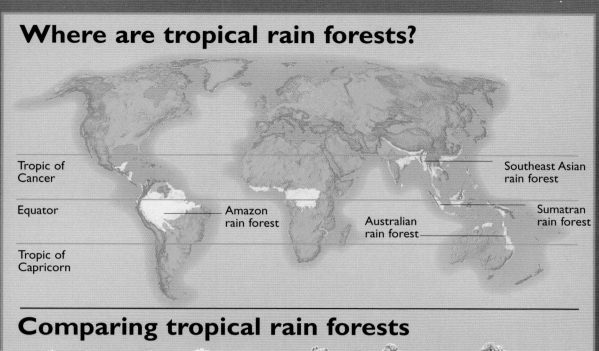

Tropic of Cancer

Equator — Amazon rain forest

Tropic of Capricorn

Southeast Asian rain forest

Australian rain forest

Sumatran rain forest

Comparing tropical rain forests

Brazil nut, sacupaia trees | Myrtle, laurel bushes | Lianas, vines | Bromeliads, orchids | Mahogany, iroko trees | Cacao | Raffia, sisal | Fungi

South America
The Amazon rain forest has a rich variety of trees both large (e.g. rubber, Brazil nut, silk-cotton, sacupaia, and sucupir), and small (myrtle, laurel, bignonia). They are all covered with lianas and epiphytes (plants that grow on other plants), such as orchids and bromeliads.

Africa
African rain forests are less varied than those of the Amazon. The trees are large hardwoods, such as mahogany, iroko, and sapele, and smaller trees such as cacao. Beneath them grow fibrous plants including raffia, sisal, and numerous fungi.

Australasia and Asia
Southeast Asian rain forests are dominated by huge dipterocarps (tea trees) along with teak and ironwood, under which grow a wealth of small trees, including fruits, such as durian, lychees, mangoes, and mulberries. Trees are covered with mosses, epiphytes, and climbers, such as strangler figs. Exotic flowers, such as rafflesia and titan arum, grow on the ground.

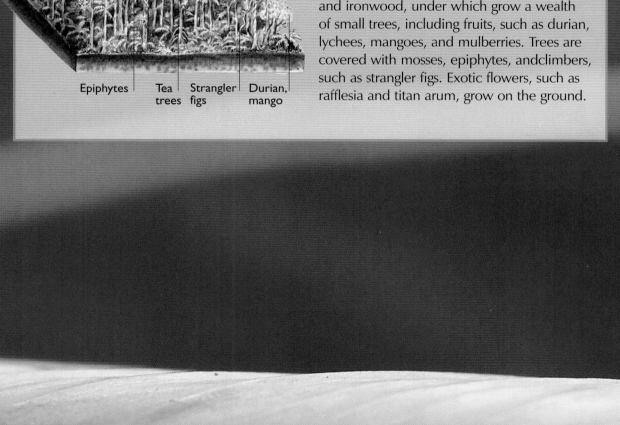

Epiphytes | Tea trees | Strangler figs | Durian, mango

Tropical rain forest environments

Rain forests are typically hot and steamy. Temperatures rarely rise above 93°F (34°C) nor fall below 68°F (20°C). There is no dry season and rain falls most afternoons. The rainfall totals over 4 in (100 mm) of rain each month.

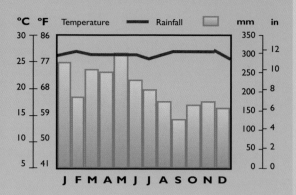

Sun and rain
Rainfall month by month and average daily temperature is shown for the Uaupés River, in the Amazon. The hottest month is often little more than 3–9°F (2–5°C) warmer than the coldest month.

Treetop pools
The dense canopy of leaves catches much of the rain. At least half the water reaching the ground is later given off by the leaves in transpiration. The trees are so damp that special "air plants" live on them. Some frogs even live in pools that collect on these air plants.

Thunderclouds
Most rain in the rain forest comes in thundershowers, which occur at least 200 days a year. Tropical warmth and humidity combine to build up huge thunderclouds each morning, which release their rain in the afternoon.

Australasian and Asian rain forests

Unlike the immense Amazon rain forest, the tropical rain forests of southern Asia, Indonesia, and Australia occupy quite small areas; and many of the larger animals, such as elephants, rhinos, and tigers, are under threat from human activity. Nevertheless, these forests remain home to an incredibly rich diversity of wildlife, including some of the world's most colorful birds and butterflies.

Wallace's Line
West of a line called "Wallace's Line," in S. E. Asia, there are deer, monkeys, pigs, cats, elephants, and rhinos. To the east, in New Guinea and Australia, are marsupials like possums, cuscuses, tree-kangaroos, and bandicoots.

Ganges forest is much depleted but is still home to tigers, rhinos, elephants, and gaurs.

Malaysia is home to 193 species of mammal, including elephants, tigers, rhinos, clouded leopards, and sun bears.

Borneo has a rich rain forest fauna, including 380 bird species, such as white-rumped shamas, and 13 primate species, such as orangutans and macaques.

Birds
In Asia, the forest canopy is full of colorful hornbills, lorikeets, sunbirds, leafbirds, and fairy bluebirds, along with wood swallows and tree swifts. On the ground run peafowl, bleeding heart doves, ground doves, pheasant, pittas, crowned pigeons, and flowerpeckers.

King of Saxony's bird of paradise
This is one of 43 kinds of dazzling birds of paradise that live in the forest canopy mostly in New Guinea and Australia, along with many other colorful birds, such as king parrots, fruit doves, and cuckoo-shrikes. The male has two long feathers growing from his head. During courtship, he holds them high and bounces up and down. As a female nears, he sweeps them before her.

Pileated gibbon
Gibbons are the smallest of the apes, but they can move through the trees with astonishing speed and agility. They have very long arms, which they use to swing over 10 ft (3 m) in a single movement. There are six species of gibbon, the largest of which is the siamang of Malaysia and Sumatra, famous for its loud whooping cry.

Primates
There are no primates in Australia, but many in southeast Asia. Best known are apes, such as gibbons and orangutans. There are also monkeys, such as rhesus macaques, 18 species of langur, and the big-nosed proboscis monkey.

Flying fox
This is actually a bat, called the greater fruit bat. It has the largest wings of any bat, spanning 6 ft (1.8 m). Unlike some bats, fruit bats have large eyes and see well in black and white, but they find the fruit they eat mainly by smell. By day, they roost in trees, taking flight only at dusk.

Insects
Besides countless tiny insects, such as termites, there are many huge ones, including giant stick insects, walking leaves, giant atlas beetles, beautiful luna moths, and birdwing butterflies.

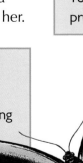

Birdwing butterfly
The Queen Alexandra's birdwing of southeast Papua New Guinea is the world's biggest butterfly, over 12 in (30.5 cm) across.

Flying creatures
As well as numerous kinds of bat, the forests of Australasia have a unique range of gliding animals, such as flying squirrels, snakes and frogs, and geckos. The most skillful are the gliding lemurs or colugos which can glide huge distances.

Reptiles and amphibians

Australasian rain forests are home to many snakes, such as venomous spitting cobras and taipans, and constrictors like the green and reticulated pythons. There are also hundreds of species of lizard, including many agamids and monitors, such as Salvador's.

Browsers and foragers

The biggest browsers and foragers are Asian elephants, but they are now very rare in the wild. So, too, are the various species of rhino found on different Indonesian islands, such as the Javan and Sumatran. Most common are wild hogs, piglike babirusas, and tapirs.

Anoa (dwarf buffalo)

Anoas are small buffaloes, standing barely 40 in (1 m) at the shoulder. They have almost no hair and enjoy bathing and wallowing in mud. They were once common on the Indonesian island of Sulawesi, but they are hunted for their horns, hide, and meat. As farms have spread, the survivors have retreated into inaccessible, swampy forest.

Grazing mammals

There are many small deer, including the tiny mouse deer (chevrotain), musk deer, tufted deer, Indian muntjac, sambar deer, and barking deer. The larger grazers are buffaloes and oxen, such as anoa and banteng. Tree kangaroos are found in Australian forests.

Komodo dragon

The Komodo dragon lives on the island of Komodo and nearby islands in Indonesia. It is the largest living lizard, growing up to 10 ft (3 m) long, and is strong enough to overpower and eat deer, wild boar, and water buffalo. Despite its bulk, it can run surprisingly fast to catch its prey, and can swim and even climb trees. It spends the night in a small hole it has dug.

Malayan tapir

Malayan tapirs have a short, flexible nose that they use to help them feed on water plants. They usually live near water and swim well.

New Guinea Among over 80 species of native mammals here, 44 are found nowhere else, including dusky pademelons and bats, such as the mastiff.

Queensland forests Here live many marsupials, including tree kangaroos and possums, and birds, such as cassowaries.

Small mammals

Among the many small mammals that live in the Australasian rain forests are marsupials, such as echidnas, bandicoots, and cuscuses. There are also numerous rodents, brush-tailed porcupines, tree shrews, and bulbuls.

Tree shrew

Tree shrews are small creatures that live in the southeast Asian rain forests. They scamper up and down trees like squirrels, but spend much of their time on the ground, feeding on ants, spiders, and seeds. Some scientists classify them as primates, others as insectivores (like shrews).

Clouded leopard

The clouded leopard is one of the most agile of all cat climbers. It can hang from branches with just its back feet, and run up and down trees like a squirrel. It often hunts by pouncing from trees and can kill prey, such as birds, pigs, and small deer, with a single bite from its very long canine teeth. It cannot roar, but it is one of the few big cats that can actually purr.

Predatory mammals

There are still tigers and leopards in the forests of southern Asia, Sumatra, and Java, but they are rare. The clouded leopard is also rare, with only about 10,000 left. Small civets, such as the masked palm civet, are still quite common.

Jungle survival

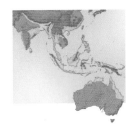

Tropical rain forests contain an incredible range of animals. In an area of just 39 sq miles (100 sq km), there may be more than 400 different bird species, 150 kinds of reptile and amphibian, 125 types of mammal, and tens of thousands of different insects. With this range of wildlife, there is a remarkable degree of interdependence. Rain forests are among the most stable and ancient of environments, and, over millions of years, a complex web of food relationships has developed between different animals and also between plants and animals.

Flies and beetles

Sheath-tailed bat

Masked palm civet

Water monitor lizard

Ants

Moon rat

Banteng

Dhole

Tree shrew

Mouse deer

Asian rain forest food chains

At the top of the food chains are the large predators. Big cats, such as leopards, and wild dogs like the dhole stalk the jungle floor. In the lower branches, there are smaller cats like the masked palm civet and clouded leopard, and snakes, such as the green python. In the canopy, there are snakes like the flying snake, and predatory birds, such as the bat hawk, crested serpent eagle, and the variable goshawk. Below each of these top predators is a food chain of species feeding upon species.

Forest floor animals
Dholes hunt in packs to bring down animals as big as banteng and water buffalo as well as small deer like mouse deer. Small predators, such as the moon rat and water monitor lizard, feed mainly on insects, such as ants and termites, that crawl on the forest floor.

Rain forest adaptation: Flying and gliding

In the rain forests of southeast Asia, a number of canopy animals have developed the ability to take to the air, both to move in the canopy and to escape predators. They are not true fliers, but have grown winglike extensions to help them glide from tree to tree, or to the ground. They include the Rhacophorus flying frogs, which can glide 165 ft (50 m), the flying squirrels, such as Thomas's and the black flying squirrel, and the Ptychozoon flying geckos.

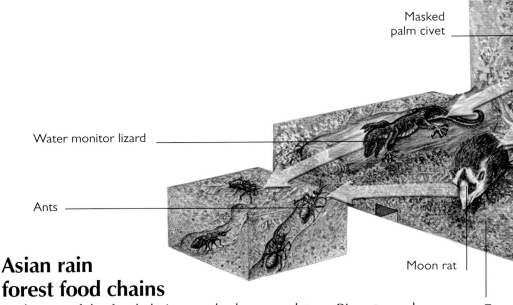

Flying squirrel

The tail is used to steer in the air.

The flying frog planes on huge webs between its toes.

Flying squirrels have gliding membranes stretched between their front and rear limbs.

The gecko has flaps on its sides and its feet.

Flying frog

Flying gecko

Bat hawk   Bar-winged flycatcher   Crested serpent eagle

Green tree
python

Shrews, snakes, and cats
Green tree pythons loop themselves
silently around tree branches to wait for
prey, such as tree shrews, mouse deer, and
civets, which they suffocate in their coils.
The shrews feed on insects and fruit. The
masked palm civet hunts at night for
rodents and lizards.

Bats and flycatchers
Bats like the sheath-tailed
bat, and birds like the bar-
winged flycatcher catch flies
in midair high above the
forest floor in the canopy.
Bats hunt by night and birds
mostly by day. Both are
preyed on by bat hawks.

Birds of prey
High up in the treetops,
birds of prey hunt. Bat
hawks swoop on birds,
such as flycatchers,
swallows, and swiftlets.
They also prey on bats,
gliding at dusk, snapping
them up as they emerge
from their bat caves.
Crested serpent eagles
feed on reptiles, such as
tree snakes. They usually
watch their prey from
branches in the canopy,
then dive through the
branches to strike.

Sumatran tiger

Sumatran tigers are the smallest of all
tigers, with a very dark coat and
striped forelegs. They eat mostly
sambar and other deer and wild pigs,
but will occasionally kill a rhino calf.
Like all tigers, they rely on ambushing
their prey, so they prefer to live in the
densest parts of the forest, where
they can find cover. There are now
only about 400 of them left in the
wild in five national parks on
Sumatra. There are just over 200 in
zoos around the world.

Wildlife at risk!

Orangutan
Orangutans are the largest of the tree-dwelling
apes, with arms over 6½ ft (2 m) long. They
once lived all over south China and southeast
Asia. But their forest habitats have been so
reduced that there are now just 12,000
individuals on Borneo and 7,000 on Sumatra.

Javan rhinoceros
The one-horned Javan rhinoceros is the rarest
of all the five species of rhino. Less than
60 individuals survive altogether in just two
locations—in Indonesia and in Vietnam. The
very similar Sumatran rhinoceros is only slightly
more numerous.

Gurney's pitta
Gurney's pitta is a small ground bird that lives
in the forests of Thailand and Burma. The
almost total destruction of its lowland forest
habitat means there are fewer than 25 pairs
remaining, and it is now the subject of a major
conservation drive.

South American rain forests

The Amazon rain forest is by far the largest continuous area of rain forest in the world—and home to a wider variety of different creatures than almost all the rest of the world put together. There are tens of thousands of known species here—from soldier ants and tiny hummingbirds to giant beetles and the biggest snakes in the world—and there are many more that are yet to be identified.

Choco-Darien
Separated by the Andes from the Amazon, this wet region has its own rich array of creatures, including Baird's tapir, Geoffrey's tamarin, and the toucan barbet.

Andes Mountains

Pacific Ocean

River Amazon

Southwest Amazon
The forest has an extraordinary number of birds and mammals, including red uakari monkeys, ocelots, capybaras, and giant otters.

River mammals
The Amazon river has its own unique range of mammals, including dolphins and sea cows (manatees), which look like seals but are unrelated. There are also rodents, such as the coypu and capybara—the world's largest rodent, which weighs up to 176 lb (80 kg).

Anaconda
The anaconda is one of the world's biggest snakes, sometimes growing up to 30 ft (9 m) long. They feed mainly on small birds and animals, catching their prey by lurking in murky waters. Anacondas kill by constriction—wrapping their coils around the victim and squeezing until it suffocates.

Amazon dolphin (bouto)
The Amazon river dolphin or bouto is the largest freshwater dolphin, reaching 8½ ft (2.6 m) in length. As it matures, it often turns vivid pink in color, but it is usually blue-gray like other dolphins. Unusually, for a dolphin, it can bend its neck to turn its head in any direction. It often swims upside down to see the riverbed.

Reptiles
The Amazon is one of the richest of all habitats for reptiles. Not only are there crocodile-like caimans and various turtles, such as the Arrau river turtle and the matamata, but also many snakes, such as the emerald tree boa, the vine snake, and the anaconda.

Woolly spider monkey
The woolly spider monkey is the largest monkey in the Amazon, and lives in the tops of the highest trees. It resembles a spider as it hangs upside down with all four limbs and tail grasping a branch. Unlike nearly all other monkeys, it has no thumb.

Amphibians
There is little standing water in the rain forest, yet many amphibians live here. Rain frogs live by small puddles, and many tree frogs live by pools in treetop plants. Toads, such as leaf and marine toads, live in damp leaf litter, as do salamanders and legless caecilians.

Poison arrow frog
In the rain forests of South and Central America live a number of different poison arrow frogs. These brightly colored tree frogs get their name from the deadly "batrachotoxin" poison secreted by their skin, which native hunters put on their arrow tips. The poison from the skin of one frog is enough to kill 100 people.

Primates
The Amazon's monkeys include spider monkeys, howlers, titis, capuchins, sakis, and uakaris, and over 30 kinds of small marmoset and tamarin. Unlike monkeys elsewhere, Amazon monkeys have flat, wide noses.

Insects

More than one million insect species are thought to live in the Amazon, including ants, fireflies, bees, cicadas, centipedes, and many kinds of vividly colored butterflies.

Acteon beetle

Of all the South American rain forest's many beetle species, none is more spectacular than the acteon beetle (*Megasoma acteon*). This is the world's biggest beetle, growing up to 3½ in (9 cm) long and 2 in (5 cm) wide—bigger even than Africa's giant goliath beetle.

Birds of the air

The Amazon air is constantly filled with the sound of myriad birds—colorful parrots, macaws, and parakeets, noisy caciques, elegant hoatzins, quetzals, jewel-like hummingbirds, giant-billed toucans, and numerous small birds, such as antbirds and woodpeckers.

Negro-Branco forests
Here in the remote heart of the Amazon, saki monkeys and jaguars and many other rare animals survive—and even the giant ground sloth may not be a myth.

Ground birds

The dense vegetation on the Amazon forest floor provides good cover for a range of ground birds, including elegant sunbitterns, quail doves, quails, nightjars, and 47 kinds of henlike tinamous. Waterbirds include cormorants, spoonbills, and ibises.

Great curassow

Curassows are a family of 50 American rain forest species that includes chacalacas and guans. Great curassows are about 40 in (1 m) long. They roost and nest in trees, but spend a great deal of time on the ground searching for fruit, leaves, and berries. The males have a loud, booming call that they use to attract females and threaten other males.

Predatory mammals

The largest predators are the big cats— jaguars, ocelots, and pumas. Jaguars and ocelots are now rare, though pumas are more common toward the Andes mountains. Smaller predators include raccoonlike coatis, ferretlike grisons, and weasels.

Three-toed sloth

Sloths are leaf-eating creatures that hang upside down in trees from their hooklike claws. They hang so securely they can sleep like this—and may even remain hanging like this after they die. They move so little that green algae grows on their fur, giving them a greenish tinge.

Herbivores; small mammals

Besides tiny deer and piglike peccaries and tapirs, there is an abundance of small mammals, including many rodents, such as agoutis, capybaras, pacas, and porcupines, a range of anteaters and sloths, the kinkajou and many bats, including the blood-drinking vampire.

Ocelot

The ocelot sleeps by day in a tree or in dense vegetation, and emerges at night to hunt on the ground for small mammals, such as deer and peccaries. Its favorite food is agouti. Ocelots are among the most beautiful of cats, and they have been hunted intensively for their pelts. Hunting is now banned, but there are very few ocelots left.

Toco Toucan

The toco toucan is the largest of the 41 species of toucans. The toco's bill can grow up to 8 in (20 cm) long—almost as long as its body. No one knows quite why it has such a large, colorful bill. It may be to attract a mate, or to gather hard-to-reach fruit. The toucan seizes fruit with the tip of its bill, then throws back its head to toss the fruit into its mouth.

Fish

There are over 1,500 known species of fish in the Amazon—and many more as yet unidentified. They include piranhas, hatchet fish, knife fish, arapaimas, and the pirarucu (the world's largest freshwater fish).

Electric eel

Electric eels are long fish that live in muddy rivers in the Amazon basin. With special muscle cells, they can generate a 650-volt electric shock—enough to stun a human. The electricity is used to detect underwater objects, signal to other eels, and stun or kill the fish they prey on.

Living on trees

It is a long way down from the tops of the trees in the Amazon rain forest—often 165 ft (50 m) or more—and the leaves and branches grow so densely that little sunlight ever penetrates to the ground. High in the treetop canopy, there is sun and rain and breezy air. Far below on the forest floor, it is still, humid, and perpetually gloomy. So striking is the difference in conditions that there are often distinct layers down through the trees. Each layer forms a different habitat, with its own range of plants and animals, each adapted to its own particular world.

Rain forest adaptations: Colorful plumage

Many of the world's most beautifully colored birds live in rain forests. In the Amazon, there are exotic cotingas and macaws, jewel-like hummingbirds and many others. Colored plumage may help birds find each other in dense jungle foliage. Male birds are especially vivid to attract females, which are often drab in comparison.

The iridescently hued hummingbird is one of 319 species of hummingbird. So gemlike are these tiny birds that in the 1800s they were actually made into jewelry.

Macaws like the scarlet macaw are the biggest and most brightly colored of all parrots.

The Andean cock-of-the-rock is the best known of over 90 kinds of cotinga. The male is bright red, but the female is brown. Though cotinga is Indian for "white-washed" from the white bellbird cotinga, many cotingas have bright plumage.

65–165 ft (20–50 m): Canopy layer

The canopy is the lush green layer of tree crowns, bathed with sun and rain and teeming with life, nourished by the abundance of fruit and nuts that grow here. Most animals in the canopy spend all their lives up there, and are well adapted to treetop life. There are fliers, such as birds, bats, and butterflies; gliders like some squirrels; and climbers, such as monkeys, sloths, beetles, ants, and spiders.

Forest floor

Large mammals, such as peccaries, and deer and birds, such as curassows, feed on the vegetation on the forest floor, foraging over a wide area rather than climbing or flying. Smaller mammals feed on insects and plant matter. Worms, centipedes, ants, termites, cockroaches, and a host of other tiny creatures live in the dank layer of rotting vegetation on the forest floor.

Layers of the rain forest

There are typically four layers in the rain forest—the forest floor; the "understory" of small trees, tree trunks, and shrubs; the "canopy" of tree crowns; and the "emergent" layer of tall trees rising above the canopy. Sometimes, the pattern of layers is disturbed by natural events. As a tree grows old and falls, for instance, it may pull with it many others tied to it by vines, creating a clearing; new trees will grow in the clearing, and the layers are eventually reestablished.

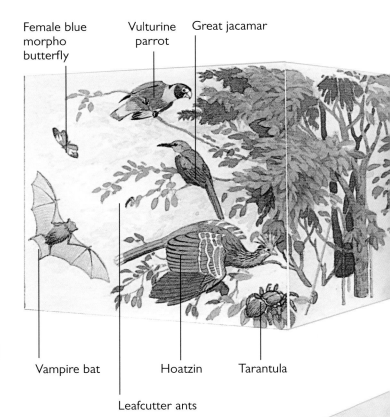

Female blue morpho butterfly

Vulturine parrot

Great jacamar

Vampire bat

Leafcutter ants

Hoatzin

Tarantula

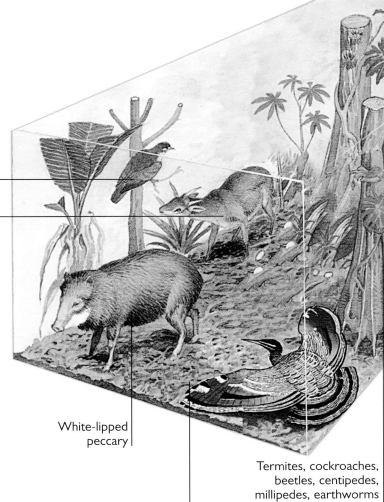

Ruddy quail dove

Pudu

White-lipped peccary

Sunbittern

Termites, cockroaches, beetles, centipedes, millipedes, earthworms

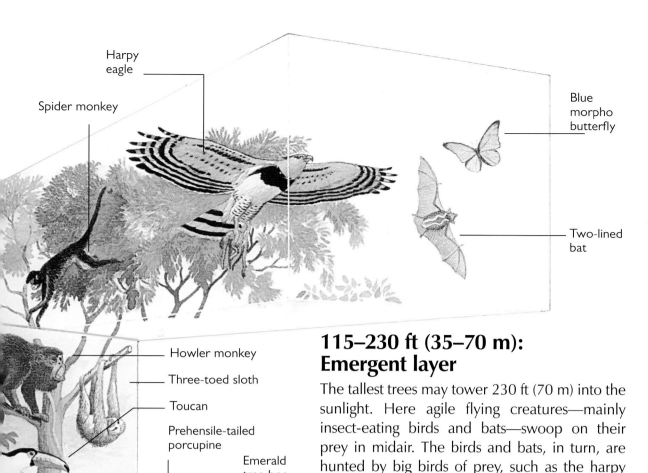

Harpy eagle

Spider monkey

Blue morpho butterfly

Two-lined bat

Howler monkey

Three-toed sloth

Toucan

Prehensile-tailed porcupine

Emerald tree boa

Olingo

Hummingbird

White fronted nun bird

St Vincent Amazon parrot

Golden toad

Poison arrow frog

Great curassow

Kinkajou

Ocelot

Upper Amazon porcupine

115–230 ft (35–70 m): Emergent layer

The tallest trees may tower 230 ft (70 m) into the sunlight. Here agile flying creatures—mainly insect-eating birds and bats—swoop on their prey in midair. The birds and bats, in turn, are hunted by big birds of prey, such as the harpy eagle. Spider monkeys may climb up for fruit.

15–65 ft (4.5–20 m): Understory layer

This is the lower layer of small trees and shrubs, and tangled vines used by climbing creatures. Little sunlight gets down here and many leaves are colored dark green or red, to make the best use of the available light. Birds, bats, monkeys, squirrels, and many kinds of snake live here. There are frogs, too, finding the water to lay their eggs in pools caught by plants high up in the trees.

Blue morpho

The blue morphos that live in the forest canopy are large butterflies, up to 6½ in (16.5 cm) across. The tops of their wings flash iridescent blue in the sunlight as they fly, but the undersides of the wings are brown, which keeps them hidden when they rest with their wings folded up.

29

Wildlife at risk!

Resplendent quetzal

The 2 ft- (60 cm-) long tail feathers of the quetzal were worn by Aztec kings. Quetzals were once common, but the expansion of farming has made the wild avocados on which they feed scarce. The birds now live only in remote areas of Central American cloud forest.

Cottontop tamarin

Tamarins are small monkeys that feed on fruit, insects, and frogs. Their forest habitat has been reduced, and tens of thousands of tamarins were taken to the U.S. for medical research. The cottontop tamarin is now one of the world's most endangered primates.

Forest clearance

Rain forest is being destroyed at an alarming rate and, with it, the habitat of countless creatures. An area of Amazon forest as big as Scotland is lost each year, as trees are cut down for timber or simply burned to clear the land. Once rain forest is cleared, it is unlikely to recover. The forest's nutrients are locked into the trees, not the soil, and once the trees go, so do the nutrients.

African rain forests

Although the African rain forests have fewer species than those of South America and Asia, they are still an astonishingly rich habitat. Among the giant hardwood trees of the Congo rain forest lives a huge variety of creatures, including monkeys, apes, and smaller primates that use their gripping hands and feet to move through the trees with amazing agility.

Eastern Guinea
Much reduced in size, this forest is still home to many monkeys, such as sooty mangabeys and dianas, and also rare pygmy hippos.

Dzanga Sangha, central Africa
One of the last areas of untouched rain forest, this is the home of rare forest elephants, bonobos, and lowland gorillas.

Zambesi

Madagascar
Cut off from mainland Africa 150 million years ago, this island has unique fauna, including lemurs and ayes-ayes.

Okapi

With their striped legs, okapis were thought to be related to zebras when they were first discovered by European explorers in the Congo in 1901. In fact, they are related to giraffes. Like giraffes, okapis have long tongues which they can use to twist and pull leaves from trees—and also to lick clean their own eyes.

Foraging mammals

The largest animals in the African rain forest are okapis and elephants, both of which can browse on leaves some way above the ground. Small foragers include the pygmy hippo and hogs, such as the red river hog and the giant forest hog, the world's biggest pig.

Small mammals

Among the many small mammals living in the rain forest are tree hyraxes, the African brush-tailed porcupine, and tree pangolins. Tree pangolins are similar to anteaters, but are covered with an armor of scales. They spend most of their lives in trees.

Colobus monkey

Agile colobus monkeys are known as "leaf-monkeys" because they eat mainly leaves. The Angolan black and white is one of nine species. In the past it was killed for its long, silky hair and it is now quite rare.

Oleander hawk (sphinx) moth

This is the most spectacular hawk moth. Big and a strong flier, it hovers in front of flowers like a hummingbird, to suck the nectar with its long proboscis.

Armored shrew

The armored shrew has an incredibly strong spine reinforced by bony flanges and rods. Mangbetu natives in the Congo call it the "hero shrew" because they can stand on its back without breaking it! In other respects it is much like other shrews, except that it moves slowly.

Insects

Like all rain forests, Africa's teem with insects, including many species of beetle (such as the giant goliath beetle), ant, termite, fly, and cockroach, including the huge Madagascar hissing cockroach that forces air out of its body noisily in order to alarm predators.

Monkeys and apes

Monkeys and apes are kings of Africa's forests, moving freely through the trees in search of fruit, leaves, and insects. Here live three of the four great apes: chimpanzee, bonobo, and gorilla. (The fourth is the orangutan.) Monkeys include monas, mangabeys, and colobus.

Birds of the air

African rain forests are home to dozens of species of hornbills (Africa's equivalent of Amazonian toucans), scores of colorful parrots and lovebirds, plus barbets, turacos, bulbuls, orioles, and blue rollers.

Red-crested turaco

Turacos spend much of their lives high up in the trees, but they are quite poor fliers. Instead, they climb and run along branches with the nimbleness of a squirrel. The beautiful plumage of the red-crested turaco is still highly prized by African tribal chiefs.

Ground birds

The largest birds in the African rain forest are those that forage on the ground for seeds, shoots, tubers, and berries. The biggest is the spectacular Congo peafowl, but the vulturine guinea fowl and the red-necked francolin are also very large birds. Less conspicuous are ground-nesters, such as the standard-winged nightjar.

Congo peafowl

The Congo peafowl is the only pheasant found in Africa and its discovery in 1936 caused a sensation, for pheasants were thought to be exclusively Eurasian. They are rare, shy birds that roam the forest floor in pairs or family groups. It is silent during the day, but when it roosts in trees at night, it screeches loudly.

Aye-aye

The Madagascan aye-aye is a nocturnal creature with long, slender fingers. It uses its long third finger to tap on tree trunks to find insects, listening for movement with its super-sensitive ears. It then probes with the same finger to draw out the insect. During the day, aye-ayes hide in treetop nests of twigs.

Grazing mammals

Africa's grassland grazers rely on speed and stamina to escape from predators. Rain forest grazers escape by being elusive. Antelopes are either small enough to dart into hiding, like royals and duikers, or are camouflaged like the bongos.

Reptiles and amphibians

Africa's rain forest is home to *Rana Goliath*, the world's biggest frog—at 12 in (30.5 cm) tall it is almost as big as the royal antelope. There are also colorful sedge frogs, chameleons, and lizards, such as Nile monitors. Snakes include pythons and tree cobras.

Eastern green mamba

The eastern green mamba is a long, slender snake that slithers along branches hunting for lizards and small birds. It is not quite as deadly as its savanna relative, the black mamba, but its poison is still lethal to humans. In the breeding season, males engage in ritual fights for females, twisting their bodies around each other.

Small primates: prosimians

Relatives of monkeys and apes, prosimians are small primates with big eyes and long tails. Like all primates, they use their hands and feet to climb. Pottos and bush babies live in all African rain forests, but lemurs, aye-ayes, and indris live only in Madagascar.

Royal antelope

The royal antelope of the west African rain forest is the world's smallest hoofed animal—less than 12 in (30.5 cm) high and with pencil-thin legs. It is a shy creature, able to vanish quickly when spotted—and can bound nearly 10 ft (3 m). It is famed in local folklore for its speed and its wisdom.

African palm civet

Civets look a little like cats, but have more pointed snouts, bushier tails, and shorter legs. They mark out their territory and attract a mate using scent from glands near the base of the tail. The base of this scent is musk, which is used to make perfumes. The African palm civet is nocturnal and hunts in the forest canopy for insects, lizards, and small mammals.

Predatory mammals

In treetops, crowned eagles are major predators; in branches, pythons are. Only near ground are mammals the main hunters. Here the leopard is the top predator, hunting young antelopes, monkeys, and apes.

31

Moving through trees

Moving through branches high above the ground is very different from moving along the ground. Many rain forest animals have developed special skills for what zoologists call "arboreal locomotion," including leaping, climbing, swinging, and gliding. Tree frogs have special pads on their toes that help them as they climb. Woodpeckers, treecreepers, and other birds have clawed feet for clinging. Squirrels and other small mammals climb with the help of claws, too. But the best climbers are monkeys, apes, and smaller primates who climb, leap, and swing with astonishing agility.

Gorilla

The gorilla is the biggest of all the apes, standing 6½ ft (2 m) tall and weighing up to 500 lb (230 kg). Despite its fierce appearance, it is a shy, gentle creature that eats only leaves and shoots. Males thump their chests to warn off intruders. Gorillas have long arms suitable for swinging, but they never do so, spending much of their time on the ground, walking on all fours on their knuckles. They climb trees at night to find a place safe from leopards, their only enemy apart from humans.

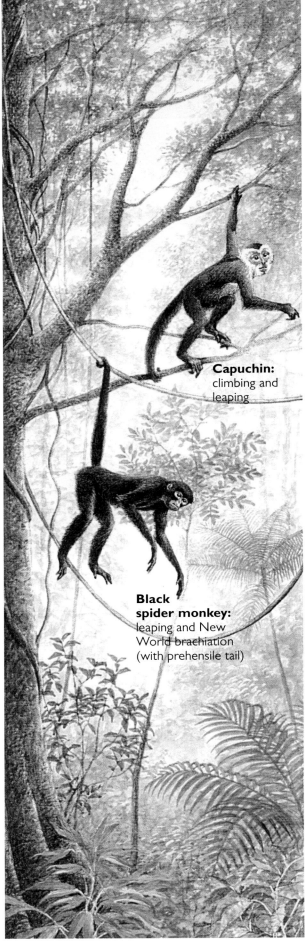

Capuchin: climbing and leaping

Black spider monkey: leaping and New World brachiation (with prehensile tail)

Rain forest adaptation: Hands for gripping

All primates are well adapted to living in trees and nearly all have hands with fingers and feet with toes for gripping branches—except for humans (whose feet cannot grip) and tree shrews (that cannot grip with their hands). American monkeys have a short thumb like every other finger. But African and Asian monkeys and apes have an opposable thumb—that is, a thumb that can bend the opposite way to the fingers to provide a very precise grip. With this precision grip, some apes can use tools, such as sticks and stones, very effectively to get food. In human hands, the opposable thumb is highly developed.

New World monkey with short thumb.

Spider monkey

Short opposable thumb for branch swinging.

Ape: gibbon

Large opposable thumb for very precise grip.

Ape: gorilla

Short opposable thumb for walking on palms.

Monkey: macaque

South America

All monkeys climb using their four long limbs. This way of moving is called quadrapedalism. Capuchins and many other American monkeys, such as sakis, titis, and marmosets, move like this—climbing, springing, and running along branches with amazing agility. Some American (New World) monkeys, like spiders and howlers, also have extra help to mobility possessed by no Asian and African (Old World) monkey—a prehensile or gripping tail. This tail is like an extra limb, giving enough support for monkeys to swing from branch to branch on their arms, a technique called "New World semi-brachiation."

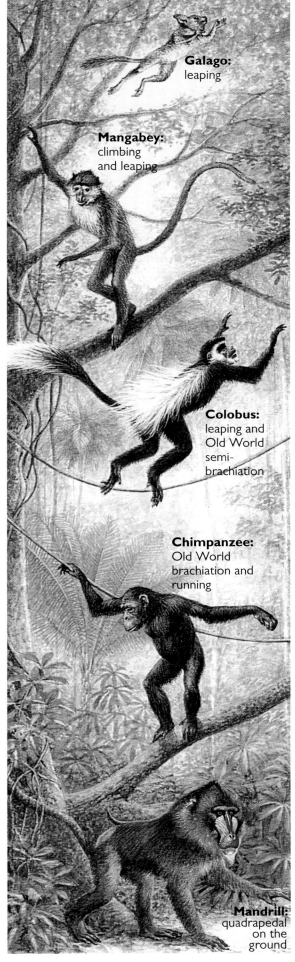

Galago:
leaping

Mangabey:
climbing
and leaping

Colobus:
leaping and
Old World
semi-
brachiation

Chimpanzee:
Old World
brachiation and
running

Mandrill:
quadrupedal
on the
ground

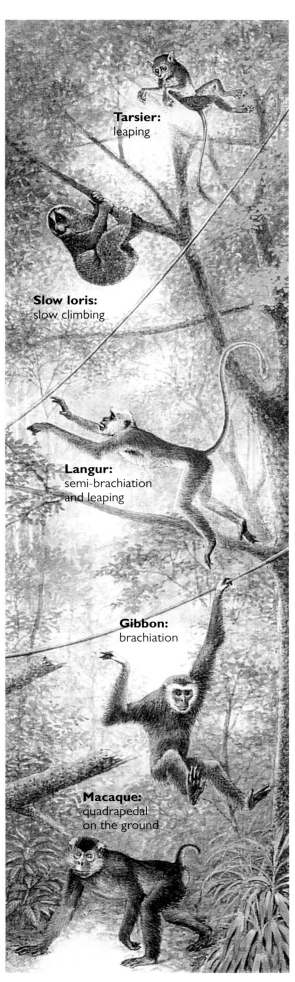

Tarsier:
leaping

Slow loris:
slow climbing

Langur:
semi-brachiation
and leaping

Gibbon:
brachiation

Macaque:
quadrupedal
on the ground

Africa

Like American monkeys, African monkeys move on all four limbs—some climbing and others, like mandrills, running on the ground. A few, like mangabeys, are slow climbers, but most African monkeys are more agile than American monkeys. The colobus is a great leaper. The colobus and a few others may also swing from their arms ("Old World semibrachiation"). Prosimians (small primates like bush babies) cling vertically to tree trunks and may leap. Apes, such as chimpanzees, have long arms and swing properly (brachiation), though they are too big to climb high. Gorillas rarely climb at all and walk on their knuckles.

Asia

Asian monkeys move on all fours like American and African monkeys. Some, like macaques, run on the ground, only rarely climbing trees. Others, like langurs, move easily through the trees using their tail as a balance, making leaps of 33 ft (10 m). Asia's two apes—the gibbon and orangutan—both brachiate (swing from their arms). While orangutans swing only when young and climb slowly when older, gibbons are the greatest of all swingers, moving from branch to branch on their long arms with amazing agility. Prosimians are clingers and leapers, but while lorises climb slowly, tarsiers leap energetically.

33

Wildlife at risk!

Pygmy hippopotamus

Pygmy hippos are only about the size of a large pig. They live in forests in west Africa and spend less of their time in the water than their large relatives. Although hunting is banned, many local people still poach them for food and there are now only a few thousand left.

Endangered chimps

Lively and intelligent, chimpanzees are our closest relatives in the animal world. Over 100,000 survive in the wild in west and central Africa, but numbers are dwindling as they are hunted for food, captured for medical research, and their habitat is slowly eroded.

Big game hunters

In the past, big game hunters came to Africa to hunt large mammals like lions and rhinos for sport. Such hunting is now largely banned, but commercial hunting for ivory, skins, and other products is harder to control and still threatens many species with extinction.

Deserts

More than one-fifth of the world's land surface is desert, where it hardly ever rains. There are deserts on all the continents except for Europe. There is a grandeur in the vast emptiness of these barren expanses, each with its own evocative name—Gobi, Sahara, Kalahari, Mojave.

•

The polar regions are called deserts because it is too cold to rain there. But the greatest deserts are those in the subtropics where the air is forever calm and clear. Here cloudless skies allow daytime sun to beat down in relentless heat— then temperatures plummet at night. With no vegetation to break the flow, winds whip across the desert, blowing dust and sand in every eye and drying up the land.

•

Satellite pictures show deserts as great brown and yellow scars on Earth's rich, green continents—seemingly devoid of life. Even close up, they can appear barren. Yet this lifelessness is an illusion—an astonishing variety of both plants and animals survive there, using an extraordinary range of tricks to cling to life in extreme conditions.

Where are deserts?

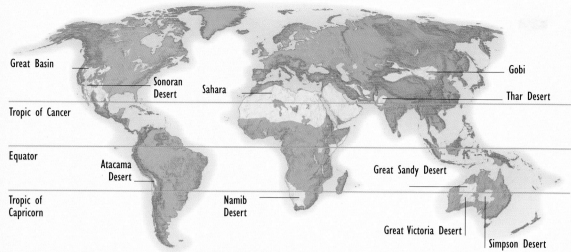

Great Basin
Sonoran Desert
Sahara
Gobi
Thar Desert
Tropic of Cancer
Equator
Atacama Desert
Great Sandy Desert
Tropic of Capricorn
Namib Desert
Great Victoria Desert
Simpson Desert

Comparing deserts

Saguaro cactus | Barrel cactus | Buffel grass | Joshua tree | Prickly pear

Date palms | Glasswort | Acacia bush | Oleander bush

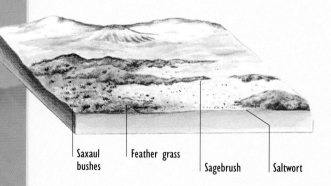

Saxaul bushes | Feather grass | Sagebrush | Saltwort

North America

North America's deserts have vast plains and towering cliffs. The Great Basin is sagebrush scrub. To the south, Joshua trees and creosote bushes punctuate the Mojave. Farther south, giant cacti like the saguaro stand like pillars in the Sonoran.

Africa

Landscapes in the Sahara vary from rocky hamadas to seas of sand dunes (ergs). It is so hot that vast areas are barren and plants often grow only near oases, where date palms may also grow. The Namib has the world's biggest dunes—up to 1,300 ft (400 m) high.

Asia

Asia's Gobi desert is hot in summer, but in winter there are no barriers to protect it from the icy air blowing in from Siberia to the north. Vegetation blooms briefly after the spring rains and survives through the early summer before the searing heat dries it out. The dominant plants are saxaul shrubs, and patches of low plants like saltwort and feather grass.

Desert environments

Deserts vary hugely, but the driest deserts get less than 4 in (100 mm) of rain a year. Areas with less than about 24 in (600 mm) are said to be semi-arid. In hot deserts rain comes in short, heavy showers that run off the land quickly—or evaporate almost instantly into the warm, dry air.

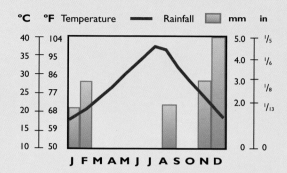

Scorching sun

All deserts are dry. Some are very hot, too, and daytime summer temperatures can soar to 122°F (50°C), although nights are cool. This graph shows conditions for In Salah, Algeria, which is exceptionally dry.

Oasis

Little rain falls on the surface, but there is often water in the desert below ground. Some is subterranean water from beyond the desert. Some is water left over from wetter times in the ancient past. Oases occur where this underground water gets to the surface.

Desert bloom

Many desert plants and seeds may lie dormant for months or even years, apparently lifeless—then burst briefly into flower when rain comes. They often germinate and bloom within hours, then die after scattering seed.

African deserts

There are three great deserts in Africa: the Namib and Kalahari in the south, and the vast Sahara that covers almost all of northern Africa. The Sahara is not only the largest desert on Earth but it is also the hottest. It is completely waterless over vast areas, yet many creatures can still survive here—tough-skinned lizards and snakes, rodents, goats and gazelles, and countless insects.

Namib coastal desert
The great sand dunes of the southern Namib seem barren, but beetles, spiders, and even springbok antelopes survive here—and below the surface live golden moles.

Zambesi

Kalahari desert
Although a desert, the sandy Kalahari has plenty of vegetation and is home to many large animals, including gemsbok antelopes, zebras, and cheetahs.

Dromedary

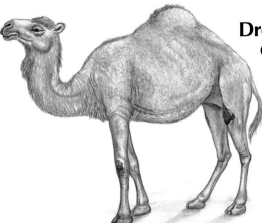

Camels cope with desert heat by letting their blood warm up during the day then cool at night. Their fur shields them from the sun. By drinking a third of their weight in water in one go, then storing it in their stomach, they can last days without water. They draw on the fat they store in their hump for food.

Browsers and foragers
The biggest creatures in the desert by far are camels, who can survive a week without water and much longer without food. On the desert fringes, anubis and hamadryas baboons manage to find enough grass seed, roots, and bulbs to survive.

Darkling beetle
Darkling beetles are among the most numerous beetles in the Namib Desert. When the damp fog rolls in from the sea, they stand on their heads so that drops of water collect on their bodies and run down toward their mouths. Many darkling beetles are white to reflect the desert sun.

Insects
Their waterproof casing helps insects and spiders to live in the Sahara. There are flying insects, such as flies, wasps, and locusts; flightless insects, such as ants, termites, and beetles (e.g. scarabs); spiders, such as wolf and jumping spiders; and many scorpions.

Small mammals
Medium-sized mammals find it hard to cope with desert heat, but small ones can burrow and hide in the shade. The Sahara has 40 species of rodent, including gerbils, mice, jerboas, and rock hares. There are also long-eared desert hedgehogs and rock hyraxes.

Fat-tailed gerbil
Like many desert rodents, this gerbil escapes the heat by resting in burrows and comes out in the cool of night to feed on seeds and insect grubs. It gets its name because it stores fat in its stubby tail. When food is plentiful, the tail swells up so much that the gerbil can barely drag it along. Then, when food is scarce, the fat is used up and the tail slims down.

Pale chanting goshawk
This small goshawk is often seen in the Namib Desert perching on a tree—or even walking about on the ground, looking very much like a secretary bird. Indeed, it spends far more time on the ground than any other hawk—perhaps to save energy—and often runs after prey at great speed.

Birds of prey
Birds can fly long distances in search of food and water, and have higher body temperatures than mammals. Many birds can survive in the Sahara. Large birds of prey include black-faced vultures, lanner falcons, and pygmy falcons.

Sahara
The world's largest desert is a mix of hamada (rocky uplands), reg (silt and gravel), and erg (seas of sand).

Mediterranean Sea

Nile

Red Sea

Predatory mammals

Although there is little plant life for food in the desert, there are other animals to eat. There are many medium-sized predators in the Sahara, including dogs, such as hyenas, jackals, and fennec foxes, and cats, such as the caracal and sandcat.

Arabian desert
Many larger animals here have been slaughtered by motorized hunting parties, but a few addax antelopes survive and there are many rodents and lizards.

Striped hyena

Unlike their larger spotted cousins, striped hyenas are solitary animals, usually hunting alone. They live only in pairs during the breeding season. They sometimes feed on carrion, such as the remains of cat kills, but also prey on lambs, small mammals, and reptiles.

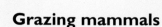

Grazing mammals

Surprisingly, many grazing animals live in the Sahara. Grevy's zebras roam the fringes, while sheep, goats, ibexes, and asses haunt mountain areas. Antelopes, such as the addax, scimitar-horned oryx, and dama, dorcas, and sand gazelles live in the heart of the desert.

Reptiles and amphibians

Reptiles are well-adapted to life in the desert. They have thick, moisture-proof skins and rely on the sun for energy. There are over 100 species in the Sahara, including lizards like the desert monitor, geckos, and skinks, as well as snakes and tortoises.

Courser

Coursers are a group of nine species of desert bird found in Africa, India, and Australia. They are strong fliers, but they are more often seen chasing the insects they catch by sprinting along the ground, or resting between bursts of running. The picture shows the cream-colored courser of Africa.

Springbok

The Namib Desert in the south of Africa has its own range of grazers. There is little rain here, yet the air is so humid from coastal fogs that mountain zebras and antelopes like the gemsbok and springbok can find enough moisture and grass to survive. The 2½ ft- (76 cm-) high springbok is known for its ability to spring up to 11½ ft (3.5 m) in the air when alarmed.

Birds of the air

In fall, birds like warblers, swallows, and martins fly south over the Sahara to escape the European winter, then fly north the following spring. Some birds, such as wheatears, even stay for the winter; others, like rock sparrows and weavers, live here all year.

Toad-headed agamid

Agamids are a huge group of lizards with chisel-shaped front teeth. The toad-headed agamid has a round head that looks rather like a toad's. Like many desert creatures, it shelters underground, digging a short tunnel, or burying itself in sand by wriggling from side to side. The picture shows it in defense mode, with its tail raised and rolled up.

Black-bellied sandgrouse

The need for water plays a key role in the life of the black-bellied sandgrouse. It roosts in small flocks on open ground, then at dawn it flies to a water hole, where several flocks may jostle for water. When it has young, it soaks its breast feathers to take water back for the chicks to drink.

Ground birds

With few trees, ground birds can cope better here than perching birds. Ostriches and guinea fowl are seen on the fringes, while houbaras and Nubian bustards live further in. Like many desert creatures, bustards get most of their water from the prey that they eat.

Desert survival

Life in the Sahara is life on the edge. The creatures that live here must be able to cope not only with the extreme heat and lack of water but also with the scarcity of food. Grazing animals and other herbivores often have to roam far and wide in search of plants to eat—and cope with the lean times when there is little growing anywhere. Predators, too, find prey scarce, and larger hunters can go many weeks without a kill.

Caracal
The fast-running caracal is the desert's biggest cat, hunting at dusk for reptiles, birds like sandgrouse, and mammals like the beira.

Fat sand rat
The fat sand rat is a gerbil that feeds on seeds. It copes with lean times by living off the thick layer of fat all over its body, built up when food is plentiful.

Spitting red cobra
Spitting cobras live near oases where they can find prey. They hunt at night for rodents, lizards, and small birds, which they kill with their venom-injecting fangs.

Ants
Honey pot ants stroke aphids and cochineal insects with their antennae to collect honeydew—a sugary substance that these insects secrete.

African desert food web

The small range of creatures in the desert means food webs here are much simpler than elsewhere. Moreover, while in other habitats many species may feed on a similar range of food and occupy similar places in the food web, food in the desert is so scarce that each kind of food may support only a single species. Predators like big cats and dogs cannot afford to be too choosy about their prey when times are lean.

Ant lion
Ant lions are large insects. Their larvae dig funnel-shaped pits to trap ants. They hide in the pits with only their jaws showing and flick sand to knock ants into the trap.

Pintail sandgrouse
During the day the pintail sandgrouse forages far and wide for seeds.

Desert adaptations: Walking on sand

Walking on soft, scorching hot sand is not easy, so many desert mammals have specially adapted feet. Desert cats like the sand cat, for instance, have fur pads on the underside of their feet to protect them from the heat. The hooves of the addax antelope are unusually large to stop them sinking into soft sand. Camels' feet are both large and padded.

Addax
Extra wide hooves spread the weight of the addax over a greater area.

Bactrian camel
Shaggy fur on the bactrian camel's foot protects it from snow as well as sand.

Dromedary camel
Thick fur on the camel's foot helps protect it from hot sand.

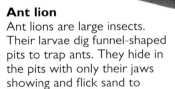

38

Sand cat
The sand cat looks like a large domestic cat. It hunts at night for rodents, lizards, and insects, sheltering in caves by day.

Lanner falcon
The lanner falcon often perches on dead trees at water holes looking for prey, or swoops down from heights of 1,640 ft (500 m). It often catches birds in flight, but if none are available it will eat lizards and small mammals.

Beira
The beira antelope eats grass and the leaves of bushes, such as mimosa, that grow in the stony hills.

Spring-tailed lizard
Small lizards like the spring-tailed lizard get the fluids their bodies need from feeding on insects.

Princely mastigure
Like other Uromastyx lizards of the Sahara, the princely mastigure has a spiny tail. It feeds on small mammals and eggs.

Desert lizards
Lizards are well-equipped to cope with desert conditions. They have thick skins that cut moisture loss to a minimum. The warm sun, which makes many mammals suffer, actually gives lizards (like all reptiles) the energy to hunt, though they become sluggish in the cold of night. Sometimes, the Saharan sun can be too hot even for lizards, so they move from one shadow to another.

Wildlife at risk!

Northern bald ibis
The northern bald ibis is now almost extinct, for reasons not fully understood, with less than 50 birds left in Algeria and Morocco. Its cousin, the sacred ibis, revered and mummified by the ancient Egyptians, is now extinct in Egypt and elsewhere in Africa.

Dama gazelle
Once numerous in the Sahara, tens of thousands of dama gazelles have been killed by hunters. The gazelles have also suffered because the grassy desert fringes where herds spend the drier part of the year are being stripped bare by livestock.

Desertification
In the last 50 years, the Sahara has expanded southward to cover a further 250,000 sq miles (650,000 sq km). This is partly due to climatic changes, but is also a result of the overgrazing of desert fringes by livestock, cutting down trees for firewood, and increasing extraction of groundwater for farming.

Asian deserts

Asia's Gobi desert is one of the world's forgotten places—a vast, parched, windswept expanse stretching across southern Mongolia into China. Unlike the ever-hot Sahara, the Gobi swings from scorching summer days—over 113°F (45°C)—to icy winters—often below -40°F (-40°C). This harshness has made it a refuge for creatures hardy enough to survive, including some of the world's rarest animals, such as the Bactrian camel.

Southern deserts
No other deserts have such scorching summers and icy winters yet many jerboas and many reptiles, such as the huge gray monitor, live here. So too does the very rare desert cheetah.

Takla Makhan
This giant high-altitude plateau is the largest sand desert in Asia.

Caucasus Mountains

Thar desert
The Thar is home not only to desert foxes and caracals, but also large grazers, such as chinkaras and blackbucks, plus many rodents and 141 species of bird, such as the rare great Indian bustard.

Mongolian agama lizard
The Mongolian agama lizard is one of over 300 plump-bodied lizards called agamids. They nearly all have thin tails, long legs, and triangular heads with chisel-shaped jaws. Like other desert agamids, the Mongolian agama is a burrowing creature, and spends the cold winter asleep deep below ground.

Reptiles
Many reptiles cope with the Gobi's extremes by burrowing. There are tortoises and many kinds of gecko and lizard, such as the gray monitor and Gobi racerunner. They are food for snakes like the lebetine viper and tatar sand boa.

Pallid harrier
Slender, long-winged pallid and pied harriers are birds of prey that nest on the ground or in bushes. They catch small mammals, such as jerboas, and birds and lizards by swooping low over the ground. The Gobi winter is too cold for the harriers, so they migrate to India by fall.

Gobi bear
The Gobi bear (*Ursus arctos pruinosus*) is the world's only desert bear, living in southwestern Mongolia, where the local people call it Mazaalai. It is actually a type of brown bear, like the North American grizzly, but is adapted to coping with the arid conditions of the Gobi. It is now very rare and close to extinction, with only 30 or so animals surviving.

Insects
The extremes of the Gobi make life difficult even for insects and other invertebrates. Nevertheless, there is a range of insects in the desert, including ants, beetles, bees, and earwigs; arachnids, such as scorpions and sun spiders; and woodlice and centipedes.

Funnel-web spider
Some funnel-web spiders like the brachyteles can cope with dry conditions on the edge of the desert because they live in burrows, and are active only at night. They spin funnel-shaped entrances to their burrows. Silk trip lines radiating from the entrance alert the spider to incoming prey.

Predatory mammals
The Gobi once had two big predators; the Gobi bear and the snow leopard, which used to venture down from the mountains of Tibet. These are now very rare, and the main hunting mammal is the marbled polecat, which hunts at night for lizards and small mammals.

Birds of prey
In summer, various birds of prey visit the Gobi, including spectacular golden and imperial eagles. All year-round, there are carrion-feeding vultures, such as the lammergeier and the giant Cinereous vulture (the European black), with its 10 ft- (3 m-) wingspan.

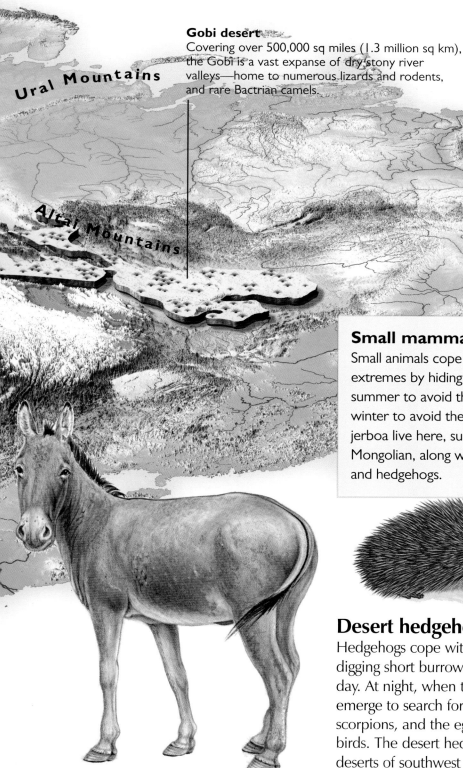

Gobi desert
Covering over 500,000 sq miles (1.3 million sq km), the Gobi is a vast expanse of dry stony river valleys—home to numerous lizards and rodents, and rare Bactrian camels.

Ural Mountains

Altai Mountains

Birds of the air
In summer, many birds visit the Asian deserts and surrounding dry steppes; they include wheatears, desert warblers, desert larks, and stone curlews. Other birds, such as Koslov's accentor and the saxaul sparrow, are here most of the year.

Desert lark
The desert lark lives in the warm deserts of southwestern Asia and India across to the Sahara, and builds its nest against a rock or tuft of grass. Its plumage is perfect camouflage against the sandy soil—vital in a habitat where there is little cover. A dark species lives on black sandy areas; a pale species lives on areas of white sand.

Small mammals
Small animals cope with the Gobi's extremes by hiding underground—in summer to avoid the heat of the day and in winter to avoid the cold. Many kinds of jerboa live here, such as the long-eared and Mongolian, along with various hamsters and hedgehogs.

Ground birds
The plants that spring up after winter in the central Asian deserts provide enough seeds to support a range of ground birds, including bustards, such as the houbara, Henderson's groundjay, Pander's groundjay, and various sandgrouses.

Desert hedgehog
Hedgehogs cope with the desert heat by digging short burrows to shelter in during the day. At night, when the air is cool, they emerge to search for invertebrates, such as scorpions, and the eggs of ground-nesting birds. The desert hedgehog lives in the deserts of southwest Asia. The long-eared hedgehog lives in the Gobi.

Kulan (wild donkey)
There are five kinds of wild donkey or kulan found in central and southern Asia. Also known as onagers, these are the onager, dzigetai (from Mongolia), kiang, khur (from India), and ashdari (the probably extinct Syrian ass). The dzigetai is the Gobi's kulan. Female dzigetai live in small herds with their young and a single male. Other males live in bachelor groups.

Pallas's sandgrouse
Like other sandgrouse, the Pallas's male brings water for its chicks from distant water holes by wading into the water to soak its special spongelike belly feathers. In the past, very cold winters would drive Pallas's sandgrouse west into Europe in huge flocks. Now, perhaps as sandgrouse numbers have dwindled, these mass movements have ceased.

Grazing mammals
In spring, places in the Gobi turn briefly green and grazing animals move in from the surrounding steppes. Besides wild horses like the kulan and Przewalski's, there are ibexes, gazelles, such as the black-tailed dzeran and Mongolian, and antelopes, such as the saiga.

Browsers and foragers
There are no oases in the Gobi, and the Bactrian camel is the only large foraging animal able to stomach the sparse vegetation and cope with the extreme conditions. The camel is always on the move, seeking tough grass, leaves, and thin branches for food.

Bactrian camel
Bactrian camels have two humps, unlike the African dromedary, and a shaggy coat to cope with icy Gobi winters. They were tamed 4,000 years ago, and it was once thought all Bactrians in the wild were feral—that is, descendants of domesticated beasts. But in the late 1800s truly wild camels were found in central Asian deserts. This wild population is small.

Wide-open spaces

The deserts and dry steppes of central Asia are one of the few places in the world where wild horses survive. They are the only remaining wild descendants of the first horselike creatures that appeared 50 million years ago. The world was wetter then, and these horse ancestors were small forest creatures. But as the world became drier and forests shrank, so bigger horses evolved that could live on dry grassland and even in deserts, where they still survive.

Horse evolution

The horse's family tree dates back 50 million years to hyracotherium, fossils of which have been found in both North America and Europe. Since then it has grown bigger, longer-legged, longer-muzzled, developed hooves instead of toes, and changed from a browser to a grazer. But it was never a steady progression, and this illustration shows just a few major stages and branches.

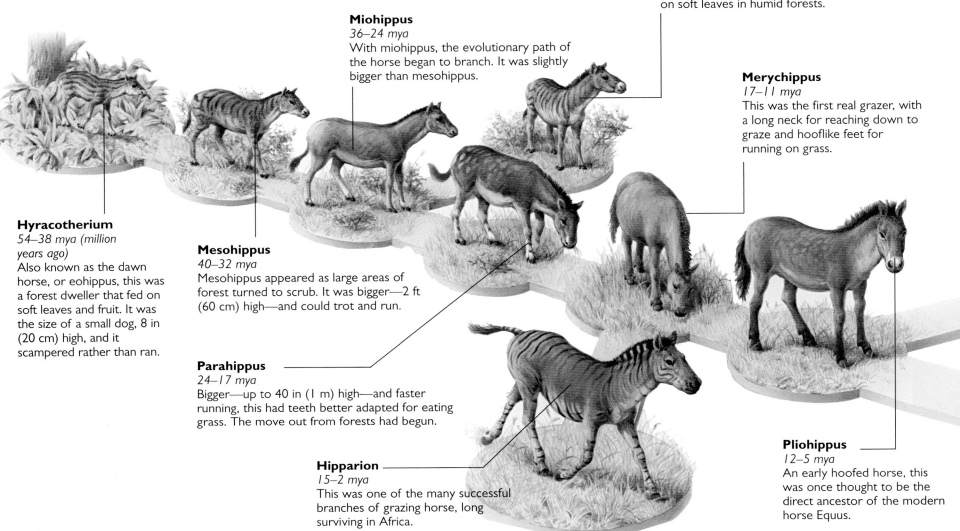

Anctitherium
25–5 mya
This successful offshoot from mesohippus survived until 5 mya in China. It browsed on soft leaves in humid forests.

Miohippus
36–24 mya
With miohippus, the evolutionary path of the horse began to branch. It was slightly bigger than mesohippus.

Merychippus
17–11 mya
This was the first real grazer, with a long neck for reaching down to graze and hooflike feet for running on grass.

Hyracotherium
54–38 mya (million years ago)
Also known as the dawn horse, or eohippus, this was a forest dweller that fed on soft leaves and fruit. It was the size of a small dog, 8 in (20 cm) high, and it scampered rather than ran.

Mesohippus
40–32 mya
Mesohippus appeared as large areas of forest turned to scrub. It was bigger—2 ft (60 cm) high—and could trot and run.

Parahippus
24–17 mya
Bigger—up to 40 in (1 m) high—and faster running, this had teeth better adapted for eating grass. The move out from forests had begun.

Hipparion
15–2 mya
This was one of the many successful branches of grazing horse, long surviving in Africa.

Pliohippus
12–5 mya
An early hoofed horse, this was once thought to be the direct ancestor of the modern horse Equus.

Desert adaptation: Rodents

Few medium-sized mammals can cope with hot, dry deserts, but deserts are home to a huge variety of tiny rodents. Rodents hide away from the sun in burrows during the day. Burrows retain the moisture of the animal's breath and stay at a steady 77–95°F (25–35°C). Desert rodents get water from their food. Some rodents have huge back legs so that they can move in leaps, and barely touch the hot ground when they come out at night.

Dwarf hamsters live in burrows in sand dunes in Central Asia, emerging at night to feed.

Dwarf hamster

Chinese hamsters are the smallest of the "ratlike" hamsters, barely 3 in (8 cm) long.

Chinese hamster

Great jerboas are one of 11 jerboa species living in the Gobi. They can jump up to 10 ft (3 m).

Great jerboa

Przewalski's horse

Most "wild" horses are descendants of escaped domestic horses—Przewalski's horse is the only living truly wild horse. It was first identified in the 1880s by Russian explorer Nicolai Przewalski. There were very few and the last one was seen in the wild in 1969. Fortunately, over 1,000 survived in zoos, and in the 1990s a handful were reintroduced to the wild in Hustain Huruu in Mongolia.

Wildlife at risk!

Snow leopard

This leopard's thick coat shields it from the cold in the mountains where it lives at altitudes of up to 19,700 ft (6,000 m). But it has suffered from both hunting and the reduction of its natural prey, such as ibexes, due to human activity. There may now be as few as 5,000.

Hippidion
5 million–8,000 years ago
Hippidion was a large offshoot of pliohippus, about 55 in (1.4 m) high, that developed when early horses spread into South America from the north five million years ago.

Equus
4 mya–present?
The first modern horse, Equus, appeared about four million years ago. It gave rise to six species: true horses, asses, onagers, and three kinds of zebra.

Zebras (*Equus burchelli*)
There are three species of zebra—the Plains (*E. burchelli*), Mountain (*E. zebra*), and Grevy's (*E. grevyi*). Each arose in different parts of Africa.

Onagers or kulans (*Equus hemionus*)
With the Asian onagers, well-adapted for life in the desert, the horse moved farthest away from its damp forest origins.

Asses (*Equus asinus*)
Asses (or donkeys) are quite similar to onagers but originated in northern Africa.

Przewalski's horse (*Equus caballus*)
The only true horse left in the wild is Przewalski's horse. Some experts think it is the ancestor of the modern horse. Others think they both descended from a common ancestor, now extinct.

Saiga antelope

With barely 330 left, the saiga antelope of Mongolia, Kalmykia and Kazakhstan is one of the world's most endangered animals. Saiga horn is used in Chinese traditional medicines along with rhino horn. As rhino hunting has been stopped, so saiga hunting has risen.

Argali

The argali is the largest living wild sheep, up to 55 in (1.4 m) high at the shoulder. Male Marco Polo argali of the Pamir range have horns 6 ft (1.8 m) long. These horns have made them the targets of illegal hunters, and the survival of the argali is now at risk.

American deserts

The southwestern corner of North America is a vast area of plains and mountains, rocky outcrops and canyons, encompassing four great deserts—the Great Basin, Mojave, Sonoran, and Chihuahuan. Each of these deserts has its own distinctive range of wildlife, from the Great Basin with its sagebrush and coyotes to the Chihuahuan with its mesquite scrub and tarantulas.

Birds of prey
Most small desert creatures are safe in their burrows, but when they come to the surface they make easy targets for birds of prey, such as prairie falcons, American kestrels, hawks, turkey vultures, golden eagles, and owls, such as the great horned and burrowing owls.

Red-tailed hawk
The red-tailed hawk is the largest hawk. The female has a wingspan of 5 ft (1.5 m). Red-tailed hawks can live in a range of habitats. In summer, they are found in northern Alaska. In winter, they are often seen soaring over the southwestern desert, scanning for prey with their sharp eyes.

Black widow spider
Black widows live in warm regions all around the world. The North American desert species is the *hesperus*. These spiders get their name because the female often kills the much smaller male during mating. The female is the U.S.'s most venomous animal, with a venom 15 times stronger than a rattlesnake's.

Insects and spiders
The teeming insect life of the deserts includes fire ants, beetles, weevils, dragonflies, butterflies, such as the western tiger swallowtail, and the Magicada cicada (which lives 17 years, longer than almost any other insect). Spiders include many large tarantulas.

Desert kangaroo rat
Kangaroo rats are rodents that hop around like a kangaroo to keep their feet off hot ground. They dig little dens under bushes, such as hopsage and blackbrush, to shelter in during the day. At night they come out to feed and stuff food into fur-lined pouches on their cheeks.

Ground birds
With so few trees, many birds in the deserts nest or feed on the ground, including Gambel's and California quails, roadrunners, inca and mourning doves, and the common poorwill. Turkeys and ring-necked pheasants are visitors to the more moist parts of the desert.

Grazing animals
The deserts are one of the last refuges for the bighorn sheep. It keeps cool here by keeping to the shade, sweating, and panting. Pronghorns live here too, and also white-tailed deer, which feed on huajillo brush, prickly pear cactus, and other shrubs.

Greater roadrunner
The roadrunner is a large ground bird of the cuckoo family that can run at 15 mph (25 km/h). It feeds mainly on insects, rodents, and lizards, but is well known as a snake-killer. It is able to dart in and stab a snake's head, grab the snake in its beak, and thrash it on the ground.

Small mammals
As in many hot deserts, there is a wealth of small mammals. Rodents, such as kangaroo rats, wood rats, and ground squirrels, stay cool by sheltering in burrows, and get their moisture from their food. Jackrabbits stay in the shade and lose heat through their big ears.

Shy mule deer
The nimble, shy mule deer is related to the white-tailed deer, and migrates into the desert from forest areas in the winter. The deer move around mostly at dawn and dusk, and on moonlit nights. In the heat of the day, they bed down in cool places. Bucks prefer to bed down on rocky ridges. Does and fawns like flatter places.

Western diamondback rattlesnake
This snake kills more people in the U.S. than any other. Like all rattlesnakes, it has horny tailpieces, which it rattles when frightened. It eats birds, small mammals, and lizards.

Reptiles and amphibians
Besides lizards, the deserts are home to rattlesnakes, whip snakes, king, coral, and gopher snakes, and also the rare desert tortoise. Amphibians survive by emerging from burrows only after rains: e.g. spadefoot toads, leopard frogs, and desert slender salamanders.

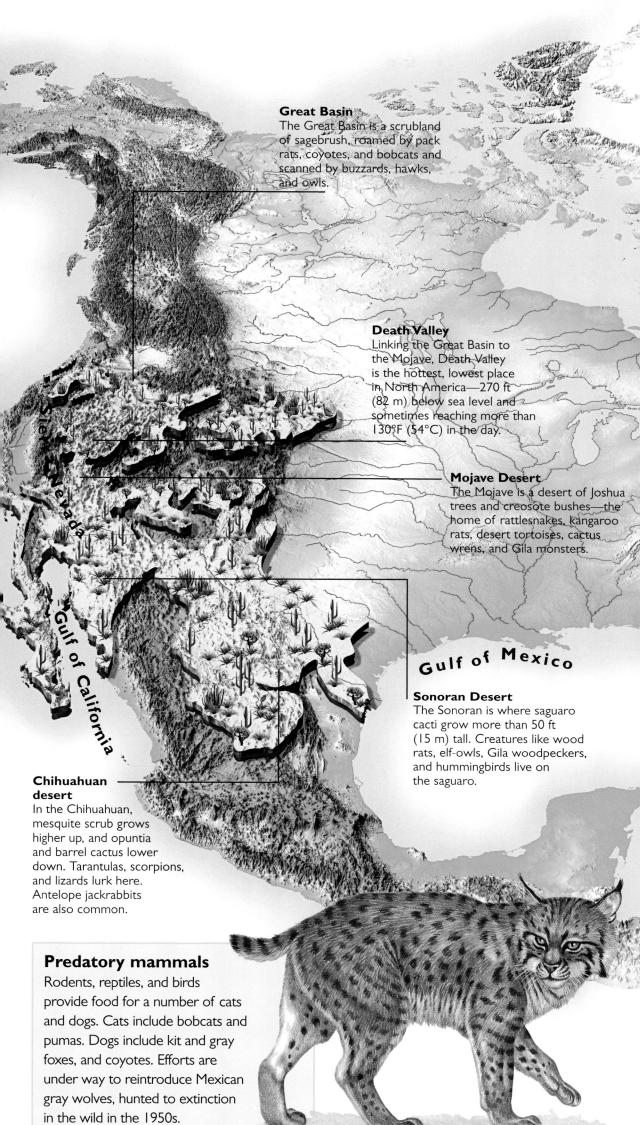

Western chuckwalla

Chuckwallas are among the largest North American lizards, second only to the Gila monster and growing up to 2 ft (60 cm) long. Despite their size, they are herbivores, and they face danger by wedging themselves into cracks, breathing in three times their normal lung capacity, to ensure a tight fit.

Lizards

The many desert lizards include swift-moving zebra lizards, fearsome-looking desert horned lizards, pretty fringe-toed lizards, desert spiny lizards, banded geckos, iguanas, and whiptails. The Gila monster is the U.S.'s largest lizard, and one of two poisonous ones. The other is the Mexican beaded lizard.

Gila woodpecker

Gila woodpeckers have an intimate relationship with the saguaro cactus. They feed on saguaro fruit and peck out cavities in the cactus to get at insects and provide a hole to raise their young. But the woodpecker's cavities rarely harm the cactus, and the bird plays a major role in dispersing its seeds.

Birds of the air

Despite the lack of trees, many birds may linger in the desert, e.g. the crowned sparrow, the warbling vireo, the rock wren, thrashers, and warblers like the hermit. Birds like the cactus wren, gilded flicker, and Gila woodpecker live here all the time.

Great Basin
The Great Basin is a scrubland of sagebrush, roamed by pack rats, coyotes, and bobcats and scanned by buzzards, hawks, and owls.

Death Valley
Linking the Great Basin to the Mojave, Death Valley is the hottest, lowest place in North America—270 ft (82 m) below sea level and sometimes reaching more than 130°F (54°C) in the day.

Mojave Desert
The Mojave is a desert of Joshua trees and creosote bushes—the home of rattlesnakes, kangaroo rats, desert tortoises, cactus wrens, and Gila monsters.

Gulf of Mexico

Sonoran Desert
The Sonoran is where saguaro cacti grow more than 50 ft (15 m) tall. Creatures like wood rats, elf-owls, Gila woodpeckers, and hummingbirds live on the saguaro.

Sierra Nevada

Gulf of California

Chihuahuan desert
In the Chihuahuan, mesquite scrub grows higher up, and opuntia and barrel cactus lower down. Tarantulas, scorpions, and lizards lurk here. Antelope jackrabbits are also common.

Predatory mammals

Rodents, reptiles, and birds provide food for a number of cats and dogs. Cats include bobcats and pumas. Dogs include kit and gray foxes, and coyotes. Efforts are under way to reintroduce Mexican gray wolves, hunted to extinction in the wild in the 1950s.

Bobcat

The bobcat may look just like a large tabby cat, but it is a fierce creature, able to kill animals as large as deer. Most of the time, however, it hunts rabbits, ground squirrels, pocket gophers, wood rats, and the occasional quail. Sometimes, bobcats raid farms for chickens and lambs—which is why many farmers hunt them. Others trap them for their pelts.

Scorching sun

Survival in hot deserts is survival against the odds for the animals that live there. Not only is there an extreme scarcity of water to cope with, but blistering heat both directly from the sun and also radiating back off the sun-scorched ground. Facing these twin threats, desert animals have developed a range of tactics. Rodents like kangaroo rats shelter in burrows during the heat of the day and gain their water from the plants they eat. Snakes, like rattlesnakes, have venom to make a kill quickly. Some animals have large ears for losing heat; others have wide mouths. Each creature has its own way of coping with the extremes.

Living with drought and heat

Lack of water is a year-round problem in the desert, and for four or five months each year, temperatures on the desert surface are too high for any creature to survive for long. This illustration shows just some of the many ways in which desert wildlife manages to stay cool, and avoid dying of thirst.

Desert adaptation:
Big ears for cooling

Desert animals have developed many techniques for losing heat. One of the most distinctive is to have large, thin ears filled with blood vessels: breezes blowing over the ears cool the blood. Black-tailed jackrabbits and kit foxes both have large ears like this.

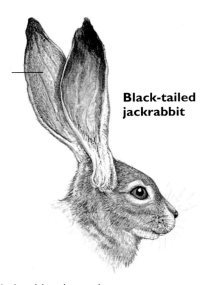

Blood vessels come near the surface and cool the blood over a large area in the jackrabbit's giant ears.

Black-tailed jackrabbit

The blood is cooled as blood vessels come near the surface inside the cool shade of the kit fox's large ears.

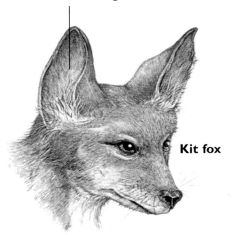

Kit fox

The elf owl avoids the heat in a hole inside the saguaro cactus.

The dark plumage of the turkey vulture soaks up heat, so it urinates on its legs to keep cool, and soars up into cooler air on thermals.

Toads, like the Sonoran green stay dormant in holes until the summer rains fill water holes. Then they emerge, breed, lay their eggs, and restock on food and water for another long wait.

Antelope jackrabbits have big ears filled with blood vessels which help the rabbit cool quickly when in the shade.

Common poorwills go into a sleep called estivation when very hot. When awake, they keep cool by gaping their beaks and fluttering their throats to evaporate water—but they must drink often to do this.

Kit foxes avoid the worst heat by curling up in burrows by day. Their paws are thickly furred to protect them from the hot ground and they have big ears to help keep them cool. They get water from their food.

Kangaroo rats shelter by day in burrows, plugging the hole to retain moisture from their breath. Chemical processes in their bodies help them turn dry seeds into water.

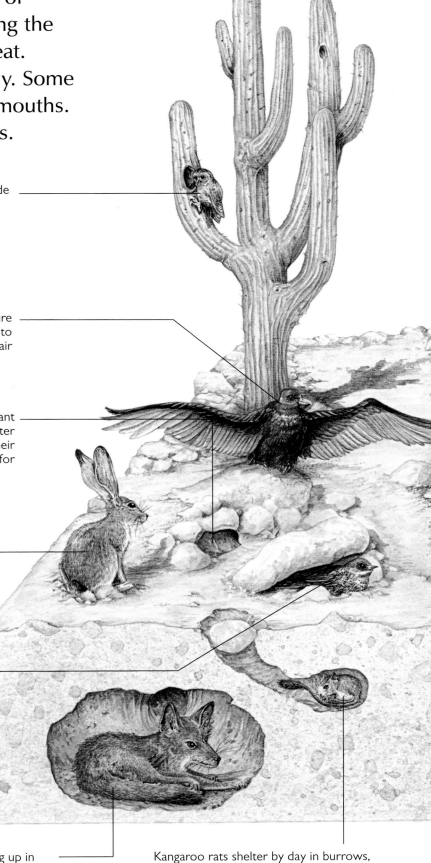

Many birds are only active in the relative cool of dusk and dawn. The kingbird is active all day, but always perches in shade under bushes.

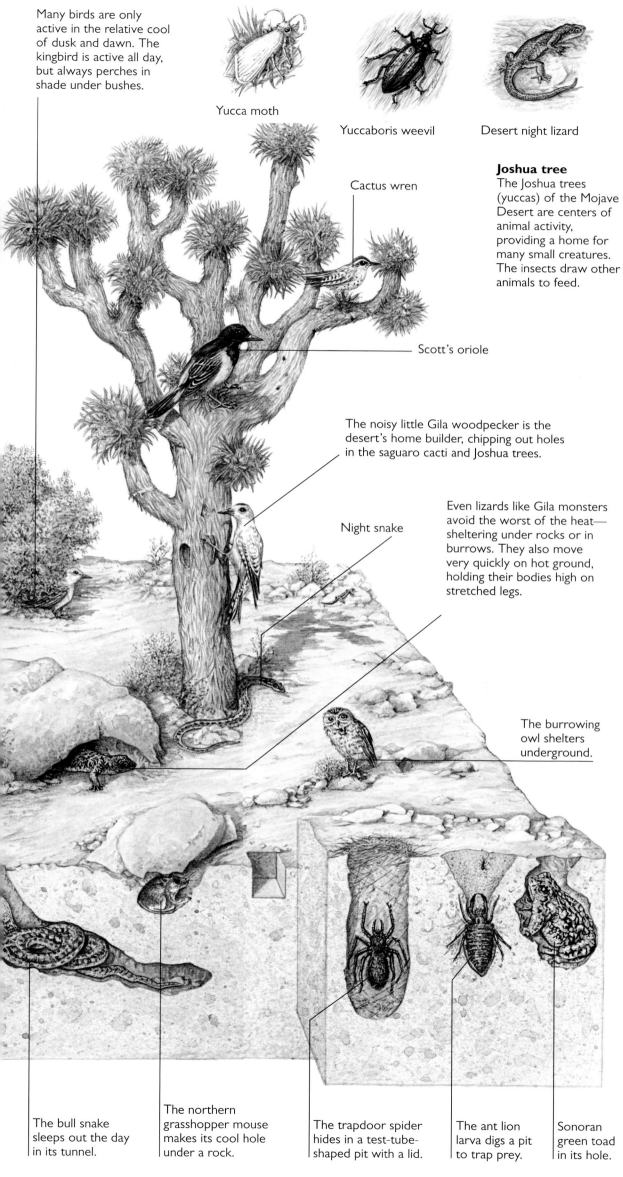

Yucca moth

Yuccaboris weevil

Desert night lizard

Cactus wren

Joshua tree
The Joshua trees (yuccas) of the Mojave Desert are centers of animal activity, providing a home for many small creatures. The insects draw other animals to feed.

Scott's oriole

The noisy little Gila woodpecker is the desert's home builder, chipping out holes in the saguaro cacti and Joshua trees.

Night snake

Even lizards like Gila monsters avoid the worst of the heat—sheltering under rocks or in burrows. They also move very quickly on hot ground, holding their bodies high on stretched legs.

The burrowing owl shelters underground.

The bull snake sleeps out the day in its tunnel.

The northern grasshopper mouse makes its cool hole under a rock.

The trapdoor spider hides in a test-tube-shaped pit with a lid.

The ant lion larva digs a pit to trap prey.

Sonoran green toad in its hole.

Wildlife at risk!

Lesser longnose bat
In the last 40 years, the lesser longnose bat (Sanborn's) has vanished from many of its old roosts, which have been vandalized. This bat pollinates and disperses seeds for many cacti, including the saguaro, so the loss of the bat could spell disaster for the saguaro.

Masked bobwhite quail
When cattle devoured the grass on the edges of the Sonoran Desert during a drought in 1892, the habitat of the masked bobwhite vanished and the bird was thought extinct. In 1964, a few were found in Mexico. It is now hoped to reestablish them in Arizona.

Mesquite bush and cattle
Once huge areas of the dry North American southwest were covered in grass. But the grass is fragile, and overgrazing by cattle can destroy it, with the soil drying out and hardening as a result. Soon, the land is colonized by tough, deep-rooted mesquite bushes. Animals that depend on the grass suffer a complete loss of habitat.

Temperate woodlands

In winter, many temperate woodlands are gaunt and cold. Deciduous trees lose their leaves to economize on the water that is hard to draw from the bitterly cold ground. Icy winds whip through bare branches, and snow may blanket the ground, leaving the wood apparently lifeless.

•

Yet come spring, the warmth of the sun starts to spread through the ground, leaf buds appear on the trees, and delicate flowers burst into bloom on the woodland floor. By summer, the trees are lush and green, and the woodland teems with life. Not all temperate woods are deciduous. Where winters are cool rather than cold—in California, around the Mediterranean, and in Australia—trees are broad-leaved (not conifers) but also evergreen. Yet even here the change from winter to summer is marked.

•

For creatures that dwell in temperate woods, survival means coping with the dramatic changing of the seasons—or, like many birds, leaving for the winter. Nevertheless, an amazing variety of animals do cope. Temperate woods may not have as many animal species as tropical forests, but they are among the richest of all animal habitats.

Where are temperate woodlands?

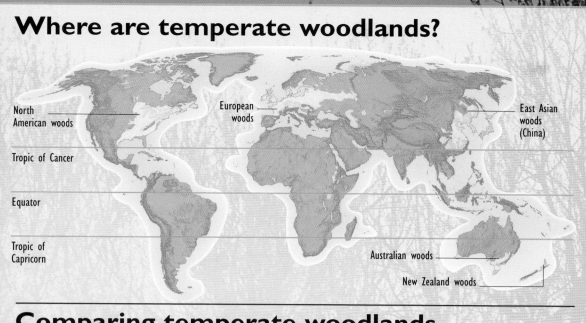

North American woods

European woods

East Asian woods (China)

Tropic of Cancer

Equator

Tropic of Capricorn

Australian woods

New Zealand woods

Comparing temperate woodlands

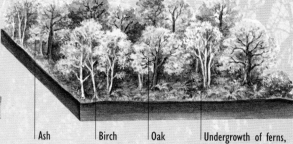

Undergrowth of sassafras | Shagbark hickory | Beech | Basswood

Ash | Birch | Oak | Undergrowth of ferns, bramble

North America

In the woods of eastern North America, trees, such as oak, beech, basswood, and hickory, spread their canopies over an undergrowth of shrubs, such as sassafras. Farther north, pine and redwood forests grow.

Eurasia

European woods vary locally, from beech woods on lime soils to oaks and birches on clay. A mixed wood may have oak, ash, and birch, with an undergrowth of thorn and bramble. Farther east, linden trees dominate.

Fir | Bamboo | Maiden-hair tree | Dawn redwood | Rhododendron, azalea bushes

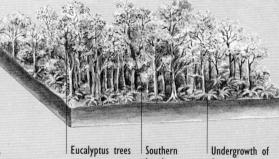

Eucalyptus trees | Southern beech | Undergrowth of ferns

China

8,000 years ago, central China was completely covered by forests of broad-leaved trees. Now these have been cleared for farms, and only pockets of woodland are left. In these grow oak and ash, as well as maidenhair and dawn redwood trees unique to China, along with dense clumps of rhododendron and azalea.

Australia

Beyond farmland on the narrow coastal plain of southeast Australia grow dense woods of gum trees (eucalyptus), mingled with dry heaths. Farther south and higher up where it is cooler and very wet—especially in Tasmania—trees change to evergreen broad-leaved southern and black beech, along with mountain ash.

Temperate woodland environments

Although not as wet as tropical forests, water is slow to evaporate in temperate woodland and there is always enough rain for trees to thrive—typically 30–60 in (760–1,500 mm) a year. In places like southeast Australia, rainfall is so high the woods are called "temperate rain forests."

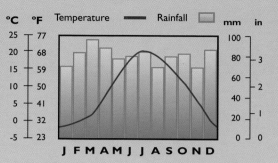

°C | °F | Temperature — Rainfall | mm | in

Sun and rain

In a typical temperate wood, such as New England, summers are warm, but winters chilly, with ground temperatures under 5°C (41°F). Frequent frosts makes it difficult for most trees to draw up water.

Woodlands in spring

In springtime, various flowers, including primroses, wood anemones, and bluebells, have a brief chance to spread across the woodland floor and bloom before the dense summer canopy of leaves closes in over them shrouding them from the sun.

Woodlands in winter

In winter, deciduous woodlands are transformed. The trees are completely bare and the wood is open to the sky. But the air is cold, and food is hard for animals to find, so only the hardiest creatures stay around.

Eurasian temperate woodlands

The supply of food in temperate woods is too seasonal for many large animals to live here. But there are many birds and small mammals—and an even greater abundance of insects and other small invertebrates. Each kind of woodland—beech, oak, mixed, pine, evergreen—attracts its own species. For example, some birds, such as redpolls, favour birch woods, while chaffinches prefer beech woods.

Rodents and small mammals
Leaves, fruit, nuts, and seeds provide a variety of food for many small mammals, and for insects which, in turn, are food for mammals. A ¼ sq mile (0.65 sq km) of woodland can support more than 5,000 mice and voles, plus many shrews, moles, hedgehogs, and squirrels.

Ground birds
The woodland floor is rich in both seeds and invertebrate life, especially in summer, providing an abundant larder for birds, such as nightingales, pheasants, and woodcocks, which wade through leaf litter probing for worms.

Ladybug
Ladybugs are brightly colored beetles that feed on tiny leaf-eating insects called aphids—which is why gardeners value them. Their bold, red color warns birds and other predators that they taste nasty. In fall, they gather to hibernate under bark or leaves.

Fat dormouse
The fat or edible dormouse has a bushy tail like a squirrel's. It even sits up to eat like a squirrel, but keeps its tail laid flat. During summer days, it sleeps in its nest high in tree branches, and comes down only to forage for nuts, seeds, and berries in the darkness. In winter, it hibernates in tree hollows or even in buildings.

Nightingale
Many birds are fine singers, but the nightingale is perhaps the most impressive. Often heard at dead of night in spring, its song is rich, varied, and loud. The nightingale is a shy bird, hiding in dense bramble undergrowth and darting out occasionally to feed on ground-living insects, such as beetles and ants.

Invertebrates
In spring, there is an explosion of invertebrate life in the wood, thriving on the new growth. The leaf litter teems with creatures, such as wood ants, centipedes, slugs, and snails, while leaves sustain beetles, may bugs, and crickets. Flies prey on other animals.

Gray wolf
The gray wolf is the largest of the dog family. Like most wolves, they live in packs made up from a pair of mature adults with a few generations of young. By working together when they hunt, they can bring down deer and other animals several times their own size.

Birds of the air
The profusion of insect life in the woodland spring draws a host of songbirds—warblers, flycatchers, chiffchaffs, and thrushes. The rich summer crop of berries, seeds, and nuts provides food for birds, such as tits, jays, and chaffinches.

Great spotted woodpecker
Like all woodpeckers, the great spotted clings to tree trunks with its strong feet and uses its long bill to drill for insects. Insects are its main food, but it also eats fruit, berries, and even nestlings of other birds. In spring, it can be heard drumming rapidly on trees to mark out its territory.

Predatory mammals
There is often too little prey in winter to sustain pure meat-eaters like big cats, though there are wildcats and lynxes. Most woodland predators, such as wolves, foxes, bears, and weasels, can survive on a range of foods in hard times.

Warm, dry woods
The woodlands around the Mediterranean are mostly evergreen, with trees, such as the cork oak and pistachio.

Browsers and foragers

Many woodland mammals mix their diet a little, and even carnivores, such as martens, often forage for fruits and nuts. The main foragers, however, are badgers and boars. Badgers feed mostly on earthworms, but also eat seeds, beetles, and fruit in fall.

Wild boar

The ancestors of domestic pigs, wild boars are sturdy animals that run fast and swim well. They tend to live alone or in small groups and they will eat almost anything—digging for bulbs and tubers, sometimes eating nuts and fruit, and at other times eating carrion.

Puss moth and caterpillar

Woodland moths feed mostly at night. By day, they sleep camouflaged in leaf litter, like lappet moths, or against tree bark, like oak tree moths. Each kind of wood attracts its own moths. Oak woods draw tortrix and puss moths. When threatened, puss moth caterpillars squirt out formic acid from their tails.

Butterflies and moths

The spring leaves of deciduous trees provide food for countless caterpillars, while adult moths and butterflies suck nectar from flowers. Purple hairstreaks flutter in oak treetops, emperors near willows, white admirals by honeysuckle. Fritillaries feed on violets on the ground.

Pockets of woodland

Much of Europe was once covered in deciduous woods, but the soil beneath the trees is so rich that much has now been cleared for farmland. Natural woods survive only in isolated pockets.

Grazing mammals

Often, only clearings have enough grass for grazing, but woodlands provide deer with shelter. Deer can also feed on tree shoots and shrubs. Woodland deer include native red, fallow, and roe deer, and introduced species, such as muntjac, sika, and Chinese water deer.

Fallow deer

Fallow deer spend the night and most of the day under the trees or in thick undergrowth, emerging at dusk and dawn to graze. Fall is rutting time. Bucks (males) herd the does (females) together and rivals fight furiously with their antlers until one retires defeated. The victor takes the harem.

Bialowieza

The Bialowieza on the Polish border is one of Europe's last great forests—home to wolves, bears, deer, and now the European bison, or wisent, which has been reintroduced from zoos.

Birds of prey

Many woodland birds and mammals fall prey to hunting birds. With short wings for weaving through trees, small hunters like sparrowhawks hunt close to the ground, ambushing prey. Big birds like golden eagles glide over woods and swoop on prey crossing clearings. Tawny and long-eared owls hunt at night.

Buzzard

The buzzard sometimes hunts by watching from a treetop perch, but more often it soars over woodland edges scanning the ground for small mammals, dropping down swiftly on to its victim. In winter, the buzzard may feed on carrion.

Woodland life

Like tropical forests, temperate woods have distinct layers, although the trees are not as tall or densely packed. The top layer is the canopy formed by the crowns of trees. Here numerous herbivores—birds, small mammals, and insects—feed on leaves and fruit. Lower down is the undergrowth of brambles and thorn, where ground birds and larger mammals find cover. The woodland floor is a deep layer of litter formed by fallen leaves, which rot slowly in the cool air. Here voles and shrews dig covered runways and there is a teeming population of insects, woodlice, centipedes, and other invertebrates.

Eurasian Badger

Badgers like to live in woods with good cover and soft, dry soil in which they can dig their setts. These huge burrow networks have a dozen or so entrances and provide a home for a male, a female or two, and cubs. Setts are passed on through the generations, and many are a century or more old. The badgers emerge at dusk to forage for earthworms, insects, plant roots, tubers, fruit, and fungi. They will even eat small mammals. In winter when food is scarce they may eat carrion.

Woodland adaptations: Songbird nest and song sites

In winter and spring especially, woods are filled with the songs of blackbirds, thrushes, and warblers. All birds call to keep in touch with each other, but male songbirds like these sing to attract a female or to proclaim their territory. Each species has its own song, which often varies through the seasons. In winter, male blackbirds sing quietly to charm females, but in spring they perch on a song post (such as a high branch) and sing out loudly to announce their territory. After finding a mate, songbird pairs build a nest, each species at a different height.

Mistle Thrush above 65 ft (20 m)

Blackbird up to 32 ft (9.8 m)

Song Thrush up to 5 ft (1.5 m)

Nightingale almost on the ground

Grasshopper Warbler almost on the ground

Willow Warbler up to 2 ft (0.6 m)

Garden Warbler up to 2–3 ft (0.6–1 m)

Woodland food web

Each tree in the wood is a world of its own, and each kind has its own range of creatures. A deciduous tree gives creatures both food and shelter and links them together in a living unit. Crucial to life in a tree are the countless insects and other small creatures in the crown that feed on the leaves and fruit, and form the base of the complex web of food dependency between the animals.

Peppered moth caterpillars eat the spring leaves of many deciduous trees. The adult is camouflaged by day against the lichen-covered bark.

Pheasants are opportunist feeders, and eat not only seeds and insects, but also lizards, small snakes, and small mammals, such as mice.

Wood mice eat berries, fruit, seeds, mushrooms, worms, and insects. They go into a torpid state in winter when food is scarce.

Long-eared owls spend the day in the abandoned nests of birds, such as crows. At night they hunt for voles, shrews, and other small nocturnal mammals, and birds.

Sparrowhawks are agile fliers that use the cover of trees to ambush birds varying in size from tiny blue tits to larger birds, such as common pheasants.

Blue tits relish the variety of food in the wood, eating all kinds of insects in summer, including caterpillars, and insects and seeds in winter.

Longhorn beetle larvae can damage trees as they tunnel through them, feeding on the living wood. Adult beetles feed on sap, pollen, nectar, or leaves.

Shrews are tiny creatures that scurry through tunnels in the leaf litter, searching for woodlice and beetles.

Woodlice are crustaceans (like crabs and lobsters), but have adapted to life on land and feed on rotting wood and vegetation.

Red foxes feed mainly on rabbits, hares, and small mammals like shrews and mice, but will eat almost anything—beetles, birds, frogs, and even garbage.

Pot worms are tiny white worms that play a key role in the soil by digesting dead organic matter. Up to 250,000 worms may be present in 1 sq yard (1.8 sq m) of soil.

Wildlife at risk!

European lynx

Because Europe has been almost entirely deforested over the centuries, there are few homes left for the lynx. Originally a woodland creature, it has been driven to refuges in mountains and scrub, especially in northern Greece, its last European stronghold. Now its very survival relies on a few specially protected areas.

Gray wolf

Europe's wolves have been subject to unremitting persecution through the ages, and they now survive in only a few pockets. Prejudice means that wolves are still threatened, but small groups have been reestablished in areas in France, Germany, and Norway.

Coppiced woodland

Few woods are entirely natural. Most are artificial or have been managed. Many woodlands are coppiced, which means that trees are cut back regularly to stimulate the growth of new, straight shoots. This helps some woodland birds and butterflies but harms others.

North American temperate woodlands

When European settlers arrived, the eastern U.S. was covered by a vast deciduous forest, in which roamed mountain lions and wolves. Much of the forest has gone, along with the lions and wolves, but pockets survive. These are home to a host of small mammals, birds, and insects. Some are able to cope with the harsh winter, often by sleeping or varying their diet. Others arrive in spring to make the most of the summer.

Cascades

Rocky Mountains

Missouri

Great Plains

Gulf of California

Sierra Madre

Rio Grande

Amphibians

Many frogs, toads, newts, and salamanders lay eggs in woodland streams and ponds and live as adults among the trees—oak toads in South Carolina, gray tree frogs in southern Canada, red efts (young eastern newts) in New Hampshire, and many more.

Spotted salamander

Spotted salamanders are among the most brightly colored woodland salamanders, often seen emerging from their winter burrows on wet spring nights. But there are many others, such as the yonahlossee of the Blue Ridge Mountains, ringed salamanders in the Missouri woodlands, marbled salamanders around the Great Lakes, and Jefferson salamanders in New England.

Insects, invertebrates

Spring leaves sustain an army of weevils and gall wasps, while a host of beetles feed on the wood of trees. But the thick leaf litter on the forest floor is one of the world's richest micro-habitats, teeming with small creatures, such as ants, centipedes, slugs, and snails.

Blue jay

Blue jays are very pretty and also very bold. Like other jays, they are noisy and aggressive, sometimes chasing songbirds and eating their eggs and nestlings. More often, though, blue jays feed on nuts and seeds, which they bury in fall, perhaps to provide a store of food for the harsh winter.

Birds of the air

Even in winter, the woods echo with the calls of birds like chickadees, titmice, woodpeckers, and even cardinals. In spring, squadrons of migrants—warblers, vireos, nuthatches, redstarts—wing in from the south to make the most of the feast of insects and new plant growth.

Sawfly

Sawflies, such as the oak slug, are a huge family of wasplike insects. Females have a sawlike tail for slicing into plants to lay eggs. When sawfly larvae emerge from their winter cocoons, they can wreak havoc as they chew through tree leaves, reducing them to skeletons.

Eastern box turtle

Box turtles get their name because their plastron (underside) is hinged, so they can fold up into a box shape to protect themselves from predators. The eastern box feeds on worms, slugs, mushrooms, and fruit. In hot summers, it may bury itself in muddy pools to keep cool.

Reptiles

Areas of wetland and fields in the woods of eastern North America provide prey and shelter for many reptiles, including wood turtles, skinks, and snakes, such as the garter snake, the rough green snake, and the copperhead.

Adirondack Mountains
In the valleys of the north, forests of sugar maple, birch, and pine are home to 54 species of mammal, including beavers, coyotes, moose, and pine martens as well as eagles and ospreys.

Allegheny Mountains
One of the few remaining pockets of the forests that once stretched right along the Appalachians. The Alleghenies provide a refuge for many creatures, such as bears, Indiana bats, and Allegheny wood rats.

Mississippi

Appalachians

Great Smoky Mountains
This is one of the last great stands of virgin deciduous wood, where tall and stately basswood, beech, and hickory trees grow.

Ground birds
Game birds, such as northern bobwhites, ruffed grouse, and introduced pheasants, grow large on seeds and berries pecked off the woodland floor and need to take off only for short flights. Ruffed grouse nest in aspens, where the female feeds on catkins as she incubates her eggs.

Turkey
Wild turkeys are large woodland birds that find their food on the ground, feeding on seeds and berries as well as plants, insects, and small reptiles. They are strong fliers over short distances. They were domesticated in Mexico over 1,000 years ago. Wild turkeys are now rare in the U.S., although they have been reintroduced in some places.

Birds of prey
Woodland trees provide perfect concealed perches for agile raptors that make sudden sallies to snatch birds and mammals. Cooper's hawks prey on bats, squirrels, and chipmunks. Sharp-shinned hawks grab small birds. Larger northern goshawks may pounce on hares.

Eastern screech owl
With their phenomenally acute directional hearing and their keen eyesight, owls can weave through the wood in almost pitch darkness and pinpoint prey, such as small nocturnal mammals, with deadly accuracy. Woodland owls include barn owls, great horned owls, and the fiercely territorial eastern screech owl, known for its eerie, rising and falling, whistling wail.

Black bear
The black bear is by far the largest woodland carnivore, up to 6 ft (1.8 m) long, weighing up to 660 lbs (300 kg), and easily able to kill small deer. But 95 percent of a black bear's diet is vegetation—grass in spring, fruits and berries in summer, nuts in fall. Sometimes, bears tear open old logs to get at worms, or forage for human food in cars and outbuildings.

Predatory mammals
In summer, woodland rabbits and hares are targets for both red foxes and bobcats. Gray foxes prey on insects and rodents—and climb with catlike agility. In hard times all three hunters turn to foods, such as fruit. In North Carolina woods, rare red wolves may be seen.

White-tailed deer
White-tailed deer are shy creatures. When threatened, they flash their white tails up to warn other deer and race for cover. They are so agile they can dart through tangled woods at 30 mph (50 km/h) and even swim rivers. Bucks develop antlers in their second fall and soon begin to fight over does with rival bucks.

Browsers and foragers
North America's only large deciduous woodland browser is the white-tailed deer. But because they feed on such a wide range of food—from leaves to fallen fruit— they can survive anywhere from the cold pine forests of Maine to the warm swamps of Florida.

Raccoon
Lively and bold, the raccoon has a "bandit" mask that reflects its opportunist way of life, eating anything from frogs to fruit. This woodland creature has adapted so well to human habitation that it can climb in windows, lift latches with its forepaws, and steal food from larders. If there is water handy, it always rinses its food clean—or at least rubs off the dirt.

Small mammals
In summer, there is a plentiful supply of insects and other invertebrates, fruit, and nuts in the woods for many small mammals, such as eastern chipmunks, voles, and Virginia opossums. They in turn are food for small carnivores, such as long-tailed weasels.

The woodland year

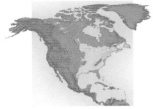

For the creatures of temperate deciduous woods, life is dominated by the seasons. No other habitat changes as much through the year, from almost arctic desolation in winter to almost tropical abundance in summer. Each creature copes in its own way, but there are four main strategies: some animals can vary their diet and lifestyle with the seasons; many birds migrate in winter; some small creatures sleep through the winter; and many insects put their development on hold until spring.

Red foxes
vary their diet, making the most of any food available.

Wild turkeys
visit the wood in winter for shelter and to feed on acorns.

Porcupines
gather in dens and come out when the weather is dry to make a short foray for bark, their winter food.

Gray squirrels
stay active all winter, relying on caches of nuts buried in fall.

Mourning cloak butterflies
spend the winter frozen alive in cracks on trees.

White-tailed deer
huddle together in areas called "deer yards" and feed on acorns.

Long-tailed weasels
turn white in winter, becoming almost invisible against the snow.

Spotted salamanders
hibernate in holes in the soil.

Winter

As the cold of winter really takes hold, warm-blooded animals can generate their own heat to avoid freezing. Cold-blooded animals must use other strategies. Insects avoid freezing by flooding their bodies with antifreeze proteins and the antifreeze fluid, glycerol. Many frogs and turtles hide in ponds under the ice. Frogs then breathe by soaking up oxygen from the water through their skin, while snapping turtles soak it up through their throat lining. Wood frogs and painted turtles actually freeze, and survive.

Winter sleep

Winter cold means animals need extra energy to function—yet food is scarce. Many small mammals survive by hibernating. So, too, do some reptiles, amphibians, and insects. Hibernation means winding down their body processes until they slip into a dormant state in which they use barely any energy. A mammal's body heat may drop below 43°F (6°C) and its heart rate to 10 beats per minute. Most hibernate in holes safe from predators. Bears do not hibernate, but doze for months in their dens.

Scarlet tanagers

Black bear

Red fox

Porcupine

Wild turkey

White-tailed deer

Ruffed grouse

Weasel

Redstarts

Groundhog

Wood frog

Spotted salamander

Snapping turtle

Spring

As spring arrives, buds appear on trees, flowers bloom, the groundhog emerges, and insects multiply. Spring azure butterflies sip on butterfly weed and monarchs lay eggs on milkweed. Birds that winter in the south, such as redstarts, vireos, tanagers, and warblers, fly in to feed on insects. Birdsong fills the air, as birds find mates and build nests.

Monarch butterfly

Woodland adaptations: Migrating birds

Most of the birds of the deciduous forest avoid the chill of winter by migrating south every fall. The route and destination vary between species, but most migrate between the same localities, using the stars and their own internal magnetic compasses to guide them with astonishing accuracy.

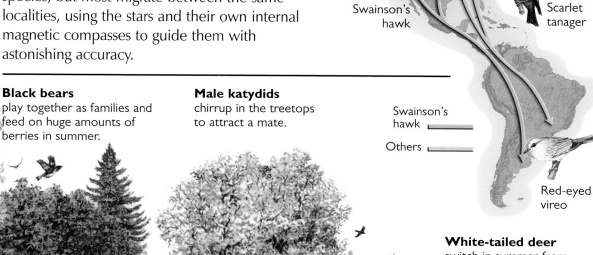

Black-and-white warbler

Swainson's hawk

Scarlet tanager

Swainson's hawk

Others

Red-eyed vireo

Black bears
play together as families and feed on huge amounts of berries in summer.

Male katydids
chirrup in the treetops to attract a mate.

White-tailed deer
switch in summer from their winter diet of acorns and twigs to green leaves and shoots. Their coats turn red.

Eastern gray squirrels
stop eating acorns in summer, and eat new growths of fungi instead.

Black bear

White-tailed deer

Eastern gray squirrel

Weasel

Chipmunk

Squirrel

Red fox

Wild turkey

Marbled salamanders
lay their eggs in dry patches in fall and guard them until they hatch in the spring rains.

Wild turkeys
head for open areas in summer and feed on berries, fruit, seeds, and insects.

Summer

In summer the trees are in full leaf. Every square yard of woodland grows 2 lb (1 kg/sq m) of plant matter. Both the plants (and the insects that feed on them) provide abundant food. All woodland animals are now at their most active. Fledgling birds begin to take to the air. Mammals born in spring grow and begin to learn how to fend for themselves.

Fall

The trees turn gold, red, yellow, and brown as they prepare for the winter drought. Songbirds flock together for the migration, taking with them the young birds born in spring. Monarch butterflies migrate, too. Animals that are staying begin to build up winter food reserves—either by eating, like deer, or by burying food "caches," as do squirrels, chipmunks, jays, and even foxes. Deer bucks seek out does and engage in mock battles with rivals.

Wildlife at risk!

Timber wolf

The timber wolf once ranged in woods from New England to the Great Lakes. It has now vanished from over 97 percent of its original range, surviving in the U.S. only in Minnesota, Michigan, and Wisconsin. With such small populations, the chances of extinction are high.

Eastern cougar

The eastern cougar is a mountain lion, native to the forests of the eastern U.S. It once roamed all over the east, but was hunted so mercilessly by settlers that it has probably been extinct for a century. Recent sightings of mountain lions in the east could be escaped pets or western cougars, not wild eastern cougars.

White-tailed deer

White-tailed deer were hunted almost to extinction in places by 1900. Then legal limits on hunting combined with deforestation reversed the decline so effectively that there are now over 15 million in North America. Deforestation replaces mature trees with bushes and shrubs so the deer can forage easily.

Asian temperate woodlands

A vast temperate forest once stretched right across the center of China through Korea and into far eastern Siberia. Most of the forest was cleared by farmers 4,000 years ago, but the remnants that survive are some of the richest and most diverse temperate forests in the world—home to a phenomenal range of plants and a host of unique animals, including the rare giant panda.

Primates

There are 18 species of monkey living in forest trees in China. Many of these, almost uniquely, live in the temperate zone, including the rare Yunnan snub-nosed, which lives in evergreen forests over 10,000 ft (3,000 m) up, where snow lies most of the winter.

Golden monkey

The golden, or snub-nosed, monkey has long, orange fur and blue patches over its eyes. It is mainly a leaf-eater and lives in high mountain forests where conifers grow alongside broad-leaved trees. Although it is hunted for its fur and for use in Chinese medicine, it is the destruction of its habitat that has put it in danger of extinction.

Red panda

Red pandas live in bamboo forests in the eastern Himalayas. They are sometimes classified as raccoons, sometimes with the giant panda. The name "panda" comes from the Nepalese for bamboo eater, but they also eat berries, acorns, and even insects and young birds.

Birds of the air

Many woodland birds fly far to avoid the winter cold, but eastern woods are often so mountainous that many, including babblers and laughing thrushes, need move to warmer places in the valleys only as winter sets in. Among the vast range of other woodland birds here are rosefinches, green-backed tits, sibias, minivets, woodpeckers, and crows.

Reptiles and amphibians

The diversity of China's woodland is matched by its amphibians and reptiles. 73 kinds of reptiles and 35 amphibians have been noted in one area. Reptiles include Reeves's turtles, blue krait snakes, and Amur and red-backed ratsnakes.

Oriental fire-bellied toad

Chinese amphibians include the biggest of all—the Chinese giant salamander, which measures over 4 ft (1.25 m) long, and the oriental fire-bellied toad, which lives in mountain streams in coastal areas. When threatened, the fire-bellied toad rears up and thrusts its fiery belly out, and emits a foul secretion through its skin.

Foraging mammals

China's most famous native animal is the giant panda, which survives now only in Sichuan, Gansu, and Shaanxi provinces, where it feeds on one type of bamboo only—unlike the more omnivorous red panda.

Asian fairy bluebird

Fairy bluebirds are brilliantly colored birds that spend most of their time high up in the branches of evergreen coral trees. Their fluting calls and their bustling search for fruit are familiar parts of the East Asian woods.

Mole shrew

Many shrews, including the rare Selanski's, Koslov's, and Gansu shrews, burrow tunnels through the thick leaf litter on the forest floor in search of insects to eat. Like moles, mole shrews (and shrew-moles) burrow right into the soil. They have tiny molelike eyes and hidden ears.

Small mammals

A huge range of small mammals are sustained by the fruits, nuts, and the abundance of insect life in the forests of the Far East, including mice, rats, and voles, such as the mandarin vole. These, in turn, provide prey for sables, Chinese minks, weasels, and martens.

Daba Shan
The mixed evergreen and oak forests that cloak Daba Shan are home to rare golden monkeys, leopards, and musk deer, as well as Reeves's pheasant and wild pigs.

Wolong
The moist mountains of Wolong are the last refuge of the giant panda, as well as home to 46 mammal species including clouded leopards and white-lipped deer, and also 225 bird species including rare pheasants.

Sichuan
Very little of the vast broad-leaved evergreen forests remain, but along the rivers black kites hunt by day and bats hunt by night. Stump-tailed macaques cling to the trees on Emei Shan mountain.

Ussuri forests
Here, on cool low coastal hills, pine grows alongside oak and walnut. This remote world is a refuge for rare Amur tigers and leopards, as well as black bears, goatlike gorals, and unique snakes like the Ussurian mamushi.

Korean woods
In oak and birch woods surviving in Korea, black bears, mandarin voles, and wolves roam. This is the home, too, of the white-bellied black woodpecker.

Insects

In every eastern forest, the ground and trees are teeming with ants, beetles, and many other insects. But China's glory is its butterflies, including the orange oakleaf (a perfect mimic of withered oak leaves), the Chinese gifu, common clippers, and the rare golden kaiser.

Predatory mammals

The rich prey of the forests supported many large predators in the past: tigers, clouded leopards, wolves, and black bears. But the shrinking of the forests—and the activities of hunters who trap them for use in Chinese medicine—have put all of these animals in grave danger.

Silkworm

Many *Bombycidae* moth caterpillars make silk, but the best known is *Bombyx mori*. The *Bombyx mori* caterpillar, or silkworm, feeds on mulberry trees and has been farmed for 4,000 years for the silk it spins to create its cocoon. Originally from China, silkworms are farmed all over the world, but are now extinct in the wild.

Takin

Takin live in dense bamboo and rhododendron thickets near the upper limits of the forest in some of the world's most rugged country, over 8,000 ft (2,400 m) up. They are clumsy-looking, solid animals, but move easily around the steep hills, looking for grass, young bamboo, and willow shoots to eat.

Ground and water birds

Nine of the world's 15 crane species—including the red-crowned crane, famed for its spectacular courting dance—hunt for fish by the rivers and lakes of the East Asian forests. Here, too, live crested shelducks, mandarin ducks, and Chinese mergansers.

Amur tiger

The Amur, Siberian, or Northeast China tiger is the largest and palest of the five tiger subspecies, and the best adapted to living in cold places. Four of the five live in China, but all are endangered, with fewer than 30 Amurs left. A few Amurs survive in Korea, and their last remaining stronghold is the pine, oak, and birch forests of Sikhote-Alin in Russia's northeast, where a few hundred have been recorded. They prey mainly on moose, wild boar, and deer.

Grazers and browsers

The forests of East Asia were once so dense and so steep that the deer living here, such as sika and eld's deer, Reeves's and Fea's muntjacs, and Siberian musks, had to be small. On open slopes high up, there are bigger white-lipped deer, blue dwarf sheep, and goatlike serows.

Copper pheasant

In among the trees of the Chinese forests strut 56 of the world's 276 species of pheasant, including some of the most splendid, such as Temminck's tragopan, monals, Reeves's pheasant, and the beautiful copper pheasant, also known as Lady Amherst's.

The lost forest

At the western edge of China, in Sichuan, the soaring Himalayas drop away into a startling landscape of high plateaus, flat basins, and deep ravines. The steep slopes are perpetually shrouded in mist, providing ample moisture for thick forests to grow. Remarkably, the special climatic conditions mean that these forests vary as much as they climb each slope as forests do from Florida to Alaska—ranging from subtropical in the valleys to alpine high up. This unique variation provides niches for the extraordinary range of animals that make western China one of the world's most special habitats.

Woodland adaptations: Giant panda

The very rare giant panda is built like a carnivore, and may be related to bears, but as the environment changed, it became vegetarian. It lives in bamboo forests above 4,500 ft (1,400 m) and feeds almost exclusively on bamboo shoots, which it grips in its forepaws to eat. To help it hold the stems, the panda's forepaw has developed an extra thumb pad.

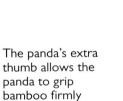

In most animals, this bone is just a wrist bone, but in the panda it has grown into an extra thumb.

The panda's extra thumb allows the panda to grip bamboo firmly while eating and to snap off shoots from the plant.

Since they spend between 12 and 14 hours a day eating, pandas sit or lie on their backs to eat. This enables them to use their paws to hold the bamboo as they chew it.

Living levels

Everywhere in the world, temperatures steadily fall as hillsides rise. But two things make Sichuan particularly special. The first is the sheer range of the changing conditions. The second is that Sichuan stands at an animal crossroads, where creatures that evolved in the Oriental tropics meet those that evolved in the Palearctic—northern Eurasia and North America. Moreover, the isolation of the deep valleys has allowed some primitive cold-climate animals, such as mole shrews, to avoid competition and survive long after they have disappeared elsewhere in the world. The various forest levels ensure there is a suitable niche for this huge range of creatures. The illustration shows some of the animals that live at different levels. Some, such as lovebirds, are limited to just one level. Others roam between them.

Musk deer

The musk deer is a small animal barely 40 in (1 m) tall that lives in bamboo forests. Males have long canine teeth instead of antlers and these are used for fighting. Musk deer have been poached heavily for the scented musk oil that male deer secrete, which is used to make perfume.

Asiatic black bear

Giant panda

Silver pheasant

Merganser

South China tiger

Golden snub-nosed monkey

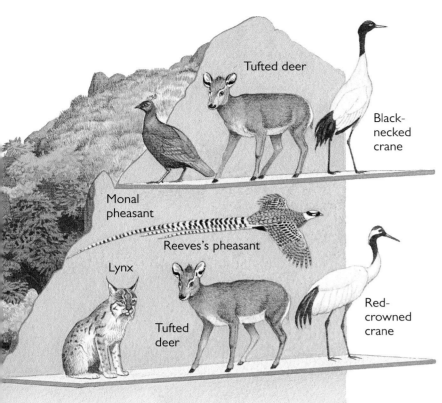

Alpine zone (above 12,000 ft/ 4,000 m)
Right at the top are open alpine meadows thinning out to bare rock just below the permanent snow line.

Tufted deer

Black-necked crane

Monal pheasant

Reeves's pheasant

Lynx

Tufted deer

Red-crowned crane

Rhododendron scrub (9,000–12,000 ft/ 3,000–4,000 m)
Near the tops of the slopes, it is too cold and dry even for conifers to survive, and the forest opens out into a scrub of rhododendron.

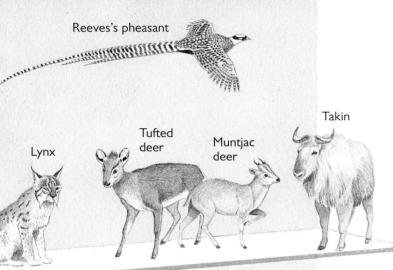

Reeves's pheasant

Takin

Lynx

Tufted deer

Muntjac deer

Cool temperate forest (6,000–9,000 ft/ 2,000–3,000 m)
At this level, the bamboos are replaced by thickets of rhododendrons and azaleas, and the conifers thin out and begin to become stunted.

Goral

Serow

Tragopan

Cloud forest (4,500–9,000 ft/ 1,400–3,000 m)
In this zone, it is cooler and wetter and frequently shrouded in a damp mist of low cloud. Here the oaks give way to dense groves of pines and fir trees mixed with tall stands of fast-growing bamboo.

Lovebird

Goral

Demoiselle crane

Serow

The lower slopes (2,000–4,500 ft/ 600–1,400 m)
The foothills support a mix of broad-leaved evergreen and deciduous trees, mostly oaks. Here and there are uniquely primitive trees: ginkgos and dawn redwoods.

61

Wildlife at risk!

Chinese alligator
The great Yangtze river and a few other rivers in China are home to the Chinese alligator. As human habitation has spread along the rivers, the alligator's survival has become increasingly threatened. There are now fewer than 500 of them left in the wild.

Giant panda
The giant panda is the best-loved of all animals in China. But its bamboo forest habitat has been destroyed by farmers and loggers, and its low reproduction rate has made it vulnerable. There are fewer than 1,000 left in the wild, and desperate measures are afoot to save them.

South China tiger
The South China tiger was hunted down by government pest controllers in the 1960s and is now the rarest of the tiger subspecies, with barely 20 left in the wild, and just 50 in captivity. Many experts think there is only a remote chance of saving it from extinction.

Australasian temperate woodlands

The far south of Australia, the island of Tasmania, and north New Zealand are so wet in places that rain forests grow, even though this is the temperate zone. Near sheltered east coasts, however, the land is warmer and drier, and here dry eucalyptus forests grow. Each area has its own range of wildlife, and isolation has made the creatures of Tasmania and New Zealand especially distinctive.

Gulf of Carpentaria

Arnhem Land

Barkly Tableland

Kimberley Plateau

Great Sandy Desert

Gibson Desert

Macdonnell Ranges

Simpson Desert

Great Victoria Desert

Southwest Australia
The warm, wandoo tree woods of the southwest are filled with birds, such as ringneck parrots and spinebills. They are also home to rare kangaroo-like bettongs and tiny, ferocious little mouselike phascogales. Rarest of all is the western swamp turtle.

Koala
The koala is one of Australia's best-known animals. It feeds at night and depends entirely on a particular type of gum or eucalyptus tree for its food. There was a time when its survival was threatened by the destruction of its native trees, but now the koala and many of its habitats are legally protected and koala numbers are recovering.

Tree-browsing mammals
In among the branches of the gum trees in the hillier areas of southern Australia and Tasmania clamber and jump many agile browsing marsupials including phalangers, brush-tailed possums, and greater gliders, which can glide 330 ft (100 m) between trees.

Insect
New Zealand has over 18,000 insect species; many are native, including thousands of kinds of beetle. But many species have been blown over by high-altitude winds from Australia, including butterflies, like the Australian painted lady.

Blue-black spider wasp
The name "spider wasp" refers to any wasp that hunts spiders to feed its young, using its sting to subdue its prey quickly. There are 4,200 species around the world, and most are blue-black in color. However, New Zealand's spider wasp is colored gold.

Tuatara
Tuataras are large, strongly built reptiles. They look like lizards, but belong to a completely different group that evolved separately over 200 million years ago. The only two species live in New Zealand. Unusually for reptiles, they can vary their body temperature to cope with cold conditions. They are also very long-lived—some are over 100 years old.

Reptiles and amphibians
New Zealand's frogs belong to a primitive group called *Leiopelma*, and have changed little in 70 million years. Eastern snake-necked turtles, oak skinks, tiger snakes, marbled geckos, and eastern brown snakes slither along the forest floor in southeast Australia.

Birds of the air

In gum tree forests, honey-eaters, which feed on insects in tree bark, are the equivalent of northern songbirds. Other birds include tiny jewel-like pardalotes, dusky robins, masked plovers, black cockatoos, and black jays.

Crimson rosella

Crimson rosellas are one of the region's many parrot species. They live mainly in the gum tree forests in southeast Australia, but escaped pets have colonized parks around Wellington, New Zealand. Green rosellas live in Tasmania. Swift parrots migrate between the two, breeding in Tasmania then returning to the mainland for winter.

Grasshoppers

New Zealand has no native mice, so their niche in the forest habitat is taken by large grasshopper-like insects called weta, and by grasshoppers, which are common in the mountain forests of South Island. Mountain grasshoppers can grow to 1¼ in (3 cm).

Weta

The word "weta" comes from *wetapunga*, a Maori name for the giant weta which means "god of ugly things." There are over 100 species of weta in New Zealand, besides the giant. Tree wetas spend the day in tree holes, with their spiked back legs sticking out. Ground wetas live in tunnels dug in the soil.

Southeast Australia
In among the scribbly gum and stringy-bark trees live extraordinary birds, such as lyrebirds and kookaburras, and many kinds of marsupial, such as koalas, quolls, bandicoots, and wombats.

Ground browsing mammals

In New Zealand, the only browsing mammals are introduced species, such as deer and chamois. But in Tasmania and southeast Australia, marsupials, including kangaroos, wallabies, and potoroos, hop around drier woodland floors.

Potoroo

Potoroos look more like giant mice than kangaroos, but they are part of the kangaroo family and bound along on their strong hind legs. Their favorite food is underground fungi, which they dig up with their forepaws, but they also eat seeds, roots, bulbs, and insects. Occasionally, they venture into gardens at night and dig up seedlings to search for fungi and insects.

New Zealand

Tasmania
Cut off from the rest of Australia, this is home to unique creatures, such as Tasmanian devils and thornbills, and rare creatures, such as pygmy possums and duckbilled platypuses.

South Island
Woods here are filled with birds, such as bellbirds, tuis, the Okarito kiwi, and the tiny rifleman.

North Island
In among soaring kauri trees live rare kokako birds, kiwis, and kakapo and kaka parrots.

Kookaburra

Famous for their raucous cry, laughing kookaburras live in the bushlands of eastern Australia. They are the largest member of the kingfisher family, but they prey on lizards, snakes, small mammals, and frogs rather than fish, often beating their victims against a rock to kill them.

Predatory mammals

New Zealand's only predators are introduced cats, dogs, and stoats. Since wolflike thylacines were wiped out in the 1930s, Tasmania has had a handful of small marsupial hunters, such as bandicoots, quolls, and devils.

Tasmanian devil

Spine-chilling screeches, black fur, and a fierce look earned this puppy-sized creature its name. Its jaws are so powerful, it can crush bone, and it eats its prey whole—bones, fur, and all. Yet it is not a hunter; it is a scavenger that feeds on the carcasses of birds, wombats, and sheep.

Superb lyrebird

The superb lyrebird is one of the two kinds of lyrebird that live in the gum tree forests. It feeds mainly on insects on the ground. When courting, males fan out their beautiful tails, which resemble a harplike instrument called a lyre. They then make an amazing array of sounds, accurately mimicking anything from other birdsongs to the whine of a chainsaw.

Ground birds

The absence of predators has meant that many New Zealand birds, including the brown kiwi, kakapo parrots, takahes, saddlebacks, and stitchbirds, have lost the power of flight. Most ground birds in Tasmania, such as pheasants, are introduced, as they could not fly there themselves.

Birds of prey

New Zealand has very few birds of prey, apart from the karearea falcon, but introduced ravens take nestlings. The open gum tree forests of southern Australia and Tasmania, however, provide good hunting for wedge-tailed eagles, whistling kites, and other raptors.

Safe on the ground

The two most remarkable features of New Zealand's wildlife are its lack of native mammals, apart from two bat species, and its abundance of flightless birds, such as kiwis and kakapos. There were no mammals because the islands of New Zealand broke away from the rest of the world's continents and became isolated 190 million years ago—long before mammals really developed elsewhere. Without mammals to prey on them, New Zealand birds had much less need to fly—and so flightless birds either survived or evolved there. New Zealand remained a safe haven for flightless birds until humans arrived bringing predatory animals, such as cats. Now most of these birds are extinct or endangered.

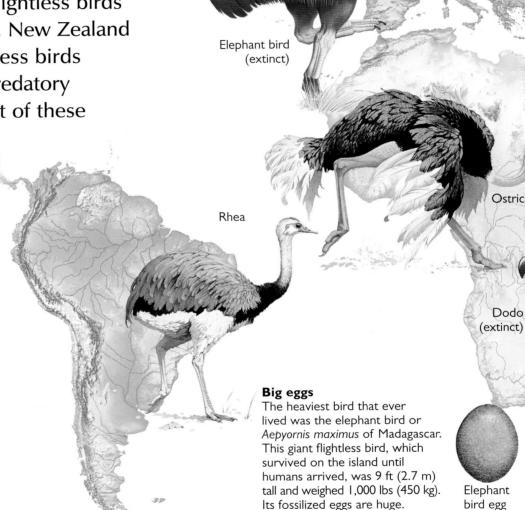

Elephant bird (extinct)

Ostrich

Rhea

Dodo (extinct)

Flightless birds

Each of the southern continents has its own large flightless bird—the South American rhea, the African ostrich, the Asian cassowary, the Australian emu, and the New Zealand kiwi, along with its now extinct giant moa. These birds, called ratites, are probably similar because they all descended from a flightless bird that evolved when the continents were joined together 100 million years ago. But some experts believe that the New Zealand birds are unique and lost the power of flight only after the islands became isolated.

Big eggs
The heaviest bird that ever lived was the elephant bird or *Aepyornis maximus* of Madagascar. This giant flightless bird, which survived on the island until humans arrived, was 9 ft (2.7 m) tall and weighed 1,000 lbs (450 kg). Its fossilized eggs are huge.

Elephant bird egg   Ostrich egg   Hen egg

Woodland streams: Duckbilled platypus

Like New Zealand, Australia's isolation has endowed it with unique creatures, such as the duckbilled platypus with its ducklike beak, webbed feet, and beaver-like tail. Along with the echidna, the platypus is the only monotreme, or egg-laying mammal. Monotremes were probably the first ever mammals and survived in Australia in isolation long after mammals that give birth to fully developed babies took over elsewhere.

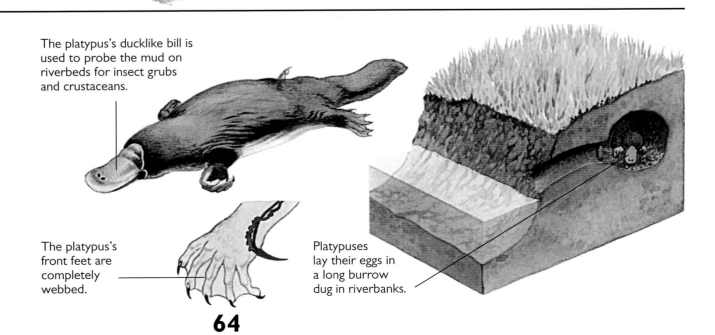

The platypus's ducklike bill is used to probe the mud on riverbeds for insect grubs and crustaceans.

The platypus's front feet are completely webbed.

Platypuses lay their eggs in a long burrow dug in riverbanks.

Gondwanaland

The world's continents are not fixed in one place but drifting slowly around the world. 100 million years ago, at a time when dinosaurs ruled the Earth and birds were just beginning to evolve, all the southern continents were joined in a huge landmass scientists call "Gondwanaland."

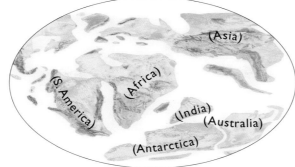

Gondwanaland breaking up about 60 million years ago.

Confucius bird

The earliest bird with a beak, dating back 130 million years, is *Confuciusornis*, fossils of which were found in Liaoning, China.

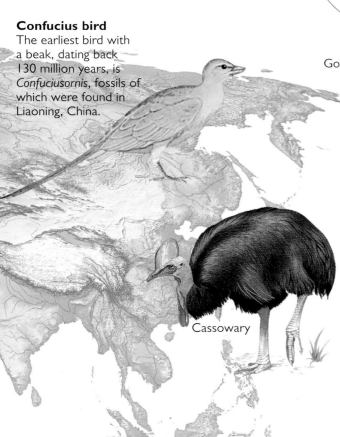

New Zealand's flightless birds

Until humans arrived, New Zealand had flightless moas, such as *Dinornis maximus*, which grew to 15 ft (4.5 m) tall, and the smaller *Emeus crassus*. The modern kiwi is the last surviving moa. New Zealand also has other, unrelated, flightless birds including the kakapo—the world's only flightless parrot—the weka, and the takahe.

Cassowary

Emu

Giant Moa
Dinornis maximus
(extinct)

Moa
Emeus crassus
(extinct)

Kakapo

Takahe

Kiwi

Koala

Among Australia's many unique creatures is the koala. Although it is sometimes called a koala bear, it is not even closely related to bears. In fact, it is a marsupial and female koalas have a pouch. Although this opens downward, young koalas never seem to fall out, even though koalas are climbing animals and the mother clambers around trees energetically. Koalas feed entirely on the leaves of gum trees (eucalyptus), sleeping by day and feeding at night. They get all their water from their food, so never need to come down from the branches.

65

Wildlife at risk!

Kakapo

New Zealand's flightless kakapo is the world's largest parrot, as big as a chicken—and the most endangered. Fewer than 130 survive, and all have been moved to offshore islands to save them from cats and dogs from which, being flightless, they cannot escape.

Eastern quoll

The eastern quoll is a lithe night hunter, like a small cat, and preys on lizards, small birds, and mammals. It has suffered greatly from the arrival of cats and dogs in Australia. It was last seen on mainland Australia in the 1960s, and now survives only in Tasmania.

Giant weta

New Zealand's giant weta is a huge insect that grows nearly 4 in (10 cm) long and weigh 2.5 oz (70 gms). The introduction of rats and stoats to the mainland has driven the giant and other wetas almost to extinction. They now survive only on mountains or offshore islands.

Temperate grasslands

Wide, open, natural grasslands once stretched far across the interiors of North America and Asia. Here, well away from coasts and their moisture-laden winds, it is too dry for trees to grow, yet there is enough rain and snow to nourish a rich growth of grass each spring. Vast tracts have been taken over for farming, but a great deal of the natural habitat remains.

•

From a distance, grassland can appear to be a monotonous, bleak place for animals to live. Even on calm summer days, a breeze usually ripples through the grasses; in winter, when snow falls, blizzards can roar unhindered across the plains.

•

But grass has hidden advantages. While most plants grow from their tips, grass grows from near the ground, so it can be grazed with minimal damage. Grazing animals, which cope with the lack of shelter by gathering in huge herds, find plentiful food. Grass puts down deep roots, too, softening the soil and making it perfect for burrowing creatures. So, while the surface is placid, there may be a hive of activity underground as little creatures sleep, eat, and dig.

Where are temperate grasslands?

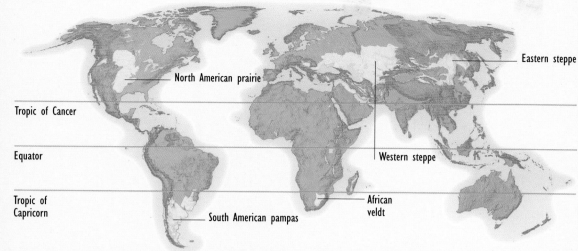

Eastern steppe

North American prairie

Tropic of Cancer

Equator

Western steppe

Tropic of Capricorn

African veldt

South American pampas

Comparing temperate grasslands

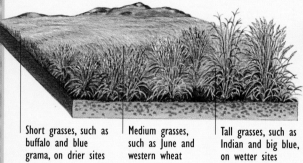

Short grasses, such as buffalo and blue grama, on drier sites | Medium grasses, such as June and western wheat | Tall grasses, such as Indian and big blue, on wetter sites

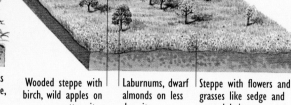

Wooded steppe with birch, wild apples on wetter sites | Laburnums, dwarf almonds on less dry sites | Steppe with flowers and grasses like sedge and crested hair

North American prairies

Hundreds of kinds of grass grow in the prairies, and as rainfall decreases to the west, so the grasses change. On the high, dry Western Plains, short grasses, such as buffalo grass and blue grama, grow. These are under 20 in (50 cm) tall, which is why it is called shortgrass prairie. Farther east is mixed grass prairie—grasses like June grass grow up to 5 ft (1.5 m) tall. In the moist east some tallgrass prairie remains, where Indian grass and big blue stem grow 10 ft (3 m) tall.

Asian steppe

The Asian steppes stretch farther across the continent than the American prairies, and so get very dry in the east. So the grasses that grow here, such as steppe feather and fescue, are short, which is why grassland with short grass may be called steppe (and grassland with tall grass, prairie). Where the ground is undulating enough to retain water, isolated trees like laburnums and dwarf almonds grow. In the moister west, clumps of wild fruit trees or birch grow, creating what is called wooded steppe.

Temperate grassland environments

Far from coasts, temperate grasslands have "continental" climates with extremes between seasons. Summers are warm and humid, with an average temperature of 64°F (18°C); winters are cool and dry, averaging 50°F (10°C). Rainfall averages 10–20 in (250–500 mm) over the year.

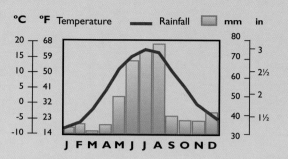

°C | °F Temperature   — Rainfall   mm   in

J F M A M J J A S O N D

Rain and snow

Most rain falls in the summer from thunderclouds, but a great deal of the grassland's moisture comes from the snow that falls in winter. This acts as a reservoir to start the growing season.

Russian steppes

Like the prairies, the steppes are places of unforgettable beauty in the spring, when the snows melt and warm sun bathes the damp ground. At this time, a carpet of flowers quickly covers the ground—countless tulips and foxgloves turning the land vivid red; sage coloring it sky blue.

The Great Plains

Thunderstorms are frequent in late summer on the prairies, and many lone trees are scorched by lightning. But more frightening still are the tornadoes, the violent corkscrew winds that often whirl beneath them.

North American temperate grasslands

Before the Europeans came, the mid-American prairies and the Great Plains to the west were an endless sea of rippling grass, roamed by huge herds of bison. Although much of the prairie is now under farmland, especially in the east, large wild areas remain. Here, although the bison and other large animals are gone, there is an abundance of small mammals, birds, and insects.

California Central Valley is known for its blooms of California poppies. Large herbivores, such as longhorn antelopes, wapiti, and mule deer, live here along with small animals, such as kangaroo rats and ground squirrels.

Prairie falcon

Prairie falcons are fast-flying birds that pursue their prey across open country. They can fly low over the ground at speeds of up to 45 mph (70 km/h) before accelerating for a quick strike. Sometimes they swoop down on prey from 3,280 ft (1,000 m) up. They feed on rodents, such as prairie dogs and chipmunks, or birds, such as horned larks, mountain bluebirds, pipits, and doves.

Birds of prey

Small mammals have to come to the surface from their burrows every now and then. Once there, with no vegetation to hide in, they make easy targets for birds of prey, such as ferruginous hawks, prairie falcons, Swainson's hawks, Mississippi kites, northern harriers, and golden eagles.

Black-tailed prairie dog

Originally named *petits chiens* (little dogs) by French explorers, prairie dogs are actually rodents, and live in vast underground colonies called "townships." There were once up to five billion prairie dogs on the prairie, but the arrival of farms has cut their numbers by 98 percent.

Ground birds

With little cover in the prairies, birds must be able to fly to escape predators, so there are few ground birds, except prairie chickens and sage grouse. In the past these survived by sheer weight of numbers. Now farming has reduced them to small groups.

Small mammals

Little shelter means the prairie's small mammals are nearly all burrowers. These include cottontail and white-tailed rabbits and many other rodents, such as ground squirrels, pocket gophers, prairie voles, pocket mice, plains harvest mice, and deer mice.

Reptiles

The cold winters on high prairies limit reptiles, most of which live in burrows to avoid predators. Lizards include short-horned, sagebrush, and northern prairie. Snakes include copperheads and blue racers.

Greater prairie chicken

Prairie chickens feed on leaves, fruit, and grain, and catch grasshoppers in summer. When courting, males move into special "booming grounds," or leks. Here on spring mornings, each male puffs out his chest and inflates air sacs on his neck to make a loud booming sound. He then struts around the lek trying to outdo his rival males.

Gopher snake

The gopher snake lives in burrows and feeds on mice and gophers, small birds, and lizards. It kills its prey by squeezing it in its coils until suffocated. It mates in spring, and the female snakes lay eggs in a burrow.

68

Grazing mammals

70 million American bison once roamed the prairies in huge herds, but they are now almost extinct in the wild. Now the prairie grazers are the agile pronghorns and white- and black-tailed deer, which rely on speed for escape rather than bulk and numbers.

The Northern shortgrass prairie stretches from Alberta to Wyoming. It is the largest grassland in North America, home to a rich variety of animals, including mammals like white-tailed deer, cougars, and bobcats, and birds, such as ferruginous hawks, sharp-tailed grouse, and mountain plovers.

The Flint and Osage Hills are the last large area of tallgrass prairie. They were once home to vast herds of bison and wapiti. Greater prairie chickens are still common.

The Western shortgrass prairie stretches from Nebraska to New Mexico and is home to a wealth of butterflies, birds, and mammals, such as prairie dogs.

Pronghorn

Named after the prong on its horn, the pronghorn looks a little like an antelope but is the only member of its family. It is one of the fastest mammals, able to reach speeds of 40 mph (65 km/h). In winter, herds of 1,000 or more may gather for shelter. In summer, they split into smaller groups.

Invertebrates

The prairie soil teems with microlife—harvester ants, nematode worms, and earthworms. In summer, the surface buzzes with insects. Honeybees hum and tiger beetles scurry, while silver-spotted skippers and other butterflies flutter, and crickets and grasshoppers chirrup. In winter, bees huddle in hives, butterflies migrate or stay as pupae; other insects hide in the soil.

Harvester ant

Huge colonies of these ants burrow in the soil, and can move as much soil as earthworms. They feed on seeds and when they find a supply, they leave scent trails to guide others.

Birds of the air

In summer, many birds, including yellow warblers, American redstarts, and vesper sparrows, fly in from the south to feast on the insects and other invertebrates that appear above-ground. Others, like chickadees and eastern kingbirds, stay all year round.

Western spadefoot toad

Spadefoot toads, such as the plain and the western, are easily missed because they spend much of their time underground, coming out at night to forage for insects. Their wedge-shaped hind feet act like spades to help them dig through loose soil. Unlike other toads, the spadefoot's bulging eyes have vertical, elliptical pupils.

Eastern meadowlark

The eastern meadowlark, which builds its nest on the ground, is well-adapted to summer on the open prairies. It walks about, flicking its tail and using its sharp beak to probe the grass for worms and other creatures. In spring, the male courts the female by showing his yellow breast and pointing his beak skyward. He defends his territory with a rich, bubbling song.

Amphibians

The melting of the winter snow and the first spring rains leave shallow sheets of water in tallgrass and mixed-grass prairie. Here, amphibians, like the plains leopard frogs, Wyoming toads, Great Plains narrow-mouthed red toads, and black-spotted newts, can lay their eggs.

Predatory mammals

The bison herds that once dominated the prairies were too intimidating for even a big predator to tackle, and today prairie predators are small. Swift foxes, coyotes, and bobcats grab rodents as they emerge from burrows, but black-footed ferrets chase them right inside.

Bobcat

Bobcats are about the size of a domestic dog, and look similar to a small lynx, but with bolder markings. They live everywhere from the deserts of Mexico to the northern forests of Canada. They tend to hunt cottontail rabbits in the south and snowshoe hares in the north, but may attack deer in winter, and occasionally eat animal remains.

Prairie prey

Life is not uniformly spread across the prairies. Instead, it clusters around hot spots, such as streams and springs, isolated trees, or sheltered valleys. But the hottest spots of all are prairie dog colonies. The prairie dog is what is called a "keystone" species—a species that is central to the well-being of the other animals in the habitat—and they have done more to shape the prairie's wildlife than perhaps any other creature. More than 200 other wildlife species have been seen on or near the colonies, and many depend on the prairie dogs for their food or habitat.

Prairie dog central

A prairie dog "town" is an elaborate burrow of tunnels where thousands of animals live together. The burrows are so big that all kinds of creatures find homes within them, from deer mice to salamanders. The prairie dogs' tireless burrowing also works over the soil, so that plants grow better. Their foraging activities and droppings promote plant growth still further, so that a rich green mix of grasses and forbs (broad-leaved plants) grows up, providing a feast for grazers, such as bison. The prairie dogs are also prey for hunters, from swift foxes to hawks.

Prairie adaptations: Butterfly country

The stunning spring and summer flowers of the prairie attract a host of butterflies, including skippers, whites, satyrs, blues, sulphurs, and red admirals. Each has its favorite plants. Most caterpillars feed on greener plants, while the adults choose sweet flowers. However, some adult butterflies feed on the same plant as the caterpillar, such as monarchs, which feed on milkweed.

One of the most common butterflies on the prairie, the silver spotted skipper, sips on the flowers of knapweed, butterfly weed, and joe-pyeweed.

Buckeye butterflies usually feed only on plantain as caterpillars. As adults, they prefer aster, knapweed, and chicory.

Clouded sulfur butterflies feed on aster, morning glory, and lantana, while their caterpillars feed on senna.

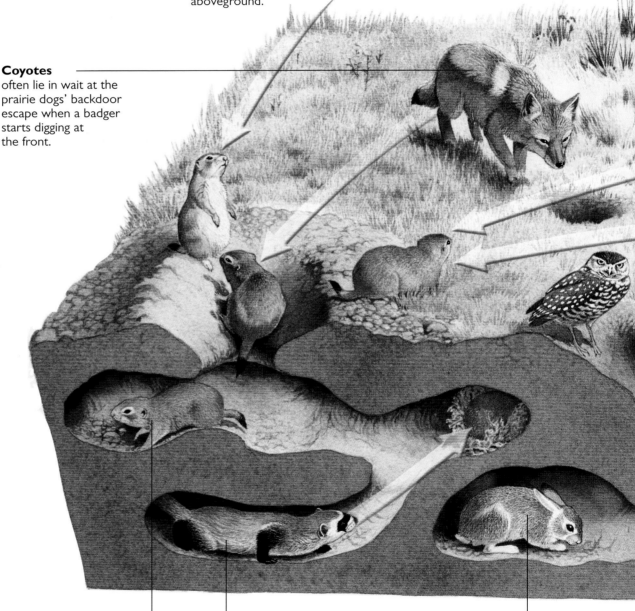

Hawks hover over prairie dog colonies and try to catch them aboveground.

Coyotes often lie in wait at the prairie dogs' backdoor escape when a badger starts digging at the front.

Prairie dogs feed aboveground during the day but use the burrows as a bolthole to escape predators, as a place to sleep at night, and to rear their young.

Black-footed ferrets feed almost exclusively on prairie dogs and, being so slender, can easily slip in and drag a victim off to their own part of the burrow.

Cottontail rabbits often live in abandoned prairie dog burrows. Both rabbits and prairie dogs eat the same plants, so if the rabbits come out during the day, the prairie dogs chase them away.

70

American bison

These massive grazing animals feed on wheat grass, buffalo grass, and other similar grasses. They got the name "buffalo" from French explorers who called them *les boeufs* when they saw them in herds of 100,000. Tens of millions of bison perished after the Europeans arrived, and by the mid-1800s the bison was close to extinction. Moves to protect them succeeded, and there are now 125,000 of them in small groups.

American bison
like the fresh plant growth stimulated by the prairie dogs' constant clipping of the grass. They wallow in the dust to get rid of insect pests.

Swift foxes
prey on prairie dogs if they are still out eating as night falls.

Mountain bluebirds
feed in winter on beetles and flies that live in prairie dog colonies. They hover over the burrows to spot their prey, or perch nearby.

American badgers
dig into prairie dog burrows at night to catch them sleeping. The prairie dogs have a backdoor escape route.

Mountain plovers
like to nest in the short grass created by prairie dog grazing, especially on bare soil where the prairie dogs dig.

Eastern tiger salamanders
are one of many amphibians happy to take advantage of the shelter provided by the township.

Burrowing owls
make their nests in old prairie dog burrows. When alarmed, their young make sounds like rattlesnakes.

Prairie rattlesnakes
occasionally move into prairie dog burrows. They sometimes prey on young prairie dogs, but adults gang up and chase the snakes away.

Badgers
may often take up residence once they have dug into a burrow to get at the prairie dogs.

Wildlife at risk!

Black-footed ferret

This is the most endangered mammal in North America. So reliant is it on prairie dogs for food, that the extermination of prairie dogs by farmers drove numbers down to just 18 in 1985. These 18 were captured and there are now 300. Some have been reintroduced into the wild.

Swift fox

Swift foxes get their name because they can run at 40 mph (65 km/h) and, as they are tiny (the size of a domestic cat), they appear even faster. Swift foxes took poison that was meant for prairie dogs and coyotes, and their habitat has almost vanished. As a result, they are now extinct in Canada and rare in the U.S.

Tallgrass prairie

Tallgrass prairie was once one of the beauties of North America, with grass growing "high as an elephant's eye" and with a profusion of flowers, songbirds, and insects. Now, there is little of it left, for the rich soil beneath it has been taken over by farms almost everywhere.

Eurasian temperate grasslands

The steppes of Asia form a seemingly endless band of waving feather and fescue grass stretching a quarter of the way around the world. Bleaker still in winter than the prairies—especially on the high Eastern Steppe beyond the Altai mountains—they bloom profusely in summer. Countless small mammals last out the winter under the ground to make the most of the summer bounty. Many more birds and grazing animals arrive in spring.

Foraging mammals

The steppes are one of the last strongholds of the wild boar, which forages over wide areas, digging up the ground with its nose to find bulbs and tubers. Boars live mostly in forest steppes where the food is more varied. Here, too, live Eurasian badgers.

Eurasian badger

Eurasian badgers are very distinctive creatures, with their long black-and-white-striped snouts. They live in family groups in huge burrows or setts with dozens of entrances—the record is 200. Every night, they emerge to hunt for earthworms, insects, and anything else that takes their fancy, usually following exactly the same route every time.

Birds of the air

In spring, many birds wing into the steppes to feed on the spring explosion of insect life: they include crested larks, chaffinches, northern starlings, and golden orioles. Great tits and Eurasian rollers nest here all year-round.

Crested lark

There are few perches in the steppes, so the crested lark, like many grassland songbirds, must deliver its song on the wing. Its song is musical and chatty, and it often mimics other birds. It arrives in spring, and spends most of the summer on the ground, searching for insects.

Pallas's cat

Pallas's cat is a predator no bigger than a small dog, 2 ft (60 cm) long. It is an elusive, solitary creature that lives in caves and rock crevices, or takes over a burrow from another creature, such as a marmot. It sleeps during the day and emerges at night to hunt for birds and small mammals, such as mice and hares.

Predatory mammals

Wolves are less common than they once were, but many smaller predators, including pine and stone martens, and Siberian polecats, feed on the abundance of rodents. Rare snow leopards inhabit the high steppes of Central Asia.

Small mammals

There is little shelter on the steppes for small mammals, but a host of rodents, such as ground squirrels, jerboas, gerbils, marmots, and pikas, live in the soil. Voles, rabbits, and hares scamper through scrub and forest steppe.

Ukrainian steppe
Here, where forest mixes with grass in the damp climate, much grassland has been lost to farming. But surviving pockets are home to a host of animals from roe deer to meadow vipers.

The Kirghiz-Kazakh steppe
This is the world's largest area of dry steppe, home to steppe marmots and pikas, saiga antelopes, and corsac foxes, as well as many birds, such as pallid harriers.

Caspian Sea

Aral Sea

Pamir Mountains

European water vole

Water voles are good swimmers and dig into riverbanks if they are near a river or stream, but they often live in the steppes far from water. Grasses and other plants are their main food, and they can survive in dry conditions by burrowing into the soil.

Locust

Grasslands are home to thousands of kinds of Orthoptera—some predators, like crickets and katydids, others plant-eaters, like grasshoppers. The most voracious plant-eaters are grasshopper species, called locusts, that form swarms. Swarms of locusts, billions-strong, occasionally appear in the steppe and devour 100,000 tons of plant matter in a day.

Insects

For most insects, grass provides quite enough shelter from the elements, and the steppes are home to a huge range of them including ants, stag beetles, and blister beetles. The spring flowers attract thousands of species of bee and butterfly, such as swallowtails.

Pallas's snake

The abundant rodent life beneath the grass provides good hunting for Pallas's snake. Like all rat snakes, it is slow-moving and relies on ambush to capture prey. Up close, it can "see" an animal's body heat through grass. It is not poisonous and kills by constriction, but when threatened it may discharge a foul liquid from its anal gland.

Birds of prey

So exposed are grassland rodents and reptiles on the surface that many birds of prey hunt here, including pallid harriers, imperial, white-tailed, and short-toed eagles, rough-legged hawks, and lesser kestrels. The growth of farming has made all of these rarer.

Steppe eagle

The steppe eagle is one of the biggest raptors, with a wingspan of over 30 in (80 cm). Like the golden eagle, it is a "booted" eagle, which means it has feathered legs. It is a superb flier and preys on rodents and reptiles, patiently cornering its victims by flying slowly, low over the grass.

Reptiles and amphibians

Rodent burrows are often taken over by grassland reptiles, such as vipers and the Mongolian racerunner lizard, which uses speed to escape when above ground. Briefly in spring, pools teem with frogs, such as the Asiatic grass frogs, which then go to ground in the heat of summer.

Saiga antelope

The saiga antelope is the steppe equivalent of the prairie's pronghorn. They are fast-running grazing animals belonging to a group of animals called goat-antelopes that also includes chamois and ibex. They live mainly in small herds, but join big herds to migrate in spring.

Grazing mammals

The rare European bison is seen only on the far western steppes, while moose venture in from the north. Here and there are small herds of roe deer. Every year, winter sees a spectacular migration of herds of Mongolian gazelles down from the high plateaus of Tibet. On the high steppes in Central Asia, ibex, Tien-Shan and Karatav mountain sheep, and argali clamber over slopes.

Great bustard

The male great bustard is the world's heaviest flying bird, weighing up to 40 lb (18 kg). In the breeding season in spring, males gather at a traditional display ground to put on a display for the females—puffing out their chests, and spreading their tails and wings to reveal white feathers. The rest of the year, bustards are on the move, searching for plants to eat.

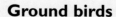

Qinghai-Tibet plateau
Too cold and remote for farming, the high mountain steppe is one of the world's few large intact ecosystems. Here live large herds of grazers, such as Tibetan antelopes (chiru), Tibetan gazelles, argali sheep, and kiang horses, as well as rare predators, such as snow leopards and lynxes.

Mongolian-Manchurian steppe
The vast steppes of East Asia are one of the world's largest areas of grassland. Huge herds of Mongolian gazelle still roam here, along with birds, such as bustards and plovers. In the marshes and reedbeds breed huge flocks of Oriental white storks and demoiselle cranes.

Ground birds

There are few trees to nest in on the steppes, but bustards and quails nest in the grass, where quails forage for insects and bustards browse on leaves and buds. Near water, white-naped cranes, flamingoes, curlews, white-headed ducks, and many others gather.

Altai Mountains
Lake Baikal
Gobi Desert

73

Life under grass

Herds of large herbivores, such as saiga and deer, are a conspicuous feature of the steppe landscape, but much of the grazing is done by unseen mouths—countless small burrowing mammals that emerge each day to feed on grass, shoots, and buds. These small mammals—mostly rodents, such as marmots, ground squirrels, and hamsters—play a crucial part in the steppe's ecosystem by bringing millions of tons of fresh soil to the surface each year as they burrow. These small mammals, in turn, are kept in check by predators, such as polecats and eagles.

Life underground

For many animals in grasslands, underground is the safest place to be. Here they are not only sheltered from the elements, especially the worst winter weather, but hidden from most predators. Rodents are the chief grassland burrowers, but there are also a few amphibians and reptiles, and a huge number of insects, such as ants, as well as earthworms and nematode worms.

Common hamster

Golden hamsters live alone in a burrow they dig 6½ ft (2 m) or more down. They are aggressive toward other hamsters and only rarely come out of their burrows to feed on seeds, nuts, and insects.

Steppe lemmings have long, waterproof fur, even covering their feet and ears, which keeps them warm when they have to emerge to forage occasionally in winter.

Common hamsters collect seeds in their cheek pouches to survive when food is hard to find. They store them in their burrows. By the end of summer, there may be 22 lb (10 kg) of food in the larder.

Grassland adaptations: The saiga antelope

The saiga antelope seems able to cope with the extremes of weather on the steppe—both the incredibly cold winters and the hot, dusty summers of the dry steppe. Among the features that help it survive are its huge, downward-pointing nostrils. These may help in winter by warming frosty air before it reaches the lungs, or help in summer by filtering out dust.

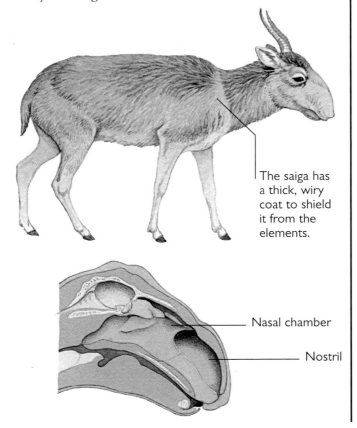

The saiga has a thick, wiry coat to shield it from the elements.

Nasal chamber

Nostril

Demoiselle crane

Early on summer mornings, demoiselle cranes can sometimes be seen striding fitfully over the ground near marshes and rivers, snapping up seeds and insects with their long beaks. Like all cranes, demoiselles mate for life and are renowned for graceful courtship dances that strengthen the bonds between mated pairs. They are still abundant worldwide, but farming and hunting has reduced their numbers in the western steppe.

Scheltopusiks
are legless lizards. When attacked, they break off their tails—which make up two thirds of their length—in several pieces. Predators are confused by all the wriggling pieces, unable to tell which is the body.

European susliks
are small mammals related to squirrels that make nests by digging deep tunnels into the soil. They feed mainly on roots, seeds, and leaves.

Bobac marmots
hibernate in deep burrows all winter. Before they go to sleep, they feed intensively to build up their body fat. This keeps them alive through the winter.

Naked mole-rats
are completely adapted for life underground. They have no tails or ear cavities, and their eyes are hidden under a layer of skin. They come to the surface only once in a lifetime to dig a new burrow.

Steppe lemmings
dig shallow temporary burrows in summer 1 ft (30 cm) deep. In winter, they live in much deeper permanent burrows, up to 3 ft (1 m) below the surface.

Southern mole voles
or mull lemmings are voles well-adapted for digging, with blunt snouts and tiny ears and eyes to keep out sand. When digging, they use their teeth to loosen the soil, and their strong paws to push it out of the way.

Wildlife at risk!

Great bustard
The great bustard was once seen on the steppes in huge numbers, but it has suffered badly from the spread of farming. Now the 10,000 or so surviving Russian birds are suffering from oil company development in their last refuge in the Volga River valley.

Siberian tiger
The biggest of all the big cats, up to 10 ft (3 m) long, the Siberian tiger was once common in the forest steppes of southeast Russia. Now there are just a handful left there. Their last stronghold is the Sikhote-Alin forests of eastern Siberia, where a few hundred survive.

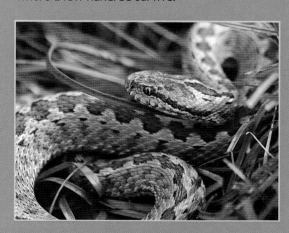

Meadow viper
The meadow or Ursini's viper is the smallest of European vipers. Unusually for vipers, it tends to be nocturnal during high summer. Loss of its open grassland habitat has made this snake very rare in eastern Europe, though it is still quite abundant further east.

Taiga and tundra

Stretching right around the world in the far north of North America and Eurasia is a vast expanse of conifer forest. Known in Russian as "taiga," and scientifically as "boreal" forest, this cool, dark green forest is one of the world's largest habitats. Beyond it to the north is open, treeless "tundra" bordering the Arctic Ocean—vast, windswept expanses of grasses, mosses, bog, and stunted trees.

•

Winters are long and severe in both taiga and tundra. Snow falls thickly in fall and never melts until spring, and in the long winter night, temperatures can plunge to -48°F (-45°C). Beneath the surface, the tundra soil stays permanently frozen, even during summer.

•

Amazingly, many creatures stay in both taiga and tundra all year-round—not only bulky, thick-coated mammals like caribou, but even tiny birds like tits—relying on the shelter and sustenance provided by the evergreen conifers. In the brief summer, snows melt, days are long and the winter residents are joined by less hardy creatures, such as songbirds and insects, emerging from winter dormancy or moving up from the south.

Where is taiga and tundra?

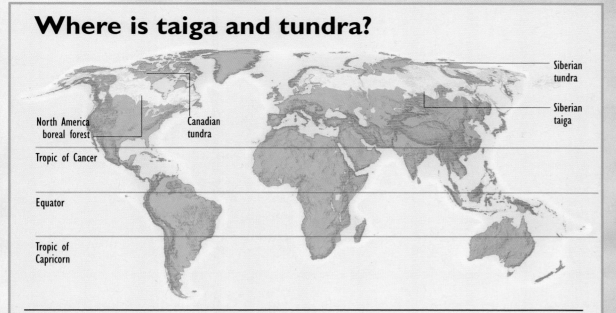

Siberian tundra

Siberian taiga

North America boreal forest

Canadian tundra

Tropic of Cancer

Equator

Tropic of Capricorn

Comparing taiga and tundra

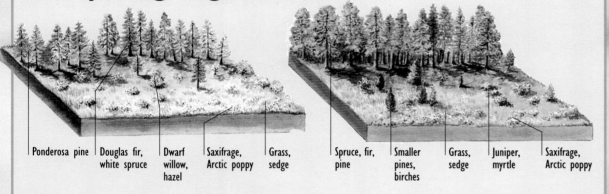

Ponderosa pine | Douglas fir, white spruce | Dwarf willow, hazel | Saxifrage, Arctic poppy | Grass, sedge

Spruce, fir, pine | Smaller pines, birches | Grass, sedge | Juniper, myrtle | Saxifrage, Arctic poppy

North America

In the south of the boreal forest, conifers, such as white pines, are mixed in with deciduous trees, such as sugar maples and American beech. Farther north, the forest is closely packed with evergreen conifers, such as jack pines, balsam firs, and white spruce. Unlike deciduous trees, the conifers in these northern forests have branches that slope down to shed heavy snow easily without breaking. In the far north, the trees become sparser and more stunted, opening out into grass and moss tundra where the only trees are tiny arctic willows and dwarf spruces and hazels. There are bogs and lakes everywhere in both taiga and tundra.

Eurasia

As in North America, deciduous maples, lindens, and ash grow alongside pines in the southern part of the Eurasian forest. Farther north, the deciduous trees disappear. Here winters are so cold that only a handful of tree species can survive, creating a vast, uniform expanse of conifers—mainly larch in Siberia, but also fir, spruce, and pine, occasionally interrupted by birches and willows. This is the true taiga, which covers vast areas of Siberia. Beyond the taiga to the north is the tundra where often little covers the ground but mosses and lichens that can survive without rooting in the frozen soil. In places, though, junipers, myrtles, and dwarf willows grow.

Taiga and tundra environments

The climate of the taiga is severe, and that of the tundra even more severe. There are typically up to six months of the year with average temperatures below freezing. Summers are often warm but usually short, with fewer than 50 to 100 frost-free days each year.

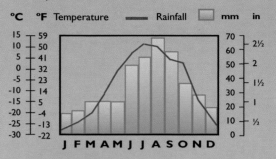

°C | °F | Temperature — Rainfall □ mm in

15 — 59
10 — 50
5 — 41
0 — 32
-5 — 23
-10 — 14
-15 — 5
-20 — -4
-25 — -13
-30 — -22

70 — 2½
60 — 2
50 —
40 — 1½
30 — 1
20 —
10 — ½
0 —

J F M A M J J A S O N D

Sun and rain

Average temperatures hover just above or below freezing, but while winter days can plummet below -40°F (-40°C), summer days may rise over 104°F (40°C). Most precipitation falls as snow.

Tundra in summer

As the snow melts in late spring, the tundra becomes boggy. But the ground turns vivid green with fresh moss and grass, while here and there a patchwork of tiny wildflowers, such as saxifrage and Arctic poppy, brings a brief color to the bleak landscape.

Taiga in winter

Snow is universal in winter in the taiga. The ground is frozen, too, making it hard for trees to draw up water, but the needlelike leaves of conifers lose very little water and so stay green on the tree ready for the brief summer.

Eurasian taiga and tundra

Stretching from Scandinavia right across Siberia, the Eurasian taiga is the world's largest forest, with open tundra to the north. Winters here are colder than anywhere on Earth except Antarctica. However, many animals survive the cold, including large, thick-coated foraging mammals, small mammals like voles and other rodents that keep warm by burrowing, and predators, such as wolves, that kill for food to keep them warm.

Amphibians
Like reptiles, amphibians are few and far between in the taiga. Nevertheless, natterjack toads and parsley frogs survive in warmer, sandy areas. Altogether there are 27 amphibian species in the Siberian taiga—most of them in the southeast.

Siberian wood frog
The Siberian wood frog and the blue moor frog are northern Siberia's only frogs, living in wet meadows, swamps, and lake shores in both taiga and tundra. The wood frog is one of the commonest of all frogs, inhabiting a wide range in huge numbers. Remarkably, it survives well inside the Arctic Circle, hibernating through winter and often putting off breeding until June.

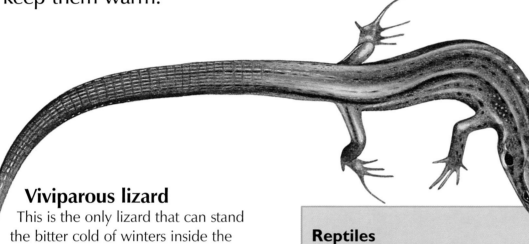

Viviparous lizard
This is the only lizard that can stand the bitter cold of winters inside the Arctic Circle, surviving by staying dormant. It gets its name, which means "live-bearing" because, common among lizards in cold places, it gives birth to live young. The young actually break out of their shells fully formed, ready to face the cold, from the moment their mother lays them.

Reptiles
Very few reptiles can survive in the cold of the taiga and tundra since they depend on the sun's warmth for energy. Nevertheless, there are more than 75 species in the Siberian taiga, including tortoises and snakes.

Birds of the air
Pinecone seeds and berries allow small birds, such as tits, wrens, nutcrackers, and crossbills, to survive in the taiga all winter. The summer eruption of insects and berries draws in migrants from the south, like waxwings and spotted woodpeckers.

Black-veined white butterfly
Moths are abundant in the pine forests of the north and their caterpillars often cause havoc in the forest by eating the pine needles. The tundra's flowers draw a number of hardier species of butterfly like the black-veined white, which feeds on flowers, such as thistles, while its caterpillar feeds on hawthorns.

Pine grosbeak
These are large finches that eat mainly berries and buds, hopping on the ground or clambering up trees. The number of these little birds that move north in summer fluctuates widely, depending on the availability of berries, such as rowan.

Insects
The springtime melting of the snow in the tundra creates bogs perfect for hatching the larvae of insects that have stayed dormant through the winter. Summer sees hordes of blackflies and mosquitoes rising from pools and tormenting the animals from which they suck blood.

Ground birds

In the taiga, grouse feed on pine needles and berries on the forest floor. In the tundra, willow ptarmigans and snow buntings peck on the ground for buds and seeds and burrow into the snow to avoid the cold.

Western capercaillie

The big, turkeylike capercaillie is the largest of all grouse, and lives only in the taiga of northern Europe. In winter, it relies on pine seeds and pine needles. In summer, it prefers leaves, bilberries, and cranberries. By the end of the short summer, capercaillie nestlings are still weak and many die in the harsh forest winter.

Wolverine

The taiga is home to many mustelids, such as sables, minks, pine martens, and fishers—all agile hunters with thick fur, some so slim they can chase prey into their burrows. The biggest mustelid is the wolverine, big as a wolf but stronger. It can run so fast over snow that it can catch large animals, such as caribou, which would outrun it in summer.

Northern hawk owl

The rodents and voles of the forest floor provide a rich source of prey for many night-hunting owls, including Tengmalm's, and the great gray, and also the eagle owl, the largest owl, as well as the Eurasian pygmy, the smallest. The northern hawk owl hunts by day, swooping from its perch to catch mice and voles.

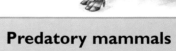

Birds of prey

There is ample prey in the taiga, even in winter, for many birds of prey. Black kites are widespread, and northern goshawks and sparrowhawks are often seen darting through trees ambushing birds. Above, imperial eagles scan the ground for small mammals, while ospreys dive for fish in taiga lakes.

Grazers and foragers

Big animals have the bulk to cope with winter, and the taiga has many deer—roe, sika, musk deer, wapiti, and moose that move to the tundra in summer to breed. In winter, deer rely on bark, stripping it from saplings.

Caribou

Known in Europe as reindeer, caribou are the only deer in which both male and female have antlers. In summer, caribou herds walk over the tundra, but in fall, they walk south to the forest. They often eat leaves and twigs, but their main food is lichen, which they find even under thick snow.

Predatory mammals

Though plant food is scarce in winter, there is enough prey to sustain both large predators like wolves, lynxes, bears, and smaller mustelids. Wolves can kill animals, like moose, much larger than themselves by hunting in packs.

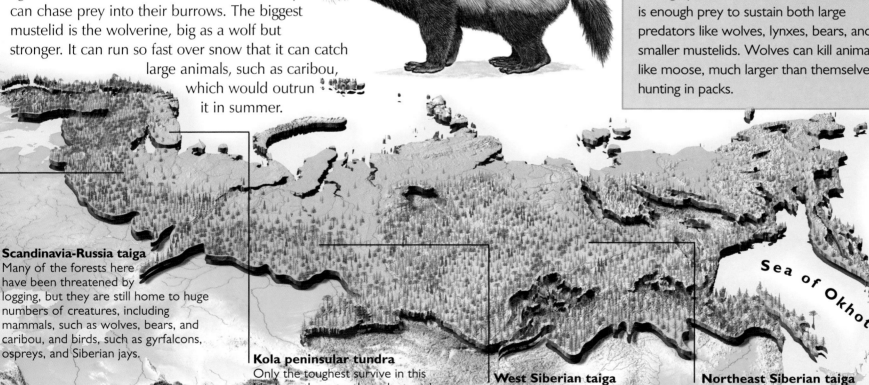

Scandinavia-Russia taiga
Many of the forests here have been threatened by logging, but they are still home to huge numbers of creatures, including mammals, such as wolves, bears, and caribou, and birds, such as gyrfalcons, ospreys, and Siberian jays.

Kola peninsular tundra
Only the toughest survive in this bleak northern tundra, where polar bears, wolverines, and Arctic foxes hunt in winter, and caribou and moose raise their young in summer.

West Siberian taiga
Almost half of West Siberia is bog, and many creatures here depend on water for food, including water voles, beavers, muskrats, and countless waterbirds, such as ducks and cranes.

Northeast Siberian taiga
This vast forest gets some of the world's coldest winters, with temperatures dropping to -94°F (-70°C). But many animals can endure the cold—mammals, such as moose, bears, red squirrels, and wolverines, and birds, such as hazel grouse, ospreys, and golden eagles.

Sea of Okhotsk

Himalayas

Tibetan Plateau

Living on pines

Compared to broad-leaved trees, conifers are hard trees for animals to live with. Not only are their needlelike leaves tough and sharp, but both leaves and wood contain an oily resin that is difficult for animals to digest. Yet many animals have managed to find a way to feed on them, eating their seeds, buds, or even their bark. Often their feeding habits have become highly specialized to make the most of the conifers. Conifers also provide shelter from the northern cold. What they lack in quality they more than make up for in quantity—conifer forests provide a vast home for those that like them.

Brown bear

With their thick fur and bulky bodies, few creatures are better adapted to cope with winter on the taiga than the bear, the animal that has become Russia's national symbol. Although bears eat most things, they eat mainly grass in spring and fruits and berries in fall. In winter, food is scarce, so bears feed themselves well in fall, then retire to the shelter of a cave or a hole, where they sleep most of the winter.

Siberian jays
are omnivorous birds, eating insects, mushrooms, and berries. In winter they often rely on pine cone seeds, which they pry out with their strong beaks.

Pine grosbeak male

Pine grosbeaks
depend heavily on conifers in winter and spring, eating pine and fir tree needles and buds, as well as extracting seeds from cones.

Male

Female

Nutcrackers,
like many other taiga birds, have strong beaks for cracking open cones to get at the seeds. Nutcrackers sometimes hoard stores of seeds for hard times.

Taiga adaptations: Creatures of Lake Baikal

Baikal is the deepest lake in the world. It is also the oldest—it formed more than 25 million years ago in a deep crack in the Earth's surface. This, combined with its long isolation from the rest of the world, has meant Baikal has developed its own unique range of creatures, such as the Coregone whitefish and the Baikal seal, the world's only freshwater seal—maybe stranded here 500,000 years ago.

Lake Baikal

Lake Baikal is more than 5,315 ft (1,620 m) deep in places.

Baikal holds a fifth of the world's freshwater.

There are 56 species of fish in the lake, including the golomoyanka, which uniquely gives birth to live young.

Baikal seal

Baikal seals are small and have only little flippers since they have no need to swim fast.

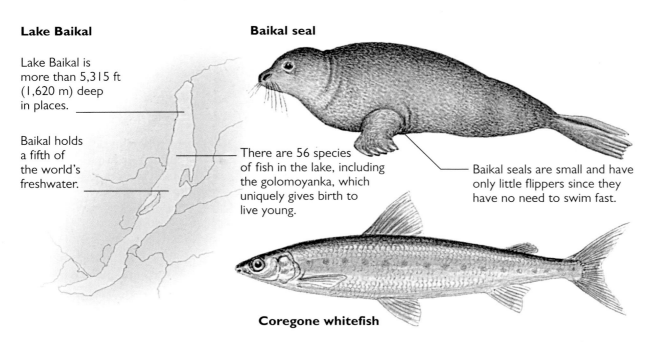

Coregone whitefish

Sables
have been hunted almost to extinction in the wild for their warm fur, essential to their survival in the Siberian winter. They climb trees well, but hunt for small animals mostly on the ground.

Hazel grouse
are among the many grouse that peck for seeds on the forest floor.

Ural owls
sleep in holes in pine trees by night, and hunt during the day for small daytime-active rodents.

Common crossbills
have unique crossed beaks that allow them to extract seeds from spruce cones. Two-barred crossbills have longer bills for dealing with larch cones.

Common crossbill

Flying squirrels
nest and roost in tree cavities and eat pine buds as well as deciduous leaves.

Siberian tit family

Siberian tit

Siberian tits
and crested tits nest in holes in pines and survive through winter by eating insects that are dormant in the bark.

Goosanders
are ducks that fly and swim fast. They hunt for fish in the taiga's many lakes and rivers, but often nest in holes in pine trees.

Red-backed voles and wood lemmings
are among many rodents that eat seeds and berries under the trees.

Goldeneye
are ducks that nest in holes in conifers, and have suffered as trees have been cleared from some areas.

Capercaillies
have strong digestive systems that allow them to survive almost entirely on pine needles in winter.

Wildlife at risk!

European bison
The European bison, Europe's largest animal, became extinct in the wild almost a century ago, but recently small populations of zoo animals have been reintroduced into the wild in various places, including the Orlovskoe forest southwest of Moscow.

Moose
European rock drawings and cave paintings reveal that moose have been hunted since the Stone Age, and they continue to be widely hunted today. Although numbers are recovering, Canada has deemed a population in Nova Scotia endangered.

Logging
The Siberian taiga is one of the world's few large, unspoiled wildernesses but, in recent years, a huge growth in demand for softwood pulp for paper has led to illegal logging on a massive scale. This, combined with a rise in mining, may destroy vast swaths of the taiga.

North American taiga and tundra

In North America, boreal forest stretches in a broad band some 500 miles (800 km) wide south of the tundra across Canada into Alaska. Winters here are bitter, and it is a vast, barely disturbed wilderness. In the far northwest, huge herds of caribou trek north in spring to their summer breeding grounds on the tundra, while the forest is home to many small mammals, birds, and insects.

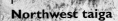

North Alaska coast
This plain is famous for the great caribou herds that arrive here each summer to raise their young.

Brooks Range

Mackenzie

Rocky Mountains

Cascade Range

Northwest taiga
Otters and beavers, moose, wolves, and bears are among the many creatures that make their homes in the mountain forests of the northwest.

American marten

Martens are nimble climbers with a doglike face and a thick, bushy tail. They sometimes forage on the ground for insects and berries, but most of the time they are up in the trees, chasing squirrels along branches at breakneck speed. They make dens in hollow trees, and produce two to four blind, helpless young in April. The babies' eyes open after about six weeks.

Predatory mammals

With warm fur and food from prey to maintain body heat, predatory mammals are well equipped to get through winter, although they often have to range far to find prey. Besides lynxes, wolves, and foxes, there are many mustelids, such as fishers and martens.

Dark-eyed junco

Dark-eyed juncos, like other sparrows, spend winter in the south, feeding on seeds. But in summer, they fly north to the boreal forest to make the most of the berries and insects. Here males court, filling the air with their musical trill, and the birds make their nests in tree roots.

Northern alligator lizard

Northern alligator lizards live not only far to the north but high up mountains. Like a number of lizards of boreal forests, they cope with the cold by giving birth to fully developed live young rather than laying eggs that need warmth to develop.

Birds of the air

In summer, 40 kinds of wood warbler arrive with birds, such as thrushes, tanagers, and grosbeaks, to feed on insects and berries. Other birds, such as chickadees, survive through winter with fluffy plumage and by gorging on seeds.

Reptiles

Reptiles cannot function without heat, so very few reptiles live in the boreal forest, and none live in the tundra. Painted and snapping turtles survive the winter under the ice in frozen ponds; eastern garter snakes go to sleep underground.

Northern flying squirrel

Flying squirrels are active throughout the winter, but need to eat a great deal to stay warm, so in fall they lay in a huge stock of nuts and dried berries in hollow trees. They glide from tree to tree mainly to escape predators.

Small mammals

Cone seeds, bark, and buds sustain many rodents, including chipmunks, groundhogs, and deer mice, that survive the winter by hibernating in burrows or in tree holes. Berries in clearings and in the tundra are also vital food. Snowshoe hares eat grass in summer but live on pine buds in winter.

Nunavut tundra
Considered a cold desert because of its lack of plants, Nunavut's tundra is still rich in wildlife. Polar bears and Arctic foxes hunt across the ice, while herds of musk oxen, caribou, and moose graze.

Hudson Bay

Lake Superior

Mid-Canada taiga
This is one of the world's last great wildlife refuges—home to countless animals, including moose, caribou, black bears, wolves, lynxes, muskrats, snowshoe hares, and many others.

Amphibians

Although amphibians find it hard to cope with the cold of the northern winter, there are frogs hardy enough to survive in the taiga's lakes and the tundra's bogs, including tiny boreal chorus frogs and mink frogs that hibernate underwater.

Moose

The moose is the world's largest deer. Males often weigh over half a ton, and their antlers can spread 6 ft (1.8 m) across. In winter, they browse in the forests on twigs and bark of waterside trees, such as willows and poplars. In summer, they wade into lakes to eat water plants.

Insects

Conifer leaves are hard to eat, and the wood oozes sticky resin that traps insects and spiders. Nevertheless, many insects thrive in the forest, including gypsy moths, sawflies, and woodwasps. Gypsy moth caterpillars eat needles. Woodwasp grubs bore into the wood.

Mosquito

The bogs formed by the spring melting of the snows in the tundra create the perfect habitat for mosquitoes. In summer, great swarms of female mosquitoes descend on large mammals, such as caribou and moose, to suck their blood. Sometimes an animal is driven so mad by the insects that it will jump off a cliff.

Foraging mammals

The scant undergrowth of the boreal forest provides little food for foragers. Nevertheless, raccoons find food by eating almost anything, while spine-covered porcupines climb trees to find new shoots in summer, and survive on soft bark and conifer needles in winter.

Oregon spotted frog

The rare Oregon spotted frog lives in marshes alongside mountain lakes. The male's breeding call in late winter sounds like a woodpecker tapping. Numbers of these rare frogs have declined dramatically as wetlands are drained and as the frogs fall prey to introduced predators, such as bullfrogs and brook trout.

Grazers and browsers

Caribou and moose are large, hardy deer that venture far north on to the open tundra in summer, then retreat to the forests in winter. But even they are not as tough as musk oxen—huge, shaggy cows that brave the most northerly tundra all year around.

Gyrfalcon

Over 2 ft (60 cm) long, the gyrfalcon is the largest of all falcons. It hunts far north over the tundra right across the Arctic from N. America to northern Siberia. It strikes birds like ptarmigans on the ground, hitting them in a surprise attack before they can take off.

Birds of prey

Birds of prey can keep out the winter cold by feeding on meat, and the boreal forest is home to owls, such as the great horned and snowy owls and raptors, such as bald and golden eagles, and red-tailed hawks. Ospreys hunt fish in the forest lakes and rivers.

Grizzly bear

Several different subspecies of brown bear live in the boreal forests of North America, including the Alaskan and the Kodiak, the biggest of them all. The grizzly bear gets its name not from its bad temper but from its "grizzled" (mottled) coat. They are mainly herbivores, but eat meat readily when they need to. To survive the winter food shortage, they sleep in holes.

Beaver home

Beavers are rodents, like prairie dogs, that are no bigger than a small dog, less than 3 ft (1 m) long. Yet, despite their size, they make a bigger impact on the northern forest environment than perhaps any other creature. They are what zoologists call a "keystone" species—a creature whose effect on the lives of others in the habitat is crucial. Beavers cut down trees with their teeth and use the logs to dam streams and create lakes where they are safe from attack. The changes they make to the environment have crucial benefits for other mammals, birds, reptiles, fish, and insects.

Felling and damming

Beavers' impact on the forest works in two ways. First, they fell trees with their teeth both to use as sticks for the dam and to feed on the bark and leaves. This creates clearings and also, because beavers prefer to cut down trees, like willows and aspens, they allow other trees to flourish. Second, as they dam the streams, beavers create large pockets of deep, still water, and also produce new wetland sites along the shore of the lake behind the dam.

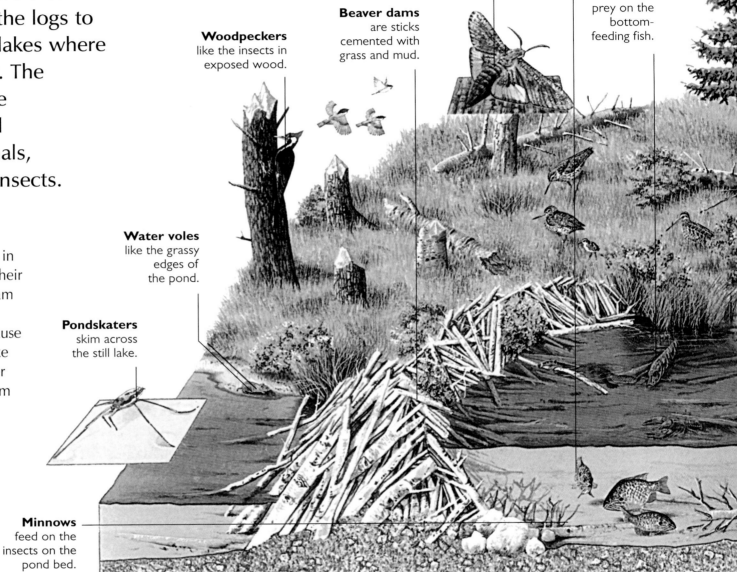

Woodpeckers like the insects in exposed wood.

Carpenter moth caterpillars move into the rotting wood and logs.

Pumpkinseeds feed on bottom-dwelling insects that like slow-moving water.

Pike prey on the bottom-feeding fish.

Beaver dams are sticks cemented with grass and mud.

Water voles like the grassy edges of the pond.

Pondskaters skim across the still lake.

Minnows feed on the insects on the pond bed.

Taiga adaptations: Cone eaters

All rodents have sharp, tough incisor teeth for gnawing into nuts, but conifers pose special problems, even for rodents. The seeds of most conifers are enclosed deep inside woody cones, protected by tough scales. The scales are open when the cones are new, but once the seeds are fertilized, the scales close up, making them hard to get at. Squirrels have become adept at finding the seeds in cones and they store up hoards of cones to help them through the winter.

The edible seeds in a cone are protected by tough wooden scales.

The squirrel has sharp incisors for gnawing into the cone.

Nimble hands allow the squirrel to turn nuts and cones to find the best angle of attack with its teeth.

Douglas fir cone

Golden-mantled ground squirrel

Red squirrel

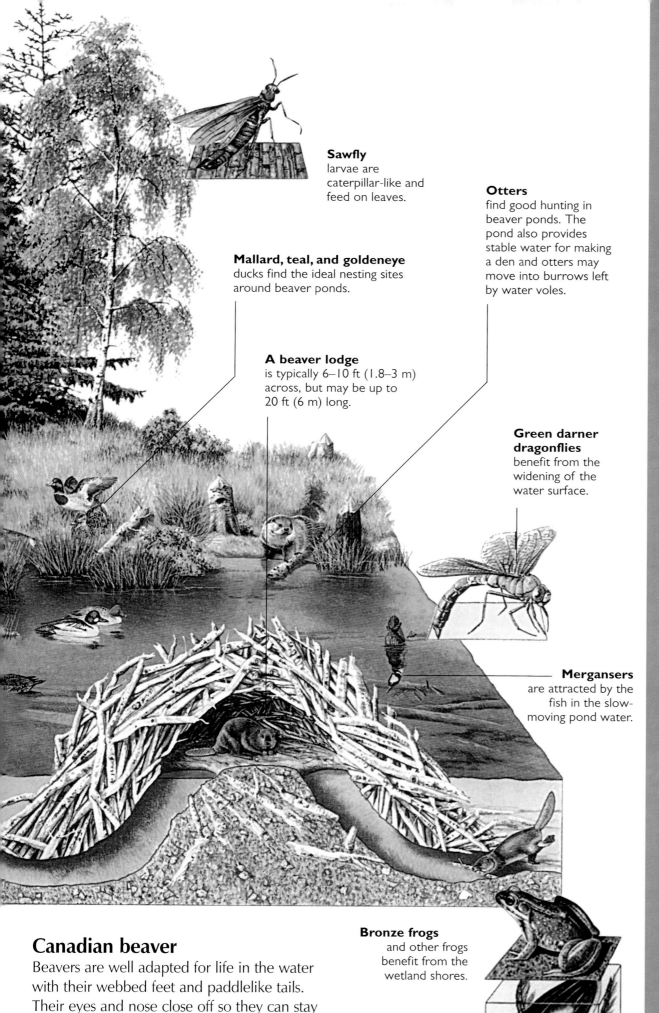

Sawfly
larvae are
caterpillar-like and
feed on leaves.

Otters
find good hunting in
beaver ponds. The
pond also provides
stable water for making
a den and otters may
move into burrows left
by water voles.

Mallard, teal, and goldeneye
ducks find the ideal nesting sites
around beaver ponds.

A beaver lodge
is typically 6–10 ft (1.8–3 m)
across, but may be up to
20 ft (6 m) long.

**Green darner
dragonflies**
benefit from the
widening of the
water surface.

Mergansers
are attracted by the
fish in the slow-
moving pond water.

Bronze frogs
and other frogs
benefit from the
wetland shores.

Diving beetles
find new prey, such
as tadpoles and
small fish.

Whirligig beetles
feed on insects that fall
on the wide pond
surface.

Canadian beaver

Beavers are well adapted for life in the water
with their webbed feet and paddlelike tails.
Their eyes and nose close off so they can stay
underwater for 15 minutes or more. They are
also master engineers. Once they have cut
down all the lakeside trees, beavers dig canals
to bring logs from farther afield. The mud they
plaster over the lodge and dam freezes like
concrete in winter to make a very solid
structure. They also build up the inside of the
lodge with mud so that their young are kept
clean and dry, even though lodge entrances are
underwater. They even make a ventilation shaft!

Wildlife at risk!

Giant carrion beetle

The giant carrion or burying beetle plays a crucial
role in forest life, feeding on corpses and helping
recycle nutrients. Its rapid decline may be due to
logging, but it may have suffered from the
extinction of the passenger pigeon that was one
of its main sources of food.

Pacific fisher

The fisher of the American northwest is related
to the otter. Despite its name, it does not eat
fish, preying instead on small mammals, such as
porcupines. Fishers are trapped for their fur and
logging destroys their forest habitat,
so now their numbers have dwindled.

Peregrine falcon

Peregrines are found worldwide, but their
numbers were devastated in the 1960s when
they ate birds that fed on seeds contaminated by
the farming pesticide DDT: 80 percent of Arctic
peregrines were lost. In 1972, DDT was banned,
and numbers are recovering.

85

Wetlands

Wetlands vary tremendously—from the bleak and lonely marshes of northern Europe, where little is heard but the sigh of the wind and the haunting cry of the curlew, to the lush, steamy mangrove swamps of southern Asia, filled with the noise of animals.

•

Every wetland is an area that is neither all water, nor all land. In swamps, there is a lot of water and very little land. In marshes, there is slightly less water and more land. Bogs are essentially waterlogged land. This balance between land and water is constantly shifting, as floods cover some of the dry places and droughts leave other areas high and dry.

•

Wetlands cover no more than six percent of the world's land surface. Yet their importance to wildlife is out of all proportion to their size and they teem with plant, fish, and bird life. Wetlands have been drained in some areas, but, because they are often hard to exploit commercially, they have become priceless refuges for many of the world's most endangered species of animals.

Comparing wetlands

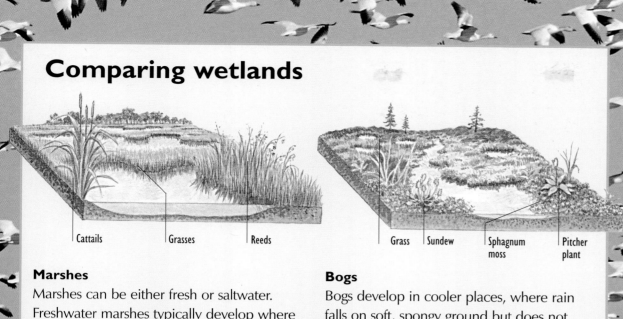

Cattails   Grasses   Reeds

Grass   Sundew   Sphagnum moss   Pitcher plant

Marshes

Marshes can be either fresh or saltwater. Freshwater marshes typically develop where rivers and lakes flood low-lying land. There are usually patches of grass, reed, and cattail, with pools of standing water.

Bogs

Bogs develop in cooler places, where rain falls on soft, spongy ground but does not drain away. Often only sphagnum moss grows on the damp, acid soil, and organic matter does not decay but accumulates as peat.

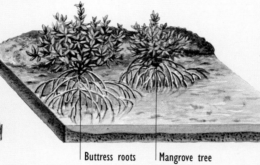

Bald cypress   Water hyacinth   Cattail

Buttress roots | Mangrove tree

Swamps

Swamps can be either fresh or saltwater. They are much wetter than marshes and there are pools and inlets for much of the year. Unlike marshes with their grasses and reeds, the main plants in swamps are trees.

Mangrove swamp

Mangrove swamps develop in the saltwater along tropical coasts. Here mangrove trees put down their buttresslike roots in pure sand, gradually spreading farther out into the water and building up the land area.

Tropical marshes

Tropical marshes are the U.S. term for treeless swamps in the tropics, such as Africa's Okavango. They develop inland where rivers seasonally flood vast, badly draining areas, yet there is too little rain for trees to grow. Tall papyrus reeds, matetite reeds, and other water plants choke meandering channels.

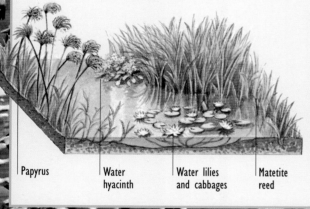

Papyrus   Water hyacinth   Water lilies and cabbages   Matetite reed

Wetland environments

Wetlands stay wet because they are constantly topped up with water. Even in cool parts of the world, they would eventually dry out if the water was not replenished. Northern bogs are kept wet by melting snow. Tropical marshes are filled by seasonal rivers.

Estonian bog

The world's largest areas of wetlands are in the cold tundra of northern Eurasia and North America. Here every hollow in the ground becomes waterlogged each spring as snow melts.

Marsh in winter

The moisture in the air over wetlands means they are often enveloped in mist, giving them an aura of mystery and helping protect wildlife. In cooler marshes in winter, the air cools quickly at night. By morning moisture in the air has condensed to form a lingering mist.

Reed beds

Few plants can survive with their roots and stems mostly underwater. The few that can, like tall reeds and tiny duckweeds, grow in wetlands throughout the world. In shallower water, sedges and rushes grow.

North American wetlands

Human activity has already destroyed half of North America's natural wetlands, and a further area the size of Chicago is lost each year. Yet there are still huge areas of wetland in the continent—from the vast bogs of northern Canada to the Florida swamps of Okefenokee and the Everglades. Here, in these precious, watery refuges survive a host of rare snakes, frogs, turtles, beavers, otters, and birds.

Alaska bogs
Alaska has twice as much wetland as all the rest of the United States, covering over half the state.

San Francisco Bay
Salt marshes are home to rare species including salt marsh harvest mice and clapper rails (wading birds).

Rocky Mountains

Rio Grande

Sierra Madre

Belted kingfisher
These small, brightly colored birds are North America's only kingfisher. They like to perch alone on trees overhanging water. But they catch fish by hovering just high enough above the water not to be seen—then diving in a flash of blue straight into the water. They also eat crayfish, frogs, snakes, and even mice. Where the water freezes over in winter, kingfishers migrate south.

Birds of prey
Large raptors, such as bald eagles and ospreys, fly over marshes scanning for fish to scoop up. Merlins and hen harriers search the land for prey, such as mice and frogs. Great blue herons and egrets wade through the water searching for fish to spear with their long beaks.

Pied-billed grebe
Grebes are diving birds, with legs set far back along their bodies and webbed feet to drive them through the water as they dive for fish. The pied-billed grebe can dive so fast it appears to vanish, earning it the nickname "water-witch." It also eats insects and snails.

Insects
A wealth of plant matter provides food for a host of insects. Few adult insects live underwater, but mayflies, caddisflies, mosquitoes, dragonflies, and damselflies develop in the water as larvae—many breathing with gills like fish. They then emerge from the water as adults.

Waterfowl
Many ducks, geese, and other waterfowl breed and feed in wetlands. Dabbling ducks like shovelers and mallards upend in the shallows to filter-feed tiny animals from the bottom mud. Diving ducks like scoters and canvasbacks dive deeper. Geese graze on grass on the shore.

Great diving beetle
The insects that have adapted to live underwater as adults are mostly predators and scavengers, such as diving beetles. Great diving beetles are hunters of small fish and insects. They breathe underwater by taking down their own air supply, tucked under their wings. Occasionally, they fly from one pond to another.

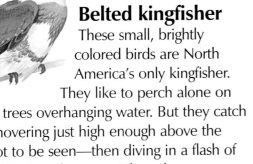

Adult

Larva

Amphibians
Wetlands are perfect for amphibians, combining water and land. Many frogs (e.g. leopard), toads (e.g. American), and newts (e.g. Eastern) breed in marshes and temporary ponds, then feed on dry land as adults. Bogs are home to four-toed salamanders and carpenter frogs.

Spring peeper
Like many "chorus" frogs, male spring peepers gather in groups in spring to belt out choruses of high, piping whistles to attract females. As adults, peepers live in trees near ponds, spending winter and dry spells under rotting vegetation.

Snapping turtle

The two American species of snapping turtle—the snapping turtle and the alligator snapping turtle—are the largest of all freshwater turtles, growing up to 200 lb (91 kg) in weight. They are fearsome predators, lying in wait on the bottom of ponds and rivers for fish, which they slice in half by their snapping jaws.

Hudson Bay bogs
One of the world's largest wetlands, these are famous for their caribou, as well as fishers, minks, and snowshoe hares.

Great Lake marshes
These are a key bird habitat not only for waterfowl, such as ducks and herons, but also for songbirds and hawks.

Hudson Bay

Prairie potholes
Appearing every spring, these marshes are home to 100 species of birds and many rare frogs.

Chesapeake Bay
This vast area of creeks and marshes is home to mammals, such as muskrats, raccoons, and beavers, and birds, such as herons and egrets.

Great Dismal Swamp
(see page 91).

Mississippi swamps
One of the world's richest freshwater fish habitats.

Gulf of Mexico

Florida swamps
Besides the Everglades, Florida has the Okefenokee cypress swamp—home to 233 kinds of birds, 49 mammals, 64 reptiles, and 37 amphibians, including rare Florida manatees and gopher tortoises.

Reptiles

North America's wetlands are home to many snakes, such as garter, water, and ribbon, and 46 species of freshwater turtle, from bog turtles to box turtles. Nearly all these turtles are endangered now, partly because they are hit by cars when they move on land.

Paddlefish

These are primitive fish that look remarkably like ancient fossil fishes. During the day, they rest at the bottom of deep pools in the rivers and wetlands of the lower Mississippi. They feed at night by filtering plankton from the water through their gaping mouths. Their long snout may help them sense the plankton.

Pumpkinseed

The pumpkinseed is a colorful fish with spots that look a little like pumpkin seeds. It lives in coolish, weedy shallows and feeds on anything from insects and their larvae to small fish. It breeds rapidly, and its abundance means it plays a key role in the habitat, becoming prey not only for all predatory fish, such as pike, but also for birds like herons and mergansers.

Fish of still waters

Habitats for fish in ponds and lakes vary considerably, from reed-choked shallows to clear deeps, and each draws its own range of fish. Blacknose dace, grass pickerels, and pumpkinseeds live in vegetation near the shore. White bass and walleyes live in deeper water.

Water mammals

Surprisingly many mammals live in the cold and wet of a marsh. Most are herbivorous rodents, such as shrews, lemmings, voles, muskrats, and beavers, which feed on plant matter. Yet there are also predators, such as bobcats, mink, otters, and rare cougars.

Muskrat

Muskrats are the largest voles, well adapted to life in water. They swim well, paddling with their webbed back feet and using their tail as a rudder. Usually, they live in small groups and burrow into riverbanks. Where the ground is flat, they build a beaver-lodge-like home from mud and plant stems.

Fish of moving waters

Rivers can be fast or slow flowing and have wide variations in temperature. Each kind of fish has its own preference. Brook trout, grayling, and sculpin live in cold, fast-flowing streams. Common carp and paddlefish prefer warmer, slower-flowing rivers.

Wading birds

Wading birds find rich pickings in wetland mud. Every fall countless waders fly down from the Arctic to spend the winter in American marshes, or rest before flying on south—stilts, avocets, snipes, woodcocks, willets, plovers, sandpipers, and many others.

Greater yellowlegs

The greater yellowlegs is a wader with long, bright yellow legs—perfect for feeding in quite deep water. It eats mainly small fish such as sticklebacks, but also insects and their larvae.
Often, these birds will form a line, wading through the water abreast as they feed. When danger approaches, one bird sounds a loud alarm call and the whole flock takes flight.

Wetland survival

Wetlands are biological superstores, providing huge quantities of food for wildlife. Billions of microscopic algae and larger plants flourish here, and wetlands can sometimes produce more plant matter each year than any other habitat in the world. Dead plant leaves and stems break down in the water to form detritus. In rivers, detritus is washed away, but in wetlands it accumulates to provide a source of food as rich for animals as living plants. Detritus and living plant matter are eaten by countless tiny water insects and their larvae, shellfish, and other fish, and these in turn provide food for larger animals.

Wetland food web

At the bottom of the wetland food chain are tiny creatures like mayfly larvae, which feed on detritus on the bottom.

They, in turn, provide food for free-swimming creatures, such as dragonfly and damselfly larvae.

All the other creatures in the wetland benefit from the sheer abundance of these minute creatures—whether they feed on them directly, like ducks, or feed on another animal that feeds on them.

Otters' main prey is fish, caught by day. But they also eat frogs, crayfish, snakes, and insects.

Soras are wading birds that feed on reedlike water plants called cattails.

Water boatmen skate across the water, feeding on algae and reeds.

Minks hunt for small mammals, frogs, fish, and crayfish.

Narrow-winged damselflies prey on small insects, such as caddisflies, and insect larvae.

Mallards eat algae and also bottom-dwelling insect larvae.

Minnows feed on algae and insects, like caddisflies and water boatmen.

Sunfish feed on algae.

Crayfish eat dead insects and fish.

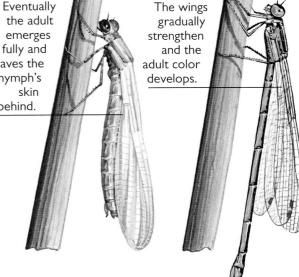

Wetland adaptations: From nymph to adult

Dragonflies and damselflies have an unusual life cycle, perfectly suited to their life as aquatic predators. Eggs are laid on water plants and hatch into nymphs. The nymphs are wingless and live under water, gradually growing bigger by preying on insects, tadpoles, and small fish. Eventually, after two or more years, the nymphs are ready to surface and emerge as winged adults.

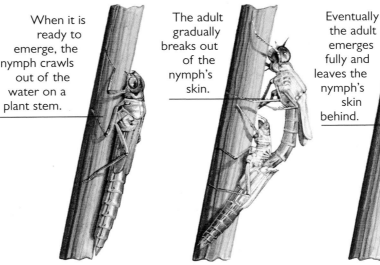

When it is ready to emerge, the nymph crawls out of the water on a plant stem.

The adult gradually breaks out of the nymph's skin.

Eventually the adult emerges fully and leaves the nymph's skin behind.

The wings gradually strengthen and the adult color develops.

Muskrats
eat water plants and also frogs, shellfish, and small fish.

Ospreys
swoop down to snatch large fish, such as sunfish, from the water.

Great blue herons
stand in the water and stab the water with their long bills for fish and frogs.

Bullfrogs
prey on insects and small fish.

Tadpoles
feed on detritus.

Pike
prey on fish, frogs, and even ducks.

Snapping turtles
prey on small mammals, fish, and birds.

Loons
feed on small fish and tadpoles.

Great Dismal Swamp

The Great Dismal Swamp is a forested wetland near the coasts of Virginia and North Carolina in the U.S., where cypress, black gum, and woodbine grow in deep pools. It covers barely a third of the area it did when given its name by Colonel William Byrd when he surveyed the area in 1728. It was once the habitat of many rare birds, including the now extinct ivory-billed woodpecker, and remains an important wildlife refuge—home to deer, raccoons, bears, and opossums.

Wildlife at risk!

Caribbean manatee

Caribbean manatees once lived in freshwater swamps and rivers as far north as the Carolinas, but hunting, pollution, and the filling of waterways has cut the U.S.'s manatee population to under 2,000. Motorboats still kill manatees, despite speed restrictions on boats.

Florida Keys white-tailed deer

The Key deer is a small subspecies of the white-tailed deer that used to wander over much of the Florida Keys. Hunting cut numbers to just 30 in 1947, when the deer became protected by law. Now the population has climbed to 700–800, but the Key deer is still vulnerable.

Florida panther

The Florida panther is a small subspecies of mountain lion that preys on white-tailed deer and hogs. As its habitat has shrunk, so numbers have plummeted. Just 30–50 survive in the wild—and a few more are killed by road traffic every year or so.

European wetlands

Europe has lost many of its wetlands over the centuries as marshes and bogs have been reclaimed for farming and building. But it still has over a fifth of the world's most important wetland wildlife sites—rare wilderness refuges in this crowded, highly developed part of the world. These are the haunts of vast flocks of wintering birds, countless frogs and toads, many water rodents, and an unimaginable number of invertebrates.

Birds of prey

Wetlands see a constant battle of wits as birds of prey swoop low and small creatures dive into the water—the best cover in open marshes. Voles are food for Montagu's harriers and rough-legged buzzards; small birds are prey for hen harriers and, in winter, merlins.

Marsh harrier

Instead of soaring, marsh harriers hunt by flying to and fro, low over the ground. If they spot a frog, small bird, or other prey, they drop suddenly to snatch it in their talons. Unusually for birds of prey, they nest on the ground, building a nest among reeds and staying all winter. Both parents look after and feed the young in spring.

Moorhen

It looks a little duck-like, but the moorhen is not a waterfowl. It does not have webbed feet, and so swims awkwardly. It can sink like a submarine when alarmed, leaving only its beak above water, and it has long toes that spread its weight so that it can walk on floating plants. It feeds on water plants and also insects, spiders, and worms.

Gray heron

Gray herons are among Europe's largest birds, standing almost 3 ft (1 m) tall. They hunt either by standing motionless in the water, waiting for prey to come by, or they stalk, treading noiselessly through the water. In flight, they are instantly identifiable by their broad, rounded wings and their necks bent double. Their call is a loud croak.

Wading birds

Wetlands are home to many long-legged birds that wade through water to hunt fish and frogs, such as cranes, herons, and bitterns. In winter, huge flocks of smaller waders walk along shores, probing the mud with long bills for food, such as curlews, godwits, lapwings, and plovers.

The Camargue
Although much reduced, the Camargue still has its famous herds of wild horses and cattle, and is a precious refuge for flamingoes, egrets, night herons, and many other birds.

Waterfowl

With their network of creeks and gentle shores, marshes make an ideal habitat for waterfowl. Snow and white-fronted geese graze on shore. Dabbling ducks like teal, pintail, and garganey, and divers like pochards feed in the water.

Broad-bodied chaser

Also known as a skimmer or darter for its fast, erratic flight, this is one of the thousands of dragonfly-like insects that breed in wetlands, living underwater as nymphs, then hunting over the surface as adults.

Amphibians

Amphibians are well adapted to make the most of the wetlands habitat, living as tadpoles in water and on land as adults. Newts, such as the smooth and palmate, spend much of their lives in water. Frogs like the huge marsh frog and common toads live more on land.

The Coto Doñana
is a haunting wilderness of marsh, heath, and dunes—home to 226 bird species and the last refuge of two very endangered species: the Spanish imperial eagle and Spain's only wildcat, the Iberian lynx.

Insects

Marshes and bogs are breeding grounds for insects. Some—caddisflies, mayflies, dragonflies—live as larvae underwater then surface as adults. Water boatmen hunt on water surfaces; diving beetles and saucer bugs hunt underwater.

Common frog

Like all adult frogs, common frogs have long, strong back legs to help them jump huge distances to escape predators. They are carnivores, catching fast-moving insects by darting out their long, sticky tongues. They live mostly on land but gather at pools to mate early in the year.

Mediterranean Sea

Reptiles

Northern marshes are too cold for reptiles except for a few, such as grass snakes and pond turtles, that live in the water. Many snakes and lizards live on dry ground in the warmer south, including sand lizards and Lataste's viper.

Pike

Pike are the most fearsome predators of European freshwaters. They lurk motionless among weeds waiting for prey, then make a lightning strike. Pike prey on many things—frogs, waterbirds, voles, and fish—and will often take prey up to half their own size.

Fish of still waters

Lakes, pools, and backwaters are home to fish, such as tench, which cruise slowly on the bottom, hunting for small creatures. Perch also live here, lying in wait among reeds for prey, such as bleak and rudd. Sticklebacks are tiny fish that build nests for their young.

Montpellier snake

This highly venomous snake lives on dry scrub in southern wetlands, such as the Nestos delta in Greece, the Coto Doñana in Spain, and the Camargue in France. It preys mainly on other reptiles, such as spiny-toed lizards and Bedriaga's skink. Unusually for a snake, it has good eyesight.

Bream

Bream live near the bottom of slow-moving waters where there are plenty of insect larvae, worms, and mollusks in the mud on which they can feed. Sometimes they seem to stand on their heads as they suck food from the mud. In June or July, large shoals gather in shallow, weed-filled water to spawn. Spawning can be so vigorous that the water appears to boil.

Eurasian otter

Few small mammals are better adapted to water than the otter, with its lithe body, waterproof fur, and webbed feet. It swims with amazing agility as it chases fishes and frogs. It hunts by night and sleeps in the day in its waterside burrow. Pollution has decimated otter numbers, but they have recovered where rivers have been cleaned up.

Fish of moving waters

The rich plant and insect life in smooth-flowing lowland rivers and creeks is food for a wealth of fish—chub, bleak, carp, roach, and bream. In faster rivers, dace and barbel feed on insects. In clear upland streams, trout, salmon fry, and minnows are common.

Water mammals

The huge bulk of plants in a marsh, and the insects around them, draw many small mammals to live here, including brown rats, bank and water voles, muskrats, and water shrews. Predators, such as red foxes and wild cats, roam the shores.

The Pripet Marshes
on the Ukraine-Belarus border remain the largest marshes in Europe, home to moose, wild boar, lynxes, beavers, and many other mammals, and a host of birds, such as black and hazel grouse, orioles, woodpeckers, owls, blue tits, and ducks.

The Danube delta
is a maze of creeks, lakes, and marshes—home to many kinds of frog, over 300 species of bird (including pelicans, water rails, cormorants, and pratincoles), and countless fish, such as sturgeons, eels, and Tyulka sprats.

The Volga delta
is a huge wetland of creeks and lakes—a feeding ground for millions of migratory birds, such as swans, herons, and ibises, and rarer species, such as great white egrets and penduline tits.

Baltic Sea

Ural Mountains

Carpathian Mountains

Volga

Danube

Adriatic Sea

Black Sea

Caucasus Mountains

93

Living in damp places

The wetlands of Europe are among the most important of all habitats for birds in this part of the world. No creature is better able to take advantage of the mix of land and water, nor cope so well with the frequent flooding. Although wetlands vary widely, a huge range of waterfowl and wading birds make their homes here. Many others find safe resting places during migration. Wetlands can look like quite uniform habitats—just grass, mud, and water—but every bird has its own special niche, exploiting a particular aspect of the habitat, and each has its own chosen nesting site.

Wetland adaptations: Bills for mud

Shorebirds walk along the shore, probing the mud and sand for food with their long bills. Each species of bird has a slightly different length and shape of bill, so that they can reach different foods and not compete. They range from plovers with short bills for feeding near the surface to godwits with long bills that probe deeply for prey, such as lugworms.

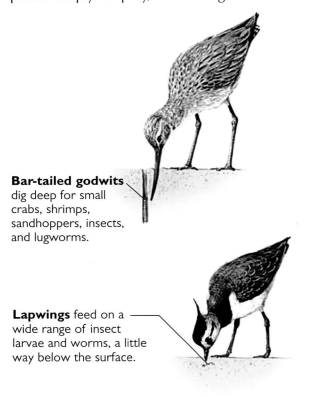

Bar-tailed godwits dig deep for small crabs, shrimps, sandhoppers, insects, and lugworms.

Lapwings feed on a wide range of insect larvae and worms, a little way below the surface.

Ringed plovers feed on small shrimps, snails, worms, and insects near the surface.

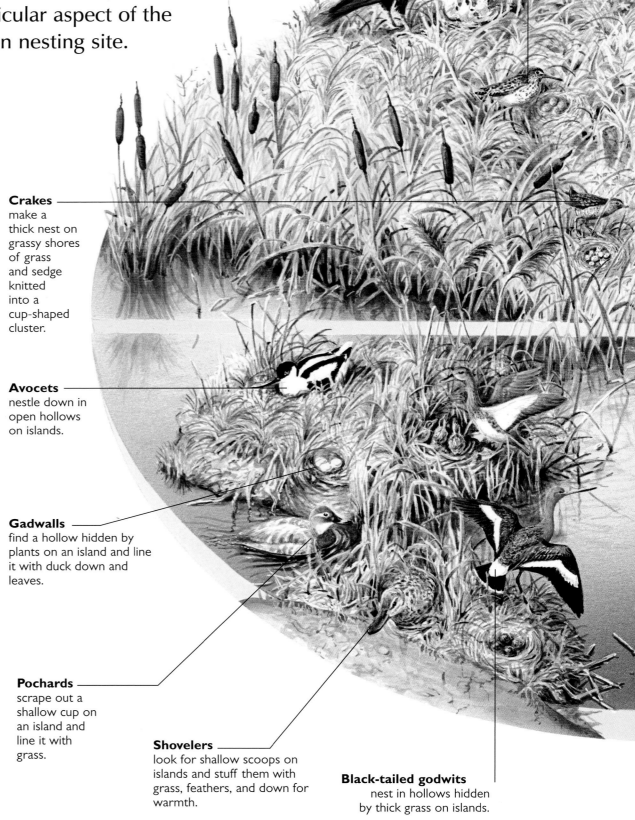

Snipe make a cup-shaped nest on muddy shores.

Redshanks make a cup-shaped nest from grasses and sedges, hidden in shoreline grass.

Harriers make a large dish-shaped nest of reeds amongst sedges.

Crakes make a thick nest on grassy shores of grass and sedge knitted into a cup-shaped cluster.

Avocets nestle down in open hollows on islands.

Gadwalls find a hollow hidden by plants on an island and line it with duck down and leaves.

Pochards scrape out a shallow cup on an island and line it with grass.

Shovelers look for shallow scoops on islands and stuff them with grass, feathers, and down for warmth.

Black-tailed godwits nest in hollows hidden by thick grass on islands.

Ospreys make large nests of branches on top of pine trees.

Gray herons make colonies of nests called heronries at the tops of trees or in reed beds. Each nest platform is 3 ft (1 m) or so across and is made of sticks and twigs.

Mallards nest in hollows in waterside trees.

Garganeys nest on the ground in drier scrubland near tussocks of grass, building their nest from twigs and grasses.

Yellow wagtails nest in drier scrubland in cup-shaped nests. They build their nests in a dip in the ground from grass and plant stems and line the nests with hair and fur.

Water rails make a large nest in reeds over mud using dead stalks and leaves.

Reed warblers nest in a deep cup of grasses woven around reed stems over the water.

Great crested grebes make their nest on a floating platform of weeds anchored among reeds.

Moorhens make a floating nest platform of dried water plants.

Coots build floating nests of reeds, often with a ramp leading into the water.

Bearded tits nest in lined reed baskets woven into reeds well above the water.

Wildlife at risk!

Slender-billed curlew

As wetlands shrink, the slender-billed curlew may become the first European bird to die out in the last 150 years. These smaller cousins of the Eurasian curlew breed in Russia and winter in the Mediterranean, but in the last few years only nine of them have been seen.

White-fronted goose

Wintering grounds of the Greenland white-fronted goose were endangered by peat digging in Scotland and Ireland. Now its nest sites are protected, but it faces a new menace as its summer breeding grounds in the Arctic are threatened by global warming.

Draining the wetlands

Over the centuries, huge areas of European and American wetlands have been "reclaimed" by draining them and turning them into farmland. Now many large wetlands are protected, but smaller wetlands and water meadows are still being drained for farms and housing.

African wetlands

Africa is surprisingly well endowed with wetlands. Over four percent is covered with permanent swamps and many large areas become swampy after heavy rain. Few large animals live in the heart of the swamps—with the exception of hippos—but many live on the fringes, while countless birds, reptiles, and insects live deep in the swamps.

Niger delta
The mangrove swamps of the Niger delta are home to hippos, manatees, swamp otters, and over 150 species of fish.

Lake Chad
This is a remarkable wetland on the fringes of the Sahara, where millions of birds, such as ibises and spoonbills, live or stop over.

Caspian Sea

Congo

Congo basin
The Congo has more species of fish (700) than anywhere but the Amazon, and the flooded forests are home to unique animals like the water genet, swamp otter, and Ruwenzori otter shrew.

Lake Tanganyika

Lake Nyasa

East African mangroves
Among the mangrove roots live animals, such as dugongs and sea turtles, as well as many fish.

The Okavango delta
This is one of the world's most important animal habitats (see pages 98–99).

Nile crocodile

This huge reptile spends most of the day basking in the sun. To catch prey, it lies still in the water and ambushes animals that come to drink, dragging them underwater, drowning them, then twisting in the water to tear their flesh. Anything from a buffalo to a stork can be killed this way. Adult crocodiles swallow stones to act as stabilizing ballast when in the water.

Reptiles, amphibians

Unlike many places, African swamps are warm enough for reptiles, including lizards, like water monitors, and snakes, like green water snakes and olive grass snakes. The land and water combination draws frogs, too, like snoring puddle frogs, reed frogs, and waterlily frogs.

Bulinus water snail

Swamps breed many tiny creatures that are parasites on animals and humans, such as the worm that causes the disease bilharzia. It lays its eggs in water, where they are swallowed by water snails. The eggs hatch in the snail.

Insects and others

The most spectacular swamp insects are large, colorful dragonflies. Warm water and dense vegetation attract mollusks and worms, too, including the swamp worm, which has a snorkel for breathing in the oxygen-poor mud.

Fish

African swamps are home to myriad fish, many of them huge. The Okavango has 65 species, including catfish, African pike, jewelfish, and tigerfish. In the Nile swamps lives the world's biggest freshwater fish, the Nile perch, 6 ft (1.8 m) long and weighing 280 lb (130 kg).

African lungfish

Swamp waters are often poor in oxygen, so some fish have developed lungs for breathing air. Lungfish were the ancestors of all backboned animals. African lungfish have gills but must come to the surface every half an hour to breathe. In droughts, they can burrow into mud and survive for months in a dormant state.

Flamingo

With their long legs, long necks, and pink plumage, flamingos are striking-looking birds, and they are often seen in huge flocks on African lakes. Uniquely for birds, they filter-feed just like many whales—straining shrimps from the water through slits in their bills.

Wading birds

Among the most spectacular sights of African wetlands and lakes are huge flocks of large wading birds stepping through shallows, feeding on fish, frogs, and snails, e.g. night herons, sacred ibises, shoebills, spoonbills, egrets, marabou storks, and hamerkops.

The Sudd
Every year a vast area of southern Sudan floods to form the Sudd, providing water and food for huge numbers of migrating birds and mammals, such as antelopes, lechwes, kobs, and Mongalla gazelles.

Nile

Large mammals
Many large mammals migrate in and out of swamps in response to seasonal fluctuations in the water level. During the dry season in the surrounding grassland, the swamps may still be swollen from floods in the mountains. Herds of elephants are joined in the swamps by giraffes and rhinos.

Hippopotamus
Hippopotamuses are permanent residents of the swamp. They are huge animals that spend their days in water and graze on land at night. They are entirely herbivorous, but strongly territorial, and are said to kill more people in Africa than any other animal. Their huge jaws with teeth 2 ft (60 cm) long are able to smash through the side of a boat.

Birds of the air
African swamps are home to a huge number of birds. The Okavango delta alone has over 400 bird species—not only water birds like pelicans and pygmy geese, but birds drawn to the wooded areas, such as parrots, barbets, bee-eaters, honeyguides, and shrikes.

Great white pelican
Pelicans are among the biggest freshwater birds, with a wingspan of up to 10 ft (3 m). They often work together when catching fish, moving in a tight semicircle to drive shoals into shallows where all the birds can feed at leisure. They scoop up huge quantities of water in their elastic bills, then let the water drain out, leaving the fish behind.

Birds of prey
The swamps full of big fish make them a paradise for fish eagles, but there is plenty of prey for other predators too, such as spotted eagles and Dickenson's kestrels. Fish are abundant for the Pel's owls that hunt fish, perhaps using their amazing night vision to catch them.

African fish eagle
Sometimes known as the "voice of Africa" for its loud, yelping call, the fish eagle is a huge bird of prey, weighing up to 8 lb (3.6 kg). It catches fish by watching quietly from waterside tree branches, then glides down to snatch it with a backward swing of one foot. It usually catches fish on the surface, but occasionally it dives in after large fish.

Marsh mongoose
An expert swimmer and diver, the marsh mongoose is probably the best equipped of all mongooses for life in the swamp. It hunts at night, swimming or trotting along the shore as it searches for crabs, fish, frogs, and snakes, which it grabs with its sharp claws. It breaks into crab shells by smashing them against a rock or tree.

Grazing mammals
At certain times of year, huge numbers of grazing animals, including kudu, impala, and buffalo, move in from the surrounding savanna to take advantage of the water and lush grazing. Some antelopes, like waterbucks, sitatungas, and lechwes, are adapted to moving around in the wetlands all year-round.

Lechwe
Lechwes are well adapted to living in watery places. They are good swimmers and can often be seen grazing in shoulder-deep water. They have wide hooves to help them wade across boggy ground, but these hooves make them very clumsy on solid earth. So they prefer to move with the seasonal fluctuations of the swamp in order to stay on soft ground.

Predatory mammals
Lions and hyenas, and occasionally wild dogs and cheetahs, roam through the woods surrounding swamps. Sometimes leopards and smaller cats called caracals can be heard prowling at night. However, few of them venture right into the swamp.

Hippo world

Botswana's Okavango delta is one of the world's biggest swamps, a placid expanse of winding channels, papyrus-fringed lagoons, and open grasslands, stretching over 5,000 sq miles (13,000 sq km). The extent of the delta varies through the year, peaking during the rainy season and when the rains reach the River Okavango in Angola. Larger animals, such as elephants, come and go with the changing of the delta, but all year-round there is an abundance of wildlife—over 400 species of bird live here, and mammals from lions to bush babies. But the Okavango is the kingdom of one animal more than any other—the hippopotamus—and it plays a key role in the life of the swamp.

Land clearance
Hippos climb out of the water at dusk to feed on grass. They consume up to 80–100 lb (36–45 kg) of grass a night. The paths they make through the bush, as they search for their favorite short grass, allow other animals easy access to the water. Their grazing keeps the grass trimmed, stimulating new growth and stopping shrubs and trees from taking over.

Wetland adaptations: Swamp feet

There are many places in swamps where the surface is very soft, and often consists of little more than soggy vegetation. To walk over these safely, some swamp creatures have developed big feet to spread their weight. Sitatunga and lechwe antelopes have splayed hooves to help them move over boggy ground, while the lily trotter has splayed toes for walking on lily leaves.

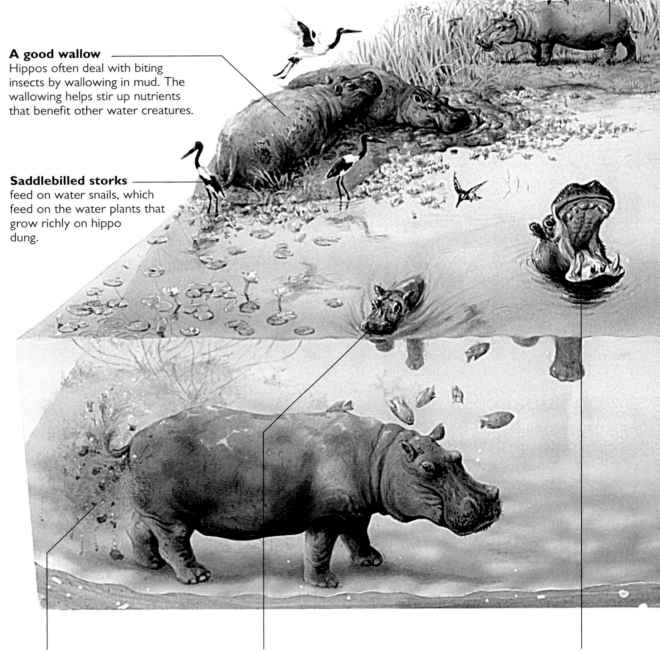

A good wallow
Hippos often deal with biting insects by wallowing in mud. The wallowing helps stir up nutrients that benefit other water creatures.

Saddlebilled storks
feed on water snails, which feed on the water plants that grow richly on hippo dung.

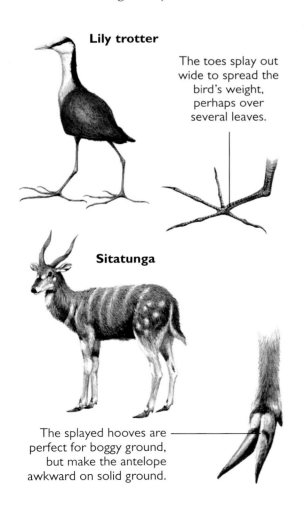

Lily trotter

The toes splay out wide to spread the bird's weight, perhaps over several leaves.

Sitatunga

The splayed hooves are perfect for boggy ground, but make the antelope awkward on solid ground.

Enriching dung
As they stand in water, hippos drop vast piles of dung that enrich the water, providing vital nutrients for both plants and micro-organisms. This benefits fish, which, in turn, provide food for larger fish, reptiles, and birds.

Born in water
Hippos are born underwater, so to reach the surface for their first breath, they must be able to swim from birth. They are naturally buoyant and often gallop gracefully along the bottom at high speed.

Huge gape
When a male hippo gives its huge yawn, it may be showing off its big canine teeth to frighten off a trespasser. Occasionally, the males fight and try to bite each other.

Hippos in water
Hippos often stay in the water with just their nostrils, eyes, and ears above the surface. They can submerge completely for half an hour by closing their nostrils and slowing their heart rate.

Cloud bathing
Hippos spend the day resting in water to keep cool and protect their skin from the sun. On overcast days, they often leave the water to bask on the bank. Hippo sweat contains a red pigment that acts as a sunblock.

Hippopotamus
Hippos are huge animals, with males weighing up to 7,000 lbs (3,200 kg). They stay semi-submerged in water during the day because of their sensitive skin, and feed on grass at night. Hippos once lived across most of southern Africa but they are now confined to reserves.

Feeding station
For hammerhead storks (hamerkops), the hippo's broad back makes the perfect feeding station, as they sift the water at dawn and dusk for fish, amphibians, insects, and crustaceans.

Feeding
Hippos feed mainly on grass, but every now and then they feed on Nile cabbage or water lettuce and so help keep the water clear. The cabbage and lettuce grows so densely over water that from a distance it can look like a lawn. As the hippos move through swamps, they break through the vegetation to create new channels or lakes.

Ground clearance
With their huge bulk, hippos have no problem trampling down patches of papyrus reeds as they climb out—and, as they do so, provide clear spaces for crocodiles to make their nests among the reeds.

Wildlife at risk!

Sitatunga
Because they follow paths created through the swamp by hippos, sitatungas are easy to trap, and are hunted widely both as trophies and for meat. Sitatungas are extinct in many places. Now water schemes and farming threaten to erode their refuge in the Okavango.

Pel's fishing owl
Pel's fishing owls are among the world's biggest owls and one of the few that feed on fish. Although still common in some places, they have become very scarce in others as their swamp and river habitats have been altered by drainage projects and dam building.

Black lechwe
Lechwes are medium-sized antelopes that feed on marshland plants and wade and swim well. They were once found in huge herds in wetlands in southern Africa. But their abundance made them easily hunted, and their wetland habitats are shrinking. The black lechwe lives only in the Bangweulu swamps of northern Zambia and is the subject of a major conservation project.

Mountains and polar regions

Mountains and polar regions are the world's coldest, most extreme environments. The heart of the polar regions and the highest mountains are so cold that they are permanently covered in ice and snow. They are also frequently covered in fog, or blasted by howling winds and blizzards.

•

Climbing a mountain in the tropics is a little like journeying from the Equator to the Poles. Temperatures drop 1.8°F (1°C) every 650 feet (200 m) up the mountainside, and the vegetation changes from tropical forest, through mixed temperate and boreal forest, before emerging on high alpine tundra and finally the snowy summit.

•

A few creatures, such as polar bears in the Arctic and yaks in the Himalayas, survive close to the ice-covered poles or high peaks. But most polar and mountain wildlife finds a way to live around the seasonally shifting edge of the ice—on the windswept tundra or farther down in the boreal forest.

Where are mountains and polar regions?

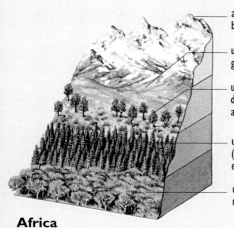

- above 8,850 ft (2,700 m)—bare rock and snow
- up to 8,850 ft (2,700 m)—grass and alpine flowers
- up to 7,870 ft (2,400 m)—dwarf shrubs, such as juniper and mountain ash
- up to 6,560 ft (2,000 m)—coniferous forest: e.g. spruce and larch
- up to 3,280 ft (1,000 m)—mixed deciduous forest

Africa

In tropical Africa, the permanent snow line is much higher. It is at about 16,400 ft (5,000 m) on east Africa's highest peaks—at 19,340 ft (5,895 m) on Mt. Kilimanjaro and 17,058 ft (5,199 m) on Mt. Kenya. Below the snow line, vegetation descends through alpine tundra to savanna. The alpine tundra is exposed to scorching sun during the day and freezing cold at night, producing plants that are unique to the region.

- above 14,760 ft (4,500 m)—bare rock and snow
- up to 14,760 ft (4,500 m) grassland with Alpine flowers
- up to 12,470 ft (3,800 m)—dwarf shrubs, such as rhododendrons
- up to 10,500 ft (3,200 m)—coniferous forest including cedar trees
- up to 6,560 ft (2,000 m)—broad-leaved forest
- up to 3,280 ft (1,000 m)—subtropical forest

Alps

The Alps are in the temperate zone nearer the Poles, where the permanent snow line is reached quite low, at 8,850 ft (2,700 m). Below that, vegetation descends in ever warmer zones down to mixed deciduous forest. These zones vary widely depending on how directly a slope faces the sun.

- above 16,400 ft (5,000 m)—bare rock and snow
- up to 16,400 ft (5,000 m)—Afro-Alpine plants including giant lobelia and senecio
- up to 13,120 ft (4,000 m)—dwarf shrubs and tree heaths including erica arborea, erica philippia
- up to 10,820 ft (3,300 m)—bamboo
- up to 8,850 ft (2,700 m)—montane forest
- up to 7,220 ft (2,200 m)—savanna grass and scrub

Himalayas

The Himalayas are the world's highest mountains, with Mt. Everest at 29,035 ft (8, 850 m) the highest of all. Above 15,000 ft (4,572 m), all the range's peaks are covered in permanent snow. Below that the vegetation descends through alpine tundra to subtropical forest. Tibet, which lies in the Himalayas, has vast, high-altitude plateaus where it is too cold and dry for anything but short alpine grasses to grow. This region is often called mountain steppe.

Mountain and polar environments

Mountain and polar habitats have much in common. The same extreme habitat is found only on the very highest mountain summits at the Equator. In the temperate zone, it is found lower down. At the Poles, it is found at ground level.

The high peaks

Steep crags, precipitous slopes, and constant cold make it hard for any plants but lichens to gain a foothold on the very tops of mountains. Mountain peaks are arctic wastelands.

Alpine flowers

In the temperate zone, there are marked seasonal changes. In spring, snow which may have fallen all over the mountain, melts up to the snow line. Up on the high meadows just below the snow line, tiny, hardy "alpine" flowers bloom. Spring in the Arctic brings similar flowers.

Cloud forest

In the tropics, the lower mountain slopes are often wrapped in clouds. Thick "cloud forest" grows here, home to many unique plants and providing a refuge for some of the world's most endangered animals, including gorillas.

Mountains

Life at high altitudes is tough, with icy winds, thin air, steep slopes, and scant vegetation. Some creatures, such as mountain goats, have adapted to these conditions. Many mountain inhabitants, like deer, are migrants, only moving up in summer. Others are refugees, like pumas, forced up because humans have eroded their natural habitat.

The Americas

Small mammals
For small mammals, the cold of mountain peaks presents special problems. Many small mammals, such as marmots, retreat to burrows and hibernate in winter. Those that stay active, like pikas, often rely on food stores built up during the fall.

Snowshoe hare
Snowshoe hares live both in high mountain forests and the boreal forests of Canada. In summer, they are brown, but in winter, they turn white to match the snow. Every nine years or so, hare numbers rise sharply, then decline as food supplies run out.

Spectacled bear
The spectacled bear is South America's only bear. It once lived down near the coast, but human activity has pushed it farther and farther up into the mountains, and it now survives only in cloud forests above 3,280 ft (1,000 m). It is mainly vegetarian, feeding on cacti and leaves.

The Rockies
stretch from the chill Brooks Range in Alaska, home to wolves and caribou, to the tropical Sierra Madre of Mexico with its parrot-filled valley forests.

Large mammals
A number of grazing animals are well-equipped to take advantage of the fresh plants that grow on almost inaccessible slopes. Ibex and bighorn and Dall sheep in North America and vicuña in the south are all agile climbers and have extra red blood cells, which help them to absorb more oxygen from thin air.

Brooks Range

Rocky Mountains

Sierra Madre

Andes Mountains

Atlas Mountains

Predatory mammals
The mountains of North America are the last refuge for predators that once roamed widely, including wolves, coyotes, bears, lynxes, and mountain lions. In the Andes, the mountain lion is the only large predator, apart from the mainly vegetarian bear.

California condor
New World vultures are big birds of prey that rely mostly on carrion for food. The best known is the rare California condor, the largest bird in North America, with wings over 10 ft (3 m) wide. There are approximately 322 left, with only 72 in the wild.

Birds of prey
Few creatures cope better at high altitudes than birds, with their warm feathers, and lungs ideal for thin air. Birds of prey can range far up and down mountains to find food. American mountains are home to many birds of prey—including hawks (e.g. Cooper's), golden eagles, and falcons.

Mountain goat
Mountain goats live near the snow line, feeding on grass and lichens. They have shaggy coats to keep them warm. Their small hooves help give them amazing balance—they can leap on to the narrowest ledges. Rough pads around the edges of the hooves stop them from slipping.

Eurasia

Insects and others

High up, springtails, athonomyiid flies, coccinellid beetles, and apollo butterflies gather to feed where alpine flowers and spores of lichen and moss lie in rock crevices. When not feeding, the springtails and flies shelter under rocks alongside centipedes, earwigs, and attid spiders.

Parnassius Apollo butterfly

Parnassius Apollo butterflies emerge in spring to feed on tiny alpine flowers high in mountains across Eurasia. They are surprisingly resistant to cold and some can even fly above the snow line. Caterpillars feed on the alpine plant sedum.

Alps

Caucasus

Hindu Kush

Himalayas

The Himalayas
are the highest mountains in the world, home to a number of unique creatures, such as the high-mountain vole, the goatlike tahr, and the rare snow leopard.

Himalayan marmot

Himalayan marmots are among the world's highest living mammals, found from 13,000 ft (4,000 m) right up to the snow line in the mountains of Nepal, India, and Tibet. They feed on grasses and flowers, and live in intricate burrows with special rest areas, "bathrooms" and rooms where they hibernate for seven months through the winter.

Small mammals

In the Himalayas and other Eurasian ranges, little rodents, such as pikas and mountain voles, stay active through the year, surviving through winter by building up stores of hay in dry places under rocks. Alpine, black-capped, and other marmots hibernate.

Birds of the air

Some birds, like snow finches, choughs, snowcocks, and ptarmigans live high up in mountains all the time, making the most of the seeds and insects, which are surprisingly abundant. Ravens and geese fly up in summer. Migrating snipe and geese may fly far overhead.

Water pipit

Birds can reach the highest peaks, soaring and gliding on mountain winds. Choughs have been seen flying over 26,250 ft (8,000 m) around Mt. Everest. Water pipits fly less high but breed well above the treeline, and often nest far above the snow line in summer.

Lammergeier

Lammergeiers are large vultures with huge wings. They feed on carrion like other vultures, but, in order to survive in the mountains, they have learned how to eat the tough parts of a carcass. When they find a big bone, they fly high up in the air and drop the bone on to a rock to smash it, so that they can get at the marrow inside.

Large mammals

Many sheep- and goatlike animals climb up to graze on the high meadows in spring, including the tahr, the markhor, the huge-horned Siberian ibex, and the argali, the largest of all wild sheep. Shaggy oxlike yaks live at heights of 19,700 ft (6,000 m) up in the Himalayas.

Chamois

The nimble chamois can run up or down almost sheer rock faces on its non-slip hooves, leap over twice its height in the air, or jump 20 ft (6 m) between dizzying crags. Even chamois just a few weeks old can perform these feats. Chamois feed on the high meadows in summer, but descend to the forests in winter.

Birds of prey

The exposed slopes of the mountains make them an ideal hunting ground for birds of prey, and the Eurasian mountains are home to many rare birds of prey, including golden eagles, mountain falcons, and buzzards. There are also many carrion-feeders, such as the Himalayan griffon and black vulture.

Polar ice

The Arctic and Antarctic are the world's most difficult habitats. For half the year, each is unimaginably cold and almost perpetually dark. But there is a brief summer when plants bloom and insects multiply and many birds fly in to make the most of the feast. A few hardy animals, like polar bears, stay all year, and there is always abundant life in the sea.

The Antarctic

Penguins
Penguins cope with the cold, snug inside waterproof feathers and layers of blubber. They cannot fly but are superb swimmers, well adapted to catching fish, the most abundant food here. There are seven Antarctic species, (e.g. Adelie, Gentoo).

Emperor
This is the world's largest penguin, up to 4 ft (1.25 m) tall. It can dive over 850 ft (250 m) to find fish and stay down for 20 minutes. It is one of the few penguins that breeds on the Antarctic ice. The female lays an egg in fall, then swims out to sea while the male keeps the egg warm on his feet through the winter. The male survives without food all winter.

Whales and seals
The Antarctic's big predators are not land mammals but seals and whales. Leopard seals prey on penguins, and toothed whales prey on seals. The abundance of fish means there are more seals here than in the Arctic, including the elephant seal—the world's biggest.

Antarctic cod
The Antarctic cod is the largest of the fish in the Southern Ocean around the Antarctic, weighing over 162 lb (70 kg). Fish could easily freeze solid in the cold polar waters, but this cod, like other fish here, has special protection in the form of antifreeze protein called glycoprotein or AFGP. This protein circulates in the fish's blood to stop ice crystals forming.

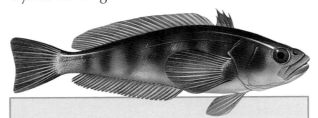

Fish
Long summer days generate lots of plankton for food, so despite the cold, the Southern Ocean teems with fish—plunder fish, ice fish, cod, and dragonfish. There are few species, but shoals are huge—and there are swarms of krill so large they can be seen by satellites.

Blue whale
Baleen whales have a comblike sieve or baleen in their mouths for straining tiny shrimplike krill from the water. Six species of baleen whale are found in Antarctica, including the southern right, the sei, and the gigantic blue whale, which is the largest creature ever—over 80 ft (24 m) long and weighing over 80 tons.

Wandering albatross
The wandering albatross is the world's largest flying bird with a wingspan of over 12 ft (3.6 m). It glides for hours on these huge wings moving barely a feather, and spends most of its life in the air, swooping down only occasionally to grab squid from the ocean's surface.

Sea birds
Penguins are Antarctica's only year-round residents, but 35 other seabird species visit in summer, including terns, petrels, gulls, and cormorants—and skuas that scavenge penguins' breeding grounds for their eggs and young.

Midge
Besides the wingless midge *Belgica antarctica*, there is one other midge in the Antarctic, and this is the only winged creature here—the midge *Parochlus steineni*. This tiny insect breeds on lakes full of aquatic mosses on the northern peninsula. Like other Antarctic insects, the midge's body contains special antifreeze proteins to stop it from freezing.

Insects
Antarctica's largest land animal is the wingless midge, only ½ in (1 cm) long. Its largest predator is a mite. There are only a few insect species, but they live in huge numbers under rocks in soil and lichens. Springtails are common around penguin colonies, feeding on plants.

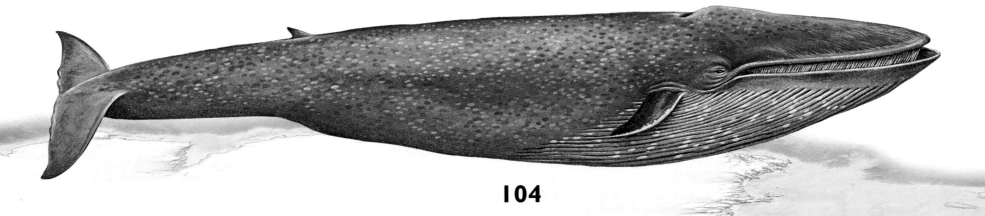

Polar bear

These are the world's largest bears, with males often weighing over 1,300 lb (600 kg). Thick fur and a layer of blubber keep out the cold. In summer, they eat berries and small rodents. In winter, females hibernate in ice dens, but males wander over the frozen sea preying on seals when they come up to breathe. Polar bears are superb swimmers.

Predators

With so little cover in the exposed Arctic landscape, predators rely on camouflage to make attacks. In winter, Arctic foxes, ermines, and least weasels all turn white to disguise them against the snow, turning brown again in spring. Even wolves are paler in winter.

Warble fly

The Arctic warble fly, known as kumak by the Inuit people, is a parasitic fly that lays its eggs in the skin of caribous. The larvae burrow into the flesh and stay there during the cold of winter. The following summer, they burrow out again, drop to the ground, and develop into adult flies.

Insects

As lakes and bogs thaw in spring, countless insects emerge from winter dormancy. Springtails and beetles crawl over the tundra. Butterflies and bees sip on Arctic flowers. In summer, huge swarms of mosquitoes and blackflies erupt to pester animals.

The Arctic

Birds of the air

As spring arrives, millions of birds flock to breed in the Arctic. Wagtails and pipits catch insects on the ground. Songbirds like wheatears feed on seeds too. Sand martins snatch insects in the air. As these birds fly north, predatory merlins and falcons are on their tails.

Ptarmigan

Of the 180 or so bird species that nest in the Arctic, just a few stay all year— including ptarmigans, snow buntings, and snowy owls. Ptarmigans are chickenlike birds that can fly but usually walk slowly, eating berries and leaves. They are brown in summer but turn snowy white in winter.

Sea birds and shore birds

In summer, the fringes of the ice melt, exposing vast areas of sea. Many birds arrive to breed on the Arctic shores, including shore birds (such as dunlins, turnstones, and knots), water-fowl (such as Brent geese), and seabirds (such as puffins, jaegers, and gulls).

Arctic tern

Many of the Arctic birds migrate long distances, but none fly as far as the Arctic tern. After breeding in the Arctic when it is summer here, they head off south to the Southern Ocean, feeding as they go. By the time they arrive, summer has come to the Antarctic. Toward the end of the Antarctic summer, they fly north again to the Arctic, completing a journey of 22,000 miles (35,000 km).

Whales and seals

The Arctic winter is hard for seals and whales because the sea freezes over, stopping them coming up for air. Some migrate in winter. Seals that stay gnaw through the ice to make breathing holes, but they must keep working to keep the holes open as the ice thickens.

Harp seal

Harp seals are fast, agile swimmers that can dive deep and stay down for up to half an hour as they hunt for cod, capelin, and other fish. As the ice sheet advances or retreats, harp seals move with it, traveling in big, noisy groups. Pups are born on the ice in early spring and are then suckled for a few weeks by their mothers, before the mothers head off north to feed.

Grazing animals

Every spring, huge herds of caribou wander north through the tundra to feed on the fresh growth, led by pregnant females. They move north each day, swimming across rivers and inlets, trekking over 600 miles (1,000 km). Calves are born en route.

Moose

The moose is the largest of all deer, the male weighing up to 1,550 lb (700 kg) and with giant antlers over 6 ft (1.8 m) across. It is well adapted for life in the far north, with long spindly legs that move easily through deep snow and a thick coat to keep out the cold.

Animal classification

The animal kingdom is divided into groups called *phyla*. One of these is called chordates. Chordates are animals that have backbones, such as tigers and tortoises. Animals without backbones, such as snails, starfish, and scorpions, are invertebrates. Nearly all the animals on Earth are invertebrates, which includes at least 1,000,000 kinds of insect. Animals are organized, or classified, into several different groups. A brown bear, for example, is one of seven kinds, or *species* of bear. Brown bears belong to the bear *family* and to the *order* of carnivores. The carnivores belong to the *class* of mammals, and mammals belong to the *phylum* of chordates. This chart shows the main animal groups.

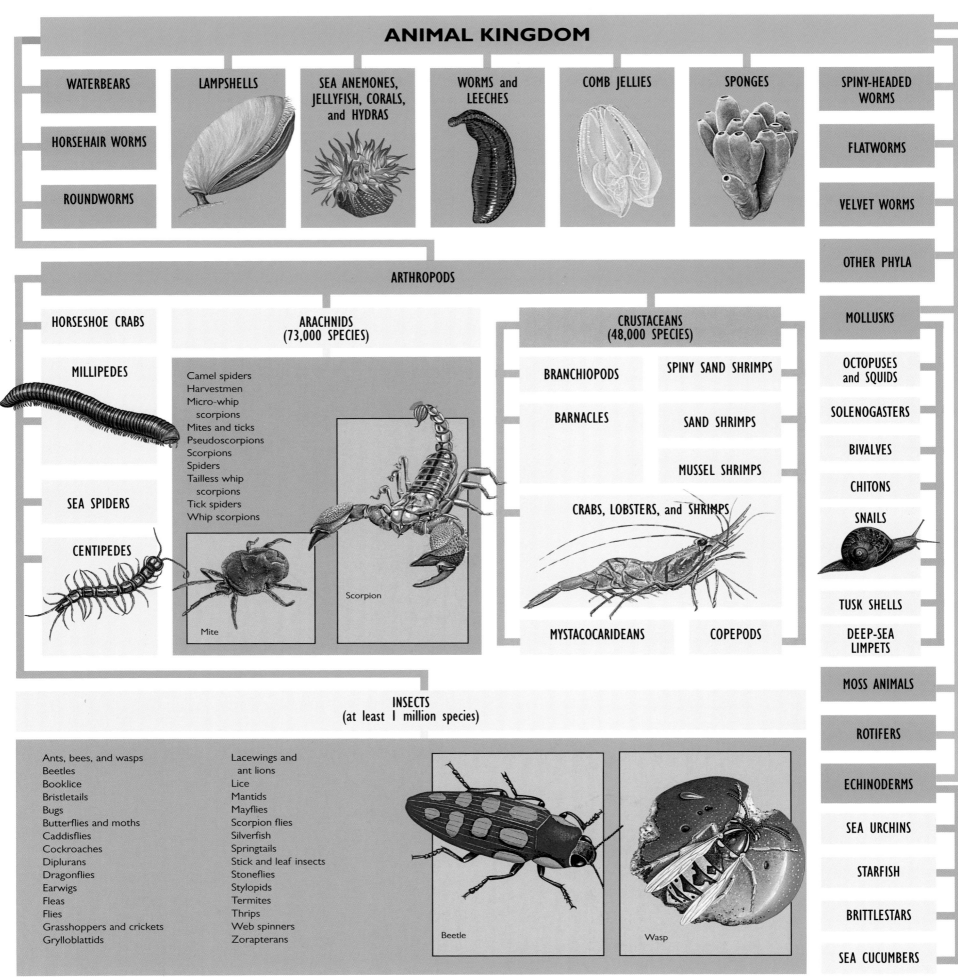

ANIMAL KINGDOM

WATERBEARS

HORSEHAIR WORMS

ROUNDWORMS

LAMPSHELLS

SEA ANEMONES, JELLYFISH, CORALS, and HYDRAS

WORMS and LEECHES

COMB JELLIES

SPONGES

SPINY-HEADED WORMS

FLATWORMS

VELVET WORMS

OTHER PHYLA

ARTHROPODS

HORSESHOE CRABS

MILLIPEDES

SEA SPIDERS

CENTIPEDES

ARACHNIDS (73,000 SPECIES)

Camel spiders
Harvestmen
Micro-whip scorpions
Mites and ticks
Pseudoscorpions
Scorpions
Spiders
Tailless whip scorpions
Tick spiders
Whip scorpions

Mite

Scorpion

CRUSTACEANS (48,000 SPECIES)

BRANCHIOPODS

BARNACLES

SPINY SAND SHRIMPS

SAND SHRIMPS

MUSSEL SHRIMPS

CRABS, LOBSTERS, and SHRIMPS

MYSTACOCARIDEANS

COPEPODS

MOLLUSKS

OCTOPUSES and SQUIDS

SOLENOGASTERS

BIVALVES

CHITONS

SNAILS

TUSK SHELLS

DEEP-SEA LIMPETS

MOSS ANIMALS

ROTIFERS

ECHINODERMS

SEA URCHINS

STARFISH

BRITTLESTARS

SEA CUCUMBERS

INSECTS (at least 1 million species)

Ants, bees, and wasps
Beetles
Booklice
Bristletails
Bugs
Butterflies and moths
Caddisflies
Cockroaches
Diplurans
Dragonflies
Earwigs
Fleas
Flies
Grasshoppers and crickets
Grylloblattids

Lacewings and ant lions
Lice
Mantids
Mayflies
Scorpion flies
Silverfish
Springtails
Stick and leaf insects
Stoneflies
Stylopids
Termites
Thrips
Web spinners
Zorapterans

Beetle

Wasp

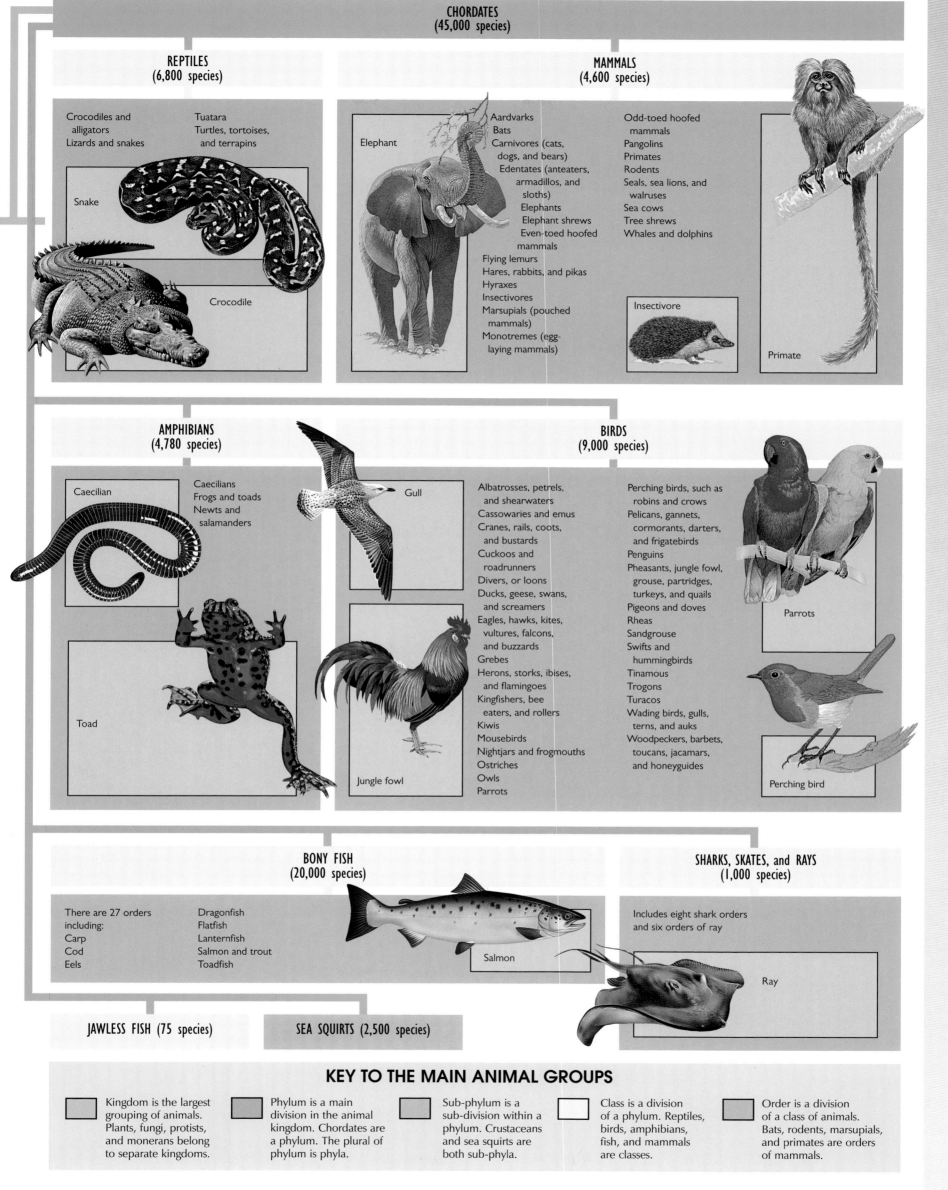

CHORDATES
(45,000 species)

REPTILES
(6,800 species)

Crocodiles and alligators
Lizards and snakes

Tuatara
Turtles, tortoises, and terrapins

Snake

Crocodile

MAMMALS
(4,600 species)

Elephant

Aardvarks
Bats
Carnivores (cats, dogs, and bears)
Edentates (anteaters, armadillos, and sloths)
Elephants
Elephant shrews
Even-toed hoofed mammals
Flying lemurs
Hares, rabbits, and pikas
Hyraxes
Insectivores
Marsupials (pouched mammals)
Monotremes (egg-laying mammals)

Odd-toed hoofed mammals
Pangolins
Primates
Rodents
Seals, sea lions, and walruses
Sea cows
Tree shrews
Whales and dolphins

Insectivore

Primate

AMPHIBIANS
(4,780 species)

Caecilian

Caecilians
Frogs and toads
Newts and salamanders

Toad

BIRDS
(9,000 species)

Gull

Albatrosses, petrels, and shearwaters
Cassowaries and emus
Cranes, rails, coots, and bustards
Cuckoos and roadrunners
Divers, or loons
Ducks, geese, swans, and screamers
Eagles, hawks, kites, vultures, falcons, and buzzards
Grebes
Herons, storks, ibises, and flamingoes
Kingfishers, bee eaters, and rollers
Kiwis
Mousebirds
Nightjars and frogmouths
Ostriches
Owls
Parrots

Perching birds, such as robins and crows
Pelicans, gannets, cormorants, darters, and frigatebirds
Penguins
Pheasants, jungle fowl, grouse, partridges, turkeys, and quails
Pigeons and doves
Rheas
Sandgrouse
Swifts and hummingbirds
Tinamous
Trogons
Turacos
Wading birds, gulls, terns, and auks
Woodpeckers, barbets, toucans, jacamars, and honeyguides

Parrots

Jungle fowl

Perching bird

BONY FISH
(20,000 species)

There are 27 orders including:
Carp
Cod
Eels

Dragonfish
Flatfish
Lanternfish
Salmon and trout
Toadfish

Salmon

SHARKS, SKATES, and RAYS
(1,000 species)

Includes eight shark orders and six orders of ray

Ray

JAWLESS FISH (75 species)

SEA SQUIRTS (2,500 species)

KEY TO THE MAIN ANIMAL GROUPS

Kingdom is the largest grouping of animals. Plants, fungi, protists, and monerans belong to separate kingdoms.

Phylum is a main division in the animal kingdom. Chordates are a phylum. The plural of phylum is phyla.

Sub-phylum is a sub-division within a phylum. Crustaceans and sea squirts are both sub-phyla.

Class is a division of a phylum. Reptiles, birds, amphibians, fish, and mammals are classes.

Order is a division of a class of animals. Bats, rodents, marsupials, and primates are orders of mammals.

Mammals

Mammals range in size from tiny shrews to gigantic blue whales. They have found a way to live in almost every habitat on Earth, because they are warm-blooded or "endothermic." This means they keep their bodies at the best temperature for body processes, whatever the conditions. A puma can live anywhere from tropical forests to snowy mountains. Even so, each mammal has its own preferred habitat.

▶ Bat, Ghost
RANGE: AUSTRALIA
HABITAT: CAVES, OLD MINE TUNNELS
This is a large carnivorous bat that feeds on insects, frogs, birds, lizards, and small bats. It uses both ears and eyes to locate prey when hunting.

▼ Aardvark
RANGE: AFRICA, SOUTH OF THE SAHARA
HABITAT: RAIN FOREST, DRY SAVANNA
Aardvark is Afrikaans for "earth pig." In fact, an aardvark is an anteater that digs into termite and ant nests with its powerful forefeet, then sweeps up the insects with its long, sticky tongue. Its big ears help it to locate insects.

▼ Anteater, Giant
RANGE: C. AND S. AMERICA
HABITAT: FOREST, SAVANNA
Like all anteaters, the giant anteater has no teeth. Instead it has a very long snout and a 2 ft- (60 cm-) long tongue for sucking termites and ants from their nests.

▼ Ape, Barbary
RANGE: GIBRALTAR AND N. AFRICA HABITAT: ROCKY AREAS, FOREST CLEARINGS
The Barbary ape is not actually an ape, but a monkey with no tail. It was once found over much of southwest Europe as well as Africa, but now its only European home is Gibraltar. It forages in trees and on the ground for leaves and fruit.

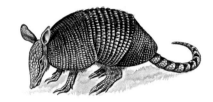

▲ Armadillo, Nine-banded
RANGE: TROPICAL AMERICA
HABITAT: DRY GRASSLAND
Armadillos dig for ants and spiders at night. When threatened they curl up into a ball so that only their armor-plated back is exposed.

▲ Armadillo, Pink fairy
RANGE: W. ARGENTINA
HABITAT: DRY GRASSLAND
This armadillo lifts its rear end with its tail while digging for ants.

▲ Baboon, Olive
RANGE: C. AFRICA
HABITAT: SAVANNA
The olive baboon is a large, ground-living monkey with a doglike muzzle. It eats mostly grass, fruit, and insects, but sometimes hunts small mammals.

▲ Badger, American
RANGE: S. W. CANADA TO C. MEXICO
HABITAT: OPEN GRASSLAND, ARID LAND
The American badger is a solitary hunter that digs out ground squirrels and prairie dogs at night. It can dig with amazing speed.

▼ Badger, Eurasian
RANGE: EUROPE AND ASIA
HABITAT: FOREST, GRASSLAND
The Eurasian badger lives in families in huge burrows called setts. It emerges at dusk to play and hunt for worms and also small animals, fruit, and nuts.

▼ Bandicoot, Brown
RANGE: AUSTRALIA
HABITAT: SCRUB, FOREST
Bandicoots are small marsupials that dig for insect larvae and plant roots. The brown bandicoot lives in dense scrub and eats fungi and scorpions.

▼ Bat, Common long-eared
RANGE: EUROPE AND N. ASIA
HABITAT: FOREST
This bat's huge, highly sensitive ears help it to fly in pitch dark by using sound echoes and also to locate its insect prey.

▼ Bat, Common vampire
RANGE: C. AND S. AMERICA
HABITAT: FOREST CAVES
The vampire bat lives only on blood, sucking it from its victims through its tongue. The victim loses only a small amount of blood, but the bat's bite may transmit diseases.

▼ Bat, Greater fruit
RANGE: SOUTHERN AND S. E. ASIA
HABITAT: FOREST
This bat has the largest wings of any bat, up to 4 ft (1.25 m) across. It roosts by day in large trees in flocks, which take to the air at night to hunt for fruit, such as bananas.

▼ Bat, Greater horseshoe
RANGE: EUROPE, ASIA, N. AFRICA
HABITAT: FOREST
Horseshoe bats get their name from the horseshoe-shaped rim on their noses which helps them amplify and direct the ultrasonic cries that they use to locate prey. The greater horseshoe is a poor flier and feeds on beetles on the ground.

▼ Bat, Spear-nosed
RANGE: TROPICAL AMERICA
HABITAT: FOREST
This bat feeds on mice, birds, and small bats, as well as the occasional insect.

108

▲ Bear, Black
RANGE: ASIA, NORTH AMERICA
HABITAT: FOREST
There are black bears in both America and Asia. The American black bear eats very little meat, living mostly on grasses and fruits in summer and nuts in fall. In October these bears retreat to their dens and sleep through the winter, though they do not go into true hibernation.

▲ Bear, Brown/Grizzly
RANGE: EUROPE, ASIA, NORTH AMERICA
HABITAT: FOREST, TUNDRA
The American grizzly and Kodiak bears are two of the various subspecies of brown bear, which also include the Siberian bear and the Gobi bear. They are very strong and amongst the largest of all carnivores.

◀ Bear, Polar
RANGE: ARCTIC OCEAN
HABITAT: COASTS, ICE FLOES
The polar bear is the top predator of the Arctic region. It lives mainly on fish, seabirds, caribou, seals, and other animals, but in the summer it also feeds on berries and leaves. Polar bears are excellent swimmers.

▼ Bear, Spectacled
RANGE: S. AMERICA
HABITAT: FOREST, SAVANNA, MOUNTAINS
The spectacled bear is the only South American bear. It lives mainly in forests, feeding on leaves, fruit, and roots, but also sometimes preys on deer and vicuña. It is a good climber and sleeps in a tree in a large nest made from sticks—either alone or in a family group.

▲ Bear, Sun
RANGE: S. E. ASIA
HABITAT: MOUNTAINS, LOWLAND FOREST
The sun bear is the smallest kind of bear, but it is still very strong. It gets its name from its habit of sunbathing in its treetop nest. It feeds mostly on insects and their larvae, which it exposes by tearing at tree bark with its strong claws. It also preys on jungle fowl and small rodents.

▶ Beaver
RANGE: NORTH AMERICA
HABITAT: RIVERS AND LAKES
Beavers are large rodents that gnaw down trees with their powerful teeth to build dams across streams and make lodges to live in during the winter. They feed on bark and twigs in winter and other plants in summer.

▲ Binturong
RANGE: S. E. ASIA
HABITAT: FOREST
This is a small carnivorous mammal related to the civet. It is the only carnivore besides the kinkajou to have a prehensile tail, which it uses as an extra limb when climbing.

▶ Bison, American
RANGE: N. AMERICA
HABITAT: PRAIRIE, OPEN WOODLAND
This huge, shaggy, cowlike creature can grow up to 10 ft (3 m) tall at the shoulders. It used to roam the American prairies in herds many thousands strong, and make annual migrations in search of good pasture. But mass slaughter by European settlers brought it almost to extinction. Now, about 20,000 live on reserves.

▼ Boar, Wild
RANGE: EUROPE, N. AFRICA, ASIA
HABITAT: FOREST, WOODLAND
The wild boar is the ancestor of the farmyard pig, but has bristly hair and males have tusks. It roots around woodland floors for plants and insects and also digs up bulbs and tubers. Wild boars are surprisingly fast, agile creatures and they can become quite aggressive if frightened.

▼ Bobcat
RANGE: NORTH AMERICA
HABITAT: SWAMP, FOREST
The bobcat is the most common North American wildcat. It is about twice the size of a domestic cat and feeds mainly on rabbits and hares, but also catches ground birds. It hunts by slowly stalking its victim. It gets its name from its stubby, "bobbed" tail.

▲ Bongo
RANGE: C. AFRICA
HABITAT: TROPICAL FOREST
The bongo is the largest forest antelope, growing up to 7 ft (2.1 m) tall. It hides among bushes during the day and comes out at dawn and dusk to feed on leaves, fruit, and bark. At night it grazes on grass. When a bongo runs, it tilts its head back to prevent its horns catching on branches.

▲ Buffalo, Asian water
RANGE: INDIA, S. E. ASIA
HABITAT: FOREST, WETLAND
American bison are sometimes called buffaloes, but true buffaloes live in the tropics and have thinner coats and flattened horns, which Asian water buffaloes use to defend themselves against tigers. The Asian water buffalo lives in southern Asia where it spends much of the day wallowing in muddy rivers. Most water buffalo are now domesticated.

▲ Bush baby, Greater
RANGE: S. AFRICA
HABITAT: FOREST, WOODED SAVANNA
This is the largest of the nine small African tree-dwelling primates known as galagos, or bush babies. These night hunters have huge eyes and ears for finding insects and reptiles in the dark.

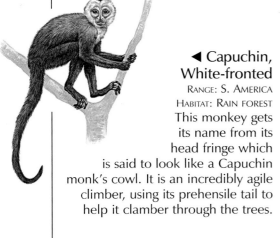

► Camel, Dromedary
RANGE: NORTH AFRICA, MIDDLE EAST
HABITAT: DRY GRASSLAND, DESERT
Camels are superbly adapted to life in hot deserts, with an amazing capacity to drink enough water to last for days and the ability to let their body temperature climb during the day.

◄ Capuchin, White-fronted
RANGE: S. AMERICA
HABITAT: RAIN FOREST
This monkey gets its name from its head fringe which is said to look like a Capuchin monk's cowl. It is an incredibly agile climber, using its prehensile tail to help it clamber through the trees.

▼ Capybara
RANGE: S. AMERICA
HABITAT: FOREST, GRASSLAND
The capybara is the largest of all rodents—the size of a sheep. It eats mainly water plants, and is a superb swimmer, with partly webbed feet.

▼ Caracal
RANGE: AFRICA, S. W. ASIA
HABITAT: DRY GRASSLAND, DESERT
Sometimes known as the desert lynx, the caracal hunts jerboas and ground squirrels at night and can bring down a bird just after take-off.

▼ Caribou
RANGE: N. EUROPE, ASIA, N. AMERICA
HABITAT: TUNDRA, TAIGA
Known in Europe as the reindeer, the caribou lives on the tundra and feeds mainly on grass in summer and lichen in winter, which it obtains by digging through snow. It is the only deer in which females as well as males have antlers. Caribou are often seen in huge herds on migration.

▼ Cat, Pallas's
RANGE: C. ASIA
HABITAT: DESERT, STEPPE, MOUNTAINS
This is a small desert cat that lives in caves or burrows taken over from other animals, such as marmots. It hunts small animals, such as mice and hares, at night.

▼ Cat, Wild
RANGE: EUROPE, AFRICA, S. W. ASIA
HABITAT: GRASSLAND, FOREST
The wild cat is an ancestor of the domestic cat and looks similar but is bigger and has a shorter, thicker tail. It climbs trees well, but stalks most of its prey on the ground, catching small rodents and ground birds. Courting males howl and screech to attract females.

▼ Chamois
RANGE: EUROPE, MIDDLE EAST
HABITAT: MOUNTAINS
The chamois is the nimblest of all mountain goats, nipping easily from crag to crag. Its hooves have special spongy pads to help them grip on slippery rocks. In summer it feeds on herbs and flowers high up; in winter it moves down to feed on lichens and pine shoots.

▼ Cheetah
RANGE: AFRICA, S. W. ASIA
HABITAT: GRASSLAND
The cheetah is the fastest land animal, able to sprint at more than 60 mph (100 km/h) for short distances. When hunting, it stalks as close as possible to its prey, then moves in for the kill with an explosive burst of speed—knocking over the victim and killing it with a bite to the throat. If the attempt fails, it usually gives up. Its prey are typically small antelopes, hares, and birds.

▲ Chevrotain, Water
RANGE: W. AFRICA
HABITAT: RAIN FOREST
This tiny mouse deer, about the size of a hare, lives in African rain forests. It rests during the day in undergrowth or a hole in the riverbank, then ventures out at night to forage.

▲ Chimpanzee
RANGE: C. AFRICA
HABITAT: RAIN FOREST, WOODED SAVANNA
Chimps are quick and very clever apes. They are very expressive and use many noises and gestures to communicate with each other. They can also use simple tools, such as sticks, to get food.

▲ Chinchilla
RANGE: N. CHILE
HABITAT: ROCKY MOUNTAINS
The chinchilla is a small rodent, with large eyes, long ears, and a bushy tail, that lives in colonies in rock crevices. It eats plants, typically sitting up to eat with the food held in its front paws.

▲ Chipmunk, Eastern
RANGE: N. AMERICA
HABITAT: FOREST
This little squirrel-like rodent lives in leafy forests in eastern North America. It is a lively animal, always on the move gathering seeds, nuts, and berries, which it stores for winter.

▼ Civet, African palm
RANGE: AFRICA SOUTH OF THE SAHARA
HABITAT: FOREST, SAVANNA
The civet is a small carnivorous animal with a doglike muzzle and a long, bushy tail. It lives in forests and grasslands and feeds at night on small lizards and rodents.

▼ Coati
RANGE: TROPICAL AMERICA
HABITAT: FOREST
The coati belongs to the same family as raccoons and red pandas, but lives in packs in the forests of tropical America. It has a long, very sensitive nose, and snuffles in the undergrowth for small animals, fruits, and seeds.

▼ Colugo
RANGE: PHILIPPINES
HABITAT: RAIN FOREST
Colugos, also known as flying lemurs, are the world's largest gliding mammals. They can glide 425 ft (130 m) on the flaps of skin between their limbs. There are two species: one from Indonesia and one from the Philippines.

▲ Coyote
RANGE: N. AND C. AMERICA
HABITAT: PRAIRIE, OPEN WOODLAND
Known by Native American tribes as the "trickster," for its cunning, the coyote has been poisoned and shot by farmers for years, but still survives. Females give birth to litters of about six pups in a burrow in the spring. The male brings the family food, including snakes, rabbits, rodents, insects, and fruit.

▲ Deer, Forest musk
RANGE: C. ASIA
HABITAT: MOUNTAINS, TEMPERATE FOREST
Musk deer are five species of small deer that live in the mountains of central Asia. Males have a pouch on their stomachs that produces a strong-smelling wax called musk. They use the scent to mark out territories, but all species of musk deer are endangered because they are hunted and farmed for their musk, which is used to make perfume.

▼ Deer, Red, or Wapiti
RANGE: MAINLY N. AMERICA, EURASIA
HABITAT: TEMPERATE WOODLAND, MOORS
Known as the red deer in Europe, the wapiti is very common. Stags have antlers up to 5 ft (1.5 m) long.

▼ Deer, Roe
RANGE: EURASIA
HABITAT: TEMPERATE WOODLAND
The small, shy roe deer usually lives alone and feeds at night, but sometimes roe deer gather in small groups in winter. Unique among deer, it has almost no tail.

▼ Deer, White-tailed
RANGE: THE AMERICAS
HABITAT: FOREST, SWAMP, GRASSLAND
The adaptable white-tailed deer lives in every habitat from the Arctic to the tropics—partly because it browses on everything from grasses to nuts and lichens.

▼ Dhole
RANGE: S. ASIA
HABITAT: RAIN FOREST
The dhole is a wild dog that lives in packs of up to 30. Dholes are not fast runners, but they can chase prey for long distances until they finally tire. A pack can pull down a buffalo or even a tiger.

▼ Dingo
RANGE: AUSTRALIA
HABITAT: DRY GRASSLAND
The dingo was introduced to Australia by people from Asia some 3,000 years ago as a hunting dog. Unlike domestic dogs, dingos cannot bark. The kangaroos they fed on are now rare, so many dingos attack sheep.

▼ Dog, Hunting
RANGE: AFRICA
HABITAT: SAVANNA, DRY GRASSLAND
Hunting dogs live and hunt in huge packs, preying on animals as large as wildebeests, seizing their legs and dragging them to the ground.

▼ Dolphin, Common
RANGE: WORLDWIDE
HABITAT: TROPICAL OCEANS
Dolphins are actually a type of whale, but they are smaller and incredibly agile. They are acrobatic and playful, and can burst right out of the water. They are also extremely intelligent.

▼ Dolphin, Ganges
RANGE: INDIA
HABITAT: RIVERS
The Ganges dolphin is one of several species of dolphin that live in rivers. It has poor eyesight and finds its food—usually small fish—by echolocation.

▲ Dormouse, Desert
RANGE: KAZAKHSTAN
HABITAT: DESERT
Dormice get their name from the Latin *dormire*, which means "to sleep," because they hibernate for long periods. Most dormice hibernate to escape cold. The desert dormouse does it to escape heat.

▲ Dugong
RANGE: INDIAN OCEAN, WESTERN PACIFIC
HABITAT: COASTAL WATERS
The dugong is also known as the sea cow because it feeds on sea grass, and has a long hind gut to digest grass just as cows have a rumen. Dugongs lie quietly on the seabed for most of the time, coming up occasionally for air.

▲ Echidna, Long-nosed
RANGE: NEW GUINEA
HABITAT: RAIN FOREST
Echidnas are, along with platypuses, the only egg-laying mammals, or monotremes. Female echidnas lay one to three eggs, which they incubate inside a temporary pouch until the eggs are ready to hatch. The long-nosed echidna is also known as the spiny anteater and feeds on ants and termites.

► Eland
RANGE: AFRICA SOUTH OF THE SAHARA
HABITAT: SAVANNA
The eland is the largest of the antelopes. Big bulls can weigh up to a ton. Both male and female have long, straight horns up to 28 in (70 cm) long, with a spiral twist. They are browsing animals, feeding at dusk and dawn in open country with scattered trees. They not only eat leaves, but also dig up roots with their hooves.

► Elephant, African
RANGE: AFRICA SOUTH OF THE SAHARA
HABITAT: RAIN FOREST, SAVANNA
The African elephant is the biggest land animal, weighing up to 6 tons. It needs to eat 660 lb (300 kg) of food a day and drink more than 26 gallons (100 liters) of water. Males have tusks of up to 10 ft (3 m) long.

▲ Elephant, Asian
RANGE: S. ASIA
HABITAT: RAIN FOREST
The Asian elephant is smaller than the African, has smaller ears, and just one fingerlike tip to its trunk—the African has two. Asian elephants live mostly in forests, feeding mainly on grass and leaves, using their trunks to pull up plants. Most Asian elephants are domesticated.

▼ Fox, Fennec
RANGE: N. AFRICA, S. W. ASIA
HABITAT: DESERT
The fennec fox is the smallest dog, but has the largest ears in proportion to its body. Its big ears help it to keep cool and also locate the small rodents, birds, and insects that it hunts at night. By day it shelters from the heat of the desert in small burrows. Fennec foxes are sociable animals and mate for life.

▲ Fox, Red
RANGE: N. AMERICA, EURASIA, INTRODUCED AUSTRALIA
HABITAT: WOODLAND, GRASSLAND
Red foxes hunt at night alone and come together only to breed and rear young. They feed on a wide range of food. Their natural habitat is forest and grassland, but many have managed to adapt to suburban gardens and even city centers.

▲ Gazelle, Thomson's
RANGE: E. AFRICA
HABITAT: SAVANNA
Gazelles are graceful, fast-running antelopes with slender legs. Thomson's gazelles live in large herds in open grassland, and have to be almost constantly on the watch to avoid predators like cheetahs.

► Gelada
RANGE: ETHIOPIA
HABITAT: MOUNTAINS
The gelada is a monkey that lives far away from trees. It feeds on plant material on the ground and even sleeps on bare rock. It has three areas of bare red skin which the male swells up when threatened.

▼ Genet, Small spotted
RANGE: S. W. EUROPE, AFRICA, S. W. ASIA
HABITAT: SAVANNA, SCRUB
Genets are small carnivores related to civets. They stalk their prey stealthily, crouching almost flat before pouncing. They catch most victims, such as rodents and reptiles, on the ground.

▼ Gerbil, Great
RANGE: S. EUROPE, ASIA, AFRICA
HABITAT: DESERT
Gerbils are good at living in dry places, getting most of their water from food and avoiding the heat by burrowing.

▼ Gerbil, Large North African
RANGE: N. AFRICA
HABITAT: DESERT
The North African gerbil lives in rough burrows dug in sand where it hides during the day, emerging at dusk to forage.

▼ Gibbon, Lar
RANGE: S. E. ASIA
HABITAT: FOREST

The Lar gibbon is one of nine species of apes called gibbon. Gibbons are great acrobats, using their long arms to swing through the forest canopy with amazing speed.

▲ Gibbon, Pileated
RANGE: THAILAND
HABITAT: FOREST

The pileated gibbon has a black cap of hair on its head. It is born white, and turns black from the head down as it grows older. It is strongly territorial and a male will scream and shout abuse at other males.

▶ Giraffe
RANGE: AFRICA SOUTH OF THE SAHARA
HABITAT: SAVANNA

The giraffe is the world's tallest animal, growing up to 20 ft (6 m). Half of its height is its incredibly long neck which enables it to reach the leaves and buds of acacia and thorn trees far above the ground. But it has to splay its long front legs in order to drink. Giraffes live in small groups of females and young led by a male.

▲ Glider, Greater
RANGE: E. AUSTRALIA
HABITAT: FOREST

The greater glider is the biggest of Australia's gliding possums, able to glide 330 ft (100 m) or more from tree to tree. Like all possums, it is a marsupial.

▲ Glider, Sugar
RANGE: N. E. AUSTRALIA, NEW GUINEA
HABITAT: FOREST

The sugar glider is a gliding possum that feeds on the sugary sap oozing from wounds on the bark of wattle and gum trees.

▲ Gopher, Plains pocket
RANGE: N. AMERICA
HABITAT: DESERT, GRASSLAND

The pocket gopher gets its name from its cheek pouches, which can be crammed full of food to take back to its burrow.

▼
Guanaco
RANGE: S. AMERICA
HABITAT: GRASSLAND, MOUNTAINS

The guanaco is related to the camel and, like camels, it kneels when lying down. It is a very hardy creature, able to survive in the scorching Atacama Desert and on snowy mountains.

▼ Guinea pig
RANGE: S. AMERICA
HABITAT: GRASSLAND, ROCKS

Guinea pigs, or cavies, are small rodents that feed on grass and leaves. Cavies are the ancestors of pet guinea pigs.

▼ Hamster, Common
RANGE: EURASIA
HABITAT: GRASSLAND, FARMLAND

Hamsters are small burrowing rodents with large cheek pouches which they use for carrying food back to their burrows.

▼ Gorilla
RANGE: C. AFRICA
HABITAT: RAIN FOREST

The gorilla is the largest primate and the largest of the great apes, weighing up to 660 lb (300 kg). Gorillas live in forests in groups led by a large male, or silverback. Despite their size, they are gentle creatures, feeding on leaves and stems which they snap off with their hands.

▼ Hare, Brown
RANGE: EURASIA, INTRODUCED AMERICAS, AUSTRALIA
HABITAT: WOODLAND, FARMLAND

Unlike rabbits, hares live above ground in a shallow depression called a form. They rely on speed to escape and can run at up to 30 mph (50 km/h). Their young, called leverets, can run soon after they are born.

▼ Hedgehog, Western
RANGE: W. EUROPE, INTRODUCED NEW ZEALAND
HABITAT: WOODLAND, FARMLAND

The hedgehog hibernates for up to six months a year. If threatened, it rolls up into a little ball and makes its 6,000 spines stand on end.

▼ Hippopotamus
RANGE: AFRICA SOUTH OF THE SAHARA
HABITAT: RIVERS OR LAKES IN GRASSLAND

The hippo is a huge creature, weighing up to 3 tons, with huge jaws. It lounges in water by day and emerges at night to feed on grass and other plants.

▼ Hippopotamus, Pygmy
RANGE: W. AFRICA
HABITAT: RAIN FOREST

The pygmy hippo is a small hippo with a narrower mouth and thinner body. It lives mainly on land and feeds on leaves and fallen fruit, which it forages for at night.

▲ Hyena, Spotted
RANGE: AFRICA SOUTH OF THE SAHARA
HABITAT: SAVANNA

The spotted hyena is the biggest, most powerful hyena. Besides feeding on carrion, it hunts in packs to bring down prey, such as zebras and antelopes.

▲ Hyena, Striped
RANGE: AFRICA, S. W. ASIA
HABITAT: DRY SAVANNA, DESERT

Hyenas look like dogs, but are an entirely separate family. The striped hyena feeds on carrion and also preys on small animals, such as sheep.

▼ Impala
RANGE: AFRICA SOUTH OF THE SAHARA
HABITAT: SAVANNA

The impala is perhaps the most agile of all antelopes, bounding 33 ft (10 m) in a single leap—just for fun as well as to escape predators. Typically, impalas live in large herds in the dry season.

▲ Indri
RANGE: MADAGASCAR
HABITAT: FOREST

The indri is the largest of the lemurs, Madagascar's unique primates, though unlike the other lemurs it has only a stumpy tail. It is also the noisiest. To claim its territory it sings a weird song, audible more than 1¼ miles (2 km) away. Indris live in family groups and forage through the trees by day for leaves, shoots, and fruit.

▼ Jackrabbit, Black-tailed
RANGE: U.S.A.
HABITAT: GRASSLAND, DESERT

The jackrabbit has long ears that help to keep it cool. It also has long, powerful back legs and bounds along at tremendous speed, up to 37 mph (60 km/h). In summer it eats green plants and grass; in winter, more woody plants.

▼ Jaguar
RANGE: C. AND S. AMERICA
HABITAT: RAIN FOREST, SAVANNA

The jaguar is the biggest South American cat. It mainly hunts peccaries and capybaras, but swims well and often hunts otters, turtles, and snakes in rivers.

▼ Jerboa, Great
RANGE: C. ASIA
HABITAT: STEPPE, DESERT

Jerboas are small, mouselike creatures with long tails and very long back legs that allow them to jump 10 ft (3 m) in a single leap. They live in burrows by day and emerge at night to feed on seeds and insects.

▼ Kangaroo rat, Desert
RANGE: S. W. U.S.A., N. MEXICO
HABITAT: DESERT

Kangaroo rats are rats with long tails and very long legs, which help them jump like kangaroos, up to 6½ ft (2 m) in a single leap. They get most of the water they need from plants and avoid the desert heat by coming out of their burrows only at night. They can travel great distances to find food.

▲ Kangaroo, Musky rat
RANGE: AUSTRALIA
HABITAT: RAIN FOREST

Rat kangaroos are tiny kangaroos that live in Australian rain forests and feed on leaves, fruit, and small animals. Unlike other kangaroos, they often move around on all four legs.

▼ Kangaroo, Red
RANGE: C. AUSTRALIA
HABITAT: DRY GRASSLAND, DESERT

This is the largest and fastest marsupial. Bounding along on its huge back legs, it can reach 37 mph (60 km/h). Females give birth to babies called joeys, which stay in the pouch for two months.

► Kinkajou
RANGE: TROPICAL C. AND S. AMERICA
HABITAT: RAIN FOREST

The kinkajou is a small tree-climber related to accoons and pandas. It uses its prehensile tail to cling on while it is grabbing food. It feeds mainly on fruit and insects.

◄ Koala
RANGE: E. AUSTRALIA
HABITAT: EUCALYPTUS FOREST

Sometimes called a koala bear, the koala is actually a marsupial. It feeds entirely on the leaves and shoots of gum trees (eucalyptus). After emerging from the pouch, baby koalas ride on their mother's back.

▲ Kudu, Greater
RANGE: AFRICA SOUTH OF THE SAHARA
HABITAT: SAVANNA, ROCKY COUNTRY

The kudu is a large antelope with gigantic horns, up to 40 in (1 m) long. It is a browser that feeds on leaves, shoots, and seeds. Its hearing and sense of smell are good but its eyesight is poor.

▼ Langur, Hanuman
RANGE: INDIA, SRI LANKA
HABITAT: FOREST, SCRUB

Langurs are agile monkeys that live in the tropical forests of southern Asia. The Hanuman of India happily lives near houses and raids them for food, but is considered sacred so it is rarely hunted.

▼ Lemming, Norway
RANGE: SCANDINAVIA
HABITAT: TUNDRA

Lemmings are said to commit mass suicide. In fact, when food is plentiful in the harsh tundra, lemming numbers rise sharply and they are forced to migrate. During their mass migration, some drown while crossing rivers.

▼ Lemur, Ring-tailed
RANGE: MADAGASCAR
HABITAT: ROCKY WOODS

Lemurs are agile, tree-climbing primates that live on Madagascar and the nearby Comoro Islands. The ring-tailed lemur has a catlike face with dark eye rings and a long, bushy, upright tail with dramatic gray and black rings. It also has glands that emit a strong scent when it is excited or disturbed.

▼ Leopard
RANGE: AFRICA, SOUTHERN ASIA
HABITAT: MOST TROPICAL ENVIRONMENTS

The leopard is the most adaptable big cat, living everywhere from dense forest to open desert. A leopard has spots; a panther is a leopard that is entirely black. The leopard is a good climber and immensely strong. It often hauls kills as large as antelopes into trees out of the reach of scavengers, such as hyenas. It typically ambushes its prey, often leaping straight out of trees.

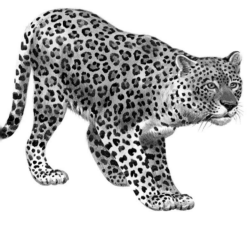

► Lion
RANGE: AFRICA SOUTH OF THE SAHARA, N. W. INDIA
HABITAT: SAVANNA

The lion is the second largest cat after the tiger, typically 6½ ft (2 m) long excluding the tail. Lions mostly live in groups called prides, consisting of about 15 animals, with three males and the rest females and their young. Prides hunt together, but it is usually the lionesses (females) that do most of the hunting.

▲ Lion, Mountain
RANGE: N., C., AND S. AMERICA
HABITAT: FOREST, GRASSLAND, MOUNTAINS

Also known as the puma or cougar, the mountain lion mainly hunts deer. Unlike lions, mountain lions hunt on their own and purr instead of roar.

► Llama
RANGE: ANDES (S. AMERICA)
HABITAT: MOUNTAINS

The llama is a relative of the guanaco, domesticated long ago, perhaps by the Incas of Peru. Unlike the alpaca, the llama is used for meat and for carrying goods.

► Loris, Slender
RANGE: S. INDIA, SRI LANKA
HABITAT: FOREST

Unlike most primates, the slender loris is very slow moving, creeping along branches on its spindly legs and ambushing insects, such as grasshoppers.

▼ Lynx
RANGE: N. AMERICA, EURASIA
HABITAT: CONIFEROUS FOREST, SCRUB

The lynx lives alone in forests and hunts hares, rodents, young deer, and birds. The North American lynx depends especially on snowshoe hares. It also has big paws for walking on snow. The tufts on the lynx's ears help it hear in dense pine forests.

▼ Macaque, Japanese
RANGE: JAPAN
HABITAT: FOREST

The Japanese macaque is the only primate apart from humans to live outside the tropics, living high up mountains in cold forests. It has unusually thick fur. In especially cold, snowy winters it sometimes lounges up to its neck in hot springs to keep warm.

▼ Manatee, American
RANGE: ATLANTIC AND CARIBBEAN COAST OF N. AND C. AMERICA
HABITAT: WARM COASTAL WATERS

The manatee looks a little like a seal but, like the dugong, it grazes on sea grass. For much of the day it lies on the seabed, just coming up to the surface every few minutes to breathe. Manatees live in family groups and often gather in large herds.

▲ Mandrill
RANGE: W. AFRICA
HABITAT: RAIN FOREST

The mandrill has a flaming red nose and blue cheeks. It is also the heavyweight of the monkey world, weighing up to 120 lb (55 kg). It feeds mostly on plants, but may kill small animals.

▲ Mangabey, Agile
RANGE: C. AFRICA
HABITAT: RAIN FOREST

The agile mangabey is a better climber than its white-cheeked cousin, but mangabeys are actually slower moving through the trees than other African monkeys.

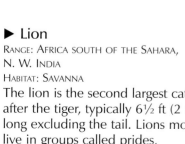

▲ Marmoset, Pygmy
RANGE: AMAZON
HABITAT: RAIN FOREST

Marmosets and tamarins look like monkeys but do not have grasping hands and feet, so they scamper along branches. The pygmy marmoset is the smallest American primate.

▲ Marten, American
RANGE: CANADA, ALASKA, N. W. U.S.A.
HABITAT: TAIGA/PINE FOREST
Martens are small, tough carnivores that live in pine forests. They are skillful climbers and adept at catching red squirrels, which they chase through the treetops. They live in dens in hollow trees or logs.

▼ Meerkat
RANGE: SOUTHERN AFRICA
HABITAT: SAVANNA
The meerkat is a small mammal that lives in burrows, linked to form a colony. It feeds on insects, spiders, scorpions, and small mammals. When above ground, some of the group always act as lookouts, sitting upright. When cool, the meerkat sits up sunning itself; when hot, it lies belly-down in its burrow.

▲ Mink, American
RANGE: N. AMERICA, INTRODUCED BRITAIN
HABITAT: WETLAND, RIVERBANKS
There are two species of mink: the North American mink and the slightly smaller European mink. Minks are usually seen near rivers or lakes, preying on waterfowl and fish, usually at night. Because of their soft, rich brown fur they have often been trapped and farmed to make fur coats. British minks have escaped from farms.

▼ Mole, Eastern
RANGE: EASTERN N. AMERICA
HABITAT: FIELDS, LAWNS, AND GARDENS
The Eastern mole spends nearly all its life underground, digging through the soil with its powerful front paws. It is almost blind but finds the earthworms and insect grubs it feeds on with its sensitive nose.

▼ Mole, European
RANGE: EUROPE, EASTERN ASIA
HABITAT: WOODLAND, FARMLAND
The mole spends most of its life burrowing tunnels underground, so is not often seen. The only signs of its activity are the soil heaps, called mole hills, it makes while tunneling.

▼ Mole, Giant golden
RANGE: SOUTH AFRICA
HABITAT: WOODLAND
The rare giant golden mole is the biggest of all moles, up to 9½ in (24 cm) long. Unlike other moles, this mole hunts aboveground for beetles, slugs, and worms—even though it is blind, and so has to rely on smell and sound alone. When frightened, it scurries for its burrow and seems to be able to find the entrance even though it cannot see.

▼ Mole, Star-nosed
RANGE: NORTHEASTERN N. AMERICA
HABITAT: WETLAND, WOODLAND
The star-nosed mole lives in wet places. Although it digs tunnels, it rarely feeds there. It has a ring of 22 fingerlike tentacles on the end of its nose, which it uses to feel for food, such as small fish, when it is underwater.

▲ Mole-rat, Naked
RANGE: N. E. AFRICA
HABITAT: DRY SAVANNA
Naked mole-rats have pink, almost furless bodies and live underground in colonies of up to 100, controlled by a single female or queen. The queen and her fat helpers are fed by "workers."

▲ Mongoose, Indian
RANGE: SOUTHERN ASIA, INTRODUCED ELSEWHERE
HABITAT: FOREST TO DESERT
The mongoose is a swift, effective predator. It catches rats, mice, and scorpions, but it is famed for the way it attacks snakes, such as cobras.

▲ Monkey, Western red colobus
RANGE: W. AFRICA
HABITAT: RAIN FOREST
Red colobuses are five species of colobus monkeys, which are very agile African monkeys that spend almost all their lives in trees. Although they have no thumbs, they are brilliant climbers and cling on with their fingers as they dart through the treetops searching for fruit, leaves, and flowers.

▲ Monkey, Diana
RANGE: W. AFRICA
HABITAT: RAIN FOREST
The Diana monkey is a noisy little monkey that lives in troops of 30 or so in the rain forest canopy. It feeds mainly on leaves, fruit, and buds soon after dawn and just before dusk. It also eats insects and birds' eggs.

▲ Monkey, Proboscis
RANGE: S. E. ASIA, BORNEO
HABITAT: RAIN FOREST, MANGROVE SWAMPS
The male proboscis monkey gives the species its name, with its very long, pink nose. This normally dangles straight down but straightens out when he honks loudly.

► Monkey, Red howler
RANGE: TROPICAL S. AMERICA
HABITAT: RAIN FOREST
The howler monkey gets its name from its incredible dawn and dusk shrieks, which can be heard echoing through the trees up to 2 miles (3 km) away. Red howlers are the biggest American monkeys.

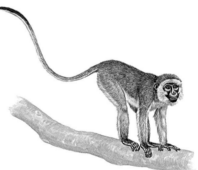

▲ Monkey, Vervet
RANGE: S. AND E. AFRICA
HABITAT: SAVANNA, WOODS
Otherwise known as the green guenon, this monkey climbs, jumps, swims well, and sleeps in trees; but it is quite happy running and foraging in open country.

► Monkey, Woolly spider
RANGE: S. E. BRAZIL
HABITAT: COASTAL FOREST
The woolly spider monkey has long limbs and a prehensile tail, which it uses as an extra limb to help it move through the trees. It has a bare face that becomes red when it is excited.

▲ Moose
RANGE: EURASIA, N. AMERICA
HABITAT: TAIGA, TUNDRA

The moose is the biggest of all deer and the antlers of bulls may be 6 ft (1.8 m) across. Moose shed the antlers in winter and grow bigger ones in spring. Bulls bellow to attract females and engage in fierce battles with rivals.

▲ Mouflon
RANGE: S. EUROPE, C. AND S. ASIA
HABITAT: MOUNTAINS

The mouflon is a tough mountain sheep, which may be an ancestor of the domestic sheep. It seems able to eat virtually any vegetation, including plants other animals find poisonous.

▶ Mouse, Deer
RANGE: N. AMERICA
HABITAT: WOODLAND, GRASSLAND

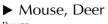

The deer mouse makes nests underground, or in trees, where it starts to breed when only seven weeks old. It is a very nimble creature and feeds on insects, seeds, and nuts.

▼ Mouse, Wood
RANGE: EASTERN EURASIA
HABITAT: WOODLAND, FARMLAND

Also known as the long-tailed field mouse, the wood mouse may be the most common European mammal, thriving everywhere from moorlands to suburban gardens. It often nests in burrows under trees and emerges at night to scurry around, foraging for seeds. It hibernates in winter.

▲ Muntjac, Chinese
RANGE: CHINA, INTRODUCED EUROPE
HABITAT: FOREST

The muntjac is the size of a big dog and is now the smallest European deer. It is known as the "barking deer" in Asia because of its barklike cry.

▲ Musk ox
RANGE: N. CANADA, GREENLAND
HABITAT: TUNDRA

The musk ox looks like a buffalo, but is actually related to the mountain goat. It lives in the Arctic tundra and has a long, shaggy coat to help it survive the bitter winter. Its big hooves stop it from sinking in soft snow.

▲ Muskrat, Common
RANGE: N. AMERICA, INTRODUCED EUROPE
HABITAT: MARSHES, riverbanks

The muskrat lives in water and eats marsh vegetation voraciously. In winter it lives in a lodge like a beaver's, only built with reeds.

◀ Myotis, Little brown
RANGE: N. AMERICA
HABITAT: FOREST, SUBURBS

This common little bat often forms nursery colonies in attics and walls of buildings. Each bat can eat more than 1,200 insects an hour.

▼ Narwhal
RANGE: HIGH ARCTIC
HABITAT: COLD OCEANS

The narwhal is a whale. The male has an extraordinary tusk, up to 10 ft (3 m) long, which is actually an extended tooth and is used to fight rival males.

▲ Numbat
RANGE: S. W. AUSTRALIA
HABITAT: FOREST

The numbat is a small marsupial, but has no pouch. The young are dragged around clinging to the mother's nipples. It feeds on termites, and licks them up with its 4 in- (10 cm-) long tongue.

▲ Okapi
RANGE: W. AFRICA
HABITAT: RAIN FOREST

The okapi looks like a horse with a zebra's stripes on its back legs. In fact, it is a relative of the giraffe and browses on leaves, twisting them off with its long tongue.

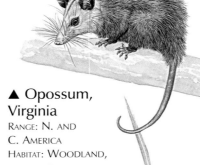

▲ Opossum, Virginia
RANGE: N. AND C. AMERICA
HABITAT: WOODLAND, FARMLAND

The Virginia opossum is one of the few marsupials outside Australia and has a kangaroo-like pouch. Scared opossums play dead.

▶ Orangutan
RANGE: SUMATRA, BORNEO
HABITAT: RAIN FOREST

The orangutan is the second largest great ape after the gorilla. Unlike gorillas, it spends most of its life in trees and builds a platform of sticks for a nest. As its rain forest habitat has shrunk, so the orangutan's survival has been threatened.

▼ Oryx, Arabian
RANGE: ARABIA
HABITAT: DESERT

The very rare Arabian oryx is well adapted to life in the desert and can endure long periods without water, getting most of its water from the plants on which it feeds. The oryx breathes deeply in the cool, moist night air to help its body make water.

▶ Otter, Eurasian
RANGE: EURASIA, N. AFRICA
HABITAT: RIVERS, LAKES, COASTS

With its streamlined body, the otter is a strong, fast swimmer, using its tail to propel it through the water. It typically lives in a burrow in the riverbank and comes out at night to hunt for fish, frogs, and voles.

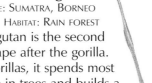

▼ Otter, Sea
RANGE: N. E. PACIFIC OCEAN
HABITAT: ROCKY COASTS

The sea otter spends most of its life at sea. It stays in shallow water close to beds of giant kelp seaweed. To eat shellfish, it floats on its back, rests a stone on its belly, and smashes the shellfish against the stone until the shell breaks.

▼ Panda, Giant
RANGE: C. CHINA
HABITAT: FOREST

The rare giant panda has the digestive system of a meat-eater, but actually feeds only on the shoots of bamboo plants, which it eats sitting down, gripping the bamboo in its front paws.

▼ Panda, Red
RANGE: S. ASIA, CHINA
HABITAT: MOUNTAIN FOREST

The red panda looks a little like a raccoon. It sleeps during the day curled up on branches with its tail wrapped around to keep it warm. It comes down to the ground at night to feed on bamboo shoots, grass, roots, fruit, acorns, and occasionally mice. When angry it rears up and hisses.

▲ Pangolin, Giant
RANGE: E. AND C. AFRICA
HABITAT: RAIN FOREST, SAVANNA

Pangolins are the only mammals covered in scales. When threatened they roll themselves up into a ball and raise their scales so the sharp edges point outward. They feed on ants and termites, which they lick up with their long, sticky tongues. They have thick eyelids to protect their eyes from ant bites and can seal off their nostrils to keep the ants out.

◄ Pangolin, Tree
RANGE: W. AFRICA
HABITAT: RAIN FOREST

Like all pangolins, the tree pangolin is covered in scales, but it is also a good climber with a long, prehensile tail. It often sleeps on the ground during the day and climbs up trees to hunt ants by smell at night.

▼ Peccary, Collared
RANGE: N., C., AND S. AMERICA
HABITAT: FOREST, GRASSLAND, DESERT

Peccaries are piglike mammals that forage for a wide range of food, from insects to prickly pear cacti. The collared peccary is the most widespread of all peccaries.

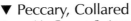

▼ Pika, Northern
RANGE: N. ASIA
HABITAT: MOUNTAINS, FOREST

The pika is like a rabbit without the big ears, but it usually lives high up in mountains. In summer it builds up little haystacks of grass among the rocks to eat during winter.

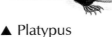

▲ Platypus
RANGE: E. AUSTRALIA, TASMANIA
HABITAT: LAKES AND RIVERS

The platypus is one of the few mammals that lays eggs. It also has webbed feet and a bill like a duck, which it uses to probe riverbed mud for insect grubs.

▲ Polecat, Western
RANGE: EUROPE
HABITAT: FOREST

The Western polecat is a small carnivore related to stoats and weasels. It hunts rodents, birds, and lizards at night.

► Porcupine, Crested
RANGE: AFRICA SOUTH OF THE SAHARA
HABITAT: FOREST, SAVANNA

This is a big rodent, armed with fearsome spines, called quills, on its back, measuring up to 12 in (30.5 cm) long. If threatened, it rattles its tail quills and charges backward, spines raised, at its foe.

▼ Possum, Brush-tailed
RANGE: AUSTRALIA, INTRODUCED NEW ZEALAND
HABITAT: WOODLAND

This is a nimble, tree-climbing marsupial that feeds mainly on leaves, flowers, and fruit. It is now quite at home in urban areas.

▲ Potoroo
RANGE: AUSTRALIA
HABITAT: DAMP SCRUB, GRASSLAND

Potoroos are small, ratlike kangaroos with soft, silky fur. Like larger kangaroos, they bound along on their strong back legs. They eat a much wider range of food than larger kangaroos, including plants, plant roots, grass, fungi, and insects, which they forage for at dusk.

▼ Prairie dog, Black-tailed
RANGE: C. U.S.A.
HABITAT: PRAIRIE

This squirrel lives in huge networks of burrows called townships. It gets its name from its doglike bark.

▼ Pronghorn
RANGE: W. U.S.A.
HABITAT: PRAIRIE

The world's fastest hoofed mammal, this can reach over 60 mph (100 km/h). Its eyes are so good it can spot movements 4 miles (6.5 km) away.

▲ Quokka
RANGE: S. W. AUSTRALIA
HABITAT: DENSE VEGETATION
Once widespread, quokkas were shot for sport and now live in few places other than Rottnest Island. This island got its name, which means "Rat's Nest," because European explorers thought the quokkas were rats.

▲ Quoll, Eastern
RANGE: S. E. AUSTRALIA, TASMANIA
HABITAT: FOREST
Quolls are a family of lithe, catlike marsupials that live in forests in Australia and New Guinea. They live in trees and hunt lizards and birds.

▲ Rabbit, European
RANGE: EUROPE, INTRODUCED ELSEWHERE
HABITAT: GRASSLAND, WOODLAND, FARMLAND
Rabbits live in burrows and breed very fast, with several litters a year. They eat grass and can also wreak havoc with farmers' crops of vegetables and grains.

▲ Raccoon
RANGE: N. AND C. AMERICA
HABITAT: WOODLAND, SUBURBS
The raccoon is a woodland creature, but has learned to scavenge from humans and is renowned for its night raids on garbage cans. Its name is Native American for "scratches with hands."

▲ Rat, Arizona cotton
RANGE:
SOUTHEASTERN U.S.A.
HABITAT: DRY GRASSLAND
Cotton rat populations sometimes expand so much that they are declared a plague. They normally feed on plants and small insects but may also feed on quail eggs.

▲ Rat, Baja California rice
RANGE: MEXICO, CALIFORNIA
HABITAT: MARSHLAND
Rice rats generally live in marshland and feed on reeds and sedges, and sometimes on fish. They sometimes also eat rice crops and can become serious pests.

▲ Rat, Brown
RANGE: WORLDWIDE
HABITAT: CITIES, HOUSES, FARMLAND
Also known as the Norway rat, the brown rat originally came from S. E. Asia, but has spread with human habitation around the world. It eats almost anything.

▲ Rat, Swamp
RANGE: S. AFRICA
HABITAT: SWAMPS
The swamp rat feeds on seeds, berries, and fruits and lives in nests made of reeds and grasses.

▼ Rhebok
RANGE: S. AFRICA
HABITAT: GRASSLAND
The rhebok is a small antelope with soft hair. The ram (male) is aggressively territorial, marking out his range by clicking his tongue, whistling, and urinating.

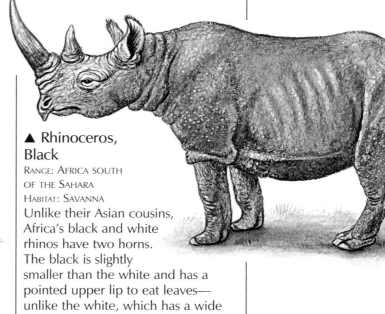

▲ Rhinoceros, Black
RANGE: AFRICA SOUTH OF THE SAHARA
HABITAT: SAVANNA
Unlike their Asian cousins, Africa's black and white rhinos have two horns. The black is slightly smaller than the white and has a pointed upper lip to eat leaves—unlike the white, which has a wide lip for grazing.

▲ Sable
RANGE: N. ASIA
HABITAT: TAIGA
This small weasel-like predator eats small mammals, fish, nuts, and berries. Its thick, soft fur insulates it against the icy Siberian winters, but has meant it is widely trapped for its fur.

▲ Saiga
RANGE: C. ASIA
HABITAT: STEPPE
The saiga is a goat-antelope with a trunklike nose that may filter out dust from the air in the summer and warm frosty air in the bitter steppe winter.

▼ Saki, Monk
RANGE: AMAZON
HABITAT: RAIN FOREST
Saki monkeys are a family of long-tailed S. American monkeys with long, coarse hair. The monk saki has long, shaggy hair around its face and neck which looks like a monk's cowl. It is a wary monkey that lives high in the forest canopy and rarely ventures down to the ground, clambering along branches on all fours. Occasionally it walks upright on large boughs and makes huge leaps from branch to branch.

▼ Sea lion, California
RANGE: W. U.S.A.
HABITAT: COASTS
The California sea lion is the trained seal—playful and brilliant at balancing and catching things in the air with its teeth. It is also very fast, able to swim at speeds of 25 mph (40 km/h), and can dive down 500 ft (150 m) for fish. Like all sea lions, it has front flippers strong enough to support its weight, and it can move quickly on land, almost galloping—unlike seals that only shuffle. It barks, wails, and bleats.

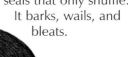

▲ Seal, Crabeater
RANGE: ANTARCTIC
HABITAT: PACK ICE FRINGES
Surprisingly the crabeater seal does not eat crabs. Instead it feeds on shrimplike creatures called krill. Its main enemy is the killer whale.

▲ Seal, Harbor
RANGE: ANTARCTIC
HABITAT: PACK ICE FRINGES
The harbor seal is also known as the common seal and is often seen basking on rocks or even swimming up river.

▲ Seal, Harp
RANGE: N. ATLANTIC, ARCTIC OCEAN
HABITAT: COLD OCEANS
The harp seal is a superb swimmer and spends most of its life at sea. It swims large distances as it migrates between its northern summer feeding grounds and warmer southern oceans.

▼ Seal, Leopard
RANGE: SOUTHERN OCEAN
HABITAT: PACK ICE, COLD OCEANS
The leopard seal is a fearsome predator with a wide mouth and sharp teeth. Its main prey are penguins, which it snatches as they move off the ice.

▼ Seal, Northern elephant
RANGE: N. AMERICA PACIFIC COAST
HABITAT: OFFSHORE ISLANDS
The elephant seal lives up to its name. Males may grow up to 20 ft (6 m) long and weigh almost 3 tons. It feeds on fish and squid and dives very deep.

▼ Seal, Ross
RANGE: ANTARCTIC
HABITAT: PACK ICE
The little Ross seal is the smallest of the Antarctic seals and also the rarest. Altogether there may be fewer than 50,000 of them. The Ross seal feeds primarily on squid, fish, and shrimplike krill, which it catches below the pack ice. It has enormous eyes adapted for hunting in the dim water under the ice. Its long flippers propel it through the water at surprising speed.

▼ Seal, Weddell
RANGE: ANTARCTIC
HABITAT: FAST ICE, INSHORE WATERS
This seal dives longer and deeper than any other seal, often staying down for an hour and reaching a depth of 2,000 ft (600 m) to feed on cod. Underwater they are lively and noisy; out of water they are quite sleepy.

▼ Serval
RANGE: AFRICA SOUTH OF THE SAHARA
HABITAT: SAVANNA
The serval hunts birds, rats, and other rodents in tall grass. Its long legs help it see over the grass but it pinpoints its prey, mainly with its astonishingly sensitive ears—then pounces on them and catches them with its front paws. Its hearing is so good that it can detect mole-rats tunneling underground. Typically it hunts at dusk and dawn.

▼ Sheep, Bighorn
RANGE: W. U.S.A., CANADA
HABITAT: MOUNTAINS, DESERTS
Male bighorn sheep live up to their name, with massive horns curling right around and weighing up to 27 lb (12 kg). Bighorns typically live in inaccessible mountain areas, but one subspecies lives in the desert and gets all its water from the plants it eats. Bighorns eat almost any plants and have a complex digestive process to get nutrients from poor quality food.

▼ Shrew, Short-eared elephant
RANGE: SOUTHERN AFRICA
HABITAT: PLAINS, ROCKY OUTCROPS
Elephant shrews are very strange shrews with very long, trunklike noses that they use to sniff out termites as well as seeds, fruit, and berries. They hop along branches on their powerful hind legs.

▼ Shrew, Short-tailed
RANGE: W. U.S.A., S. W. CANADA
HABITAT: FOREST, GRASSLAND
This shrew is the biggest North American shrew, but it is only 2½ in (6 cm) long. Many predators will not touch it, though, because it tastes horrible. It also moves so fast it looks as if it is on wheels. Sometimes shrews will fight each other to the death over territory.

► Sifaka, Verreaux's
RANGE: MADAGASCAR
HABITAT: FOREST
Sifakas are lemurs—small primates that live only in the forests of Madagascar and have very long prehensile tails. This sifaka moves very languidly and spends much of its day sunbathing.

◄ Skunk, Striped
RANGE: N. AMERICA
HABITAT: GRASSLAND, WOODLAND
When threatened, the striped skunk raises its tail and stamps its feet. If this fails, it turns around and emits a jet of foul smelling liquid from its anal glands.

▼ Sloth, Three-toed
RANGE: AMAZON
HABITAT: RAIN FOREST
The slowest of all mammals, the sloth moves barely 6½ ft (2 m) a minute flat out, hanging upside down from branches.

▼ Solenodon, Cuban
RANGE: CUBA
HABITAT: WOODS
This strange shrewlike animal forages on the forest floor for insects and fungi, but it also has a venomous bite that it can use to kill lizards, frogs, and small birds.

▲ Springbok
RANGE: SOUTHERN AFRICA
HABITAT: SAVANNA, DESERT
Springbok once formed herds 10 million strong and 100 miles (160 km) long as they trekked to find water in times of drought. Millions have been slaughtered, but quite large herds are still seen.

▲ Springhare
RANGE: SOUTHERN AFRICA
HABITAT: SAVANNA
The springhare is a small rodent about the size of a hare with powerful back legs. When frightened or on the move, the springhare bounds along like a kangaroo, leaping over 10 ft (3 m) at a time using its big, bushy tail as balance. When feeding it stands on all fours.

▲ Squirrel, European red
RANGE: EURASIA
HABITAT: CONIFEROUS WOODLANDS
The red squirrel is a rodent that lives in nests called dreys, which it builds in trees. It is an agile creature, using its sharp claws to grip as it scampers head first up and down trees. In fall, when food is plentiful, it buries stores of acorns for winter when its summer food of fungi and fruit is scarce, to supplement its main diet of pine cone seeds.

▼ Squirrel, Gray
RANGE: EASTERN N. AMERICA, INTRODUCED EUROPE
HABITAT: HARDWOOD FORESTS
A native of the oak, hickory, and walnut forests of eastern N. America, this squirrel eats a lot of acorns, hickory nuts, and walnuts. Here its numbers are controlled by predators, such as owls, foxes, and bobcats. It was introduced into Europe in the 1800s and has flourished away from its natural predators.

▼ Squirrel, Red giant flying
RANGE: SOUTHERN ASIA
HABITAT: RAIN FOREST
The large flap of skin between the limbs of this squirrel allows it to glide up to 1,500 ft (460 m) between trees. This way it can move around the forest canopy without ever coming down to the ground. Typically this squirrel rests in hollow trees by day and emerges at dusk to forage for nuts, fruit, soft twigs, leaves, and flower buds. Young squirrels are never seen on their mother's back, so it is assumed that they are placed in a safe refuge while the mother searches for food.

▼ Stoat
RANGE: N. AMERICA, EURASIA, INTRODUCED NEW ZEALAND
HABITAT: FOREST, TUNDRA
The stoat is a fierce little predator that kills rodents and rabbits with a swift bite to the back of the prey's neck. It often kills rabbits three times its own size. In winter many stoats turn creamy white, so that they are less visible against snow. In this winter coat they are called ermine.

▶ Tamandua, Northern
RANGE: C. AMERICA, AMAZON
HABITAT: RAIN FOREST
The tamandua is a smaller relative of the giant anteater and lives in trees rather than on the ground. It breaks open nests to feed on tree-living ants. Its slender tail is prehensile and enables it to hang on to branches while it eats. If attacked, the tamandua braces itself on a branch with its tail and hind limbs then lashes out with its powerful front claws.

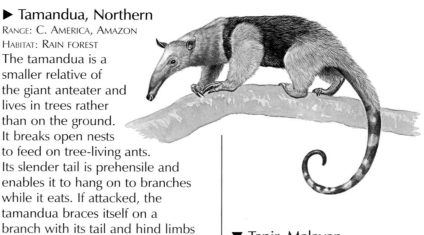

▲ Tamarin, Emperor
RANGE: AMAZON
HABITAT: RAIN FOREST
Tamarins are small monkeys that live in the rain forests of South and Central America. They do not have gripping hands and cannot swing like other monkeys. Instead they scamper along branches like squirrels.

▶ Tamarin, Golden lion
RANGE: SOUTHEASTERN BRAZIL
HABITAT: COASTAL FOREST
The golden lion tamarin with its extraordinary orange-gold, silky fur has become severely threatened as the forests on the Atlantic coast of Brazil have been cut down. Sadly, many of these beautiful creatures have also been caught and sold as pets. International efforts are afoot to save them.

▼ Tapir, Malayan
RANGE: S. E. ASIA
HABITAT: RAIN FOREST
There are four species of tapir: three in South America and one, the Malayan tapir, in Southeast Asia. They are all shy creatures with piglike bodies and long snouts, which they use to feel for food in much the same way as an elephant does with its trunk.

▶ Tarsier, Western
RANGE: SUMATRA, BORNEO
HABITAT: FOREST SCRUB
Tarsiers are tiny primates with amazingly long tails, fingers, and toes and gigantic eyes which help them find prey, such as insects, by staring through the gloom of dusk. They are great jumpers.

▼ Tasmanian devil
RANGE: TASMANIA
HABITAT: WOODLAND
Although no bigger than a small dog, the Tasmanian devil is the most fearsome marsupial hunter, wrongly famed for killing sheep. In fact it feeds mainly on dead birds, wombats, and dead sheep.

▲ Tenrec, Streaked
RANGE: MADAGASCAR
HABITAT: SCRUB, FOREST
Tenrecs are small, shrewlike, insect-eating mammals that live on Madagascar and the nearby Comoro Islands. The streaked tenrec has spines that protect it like a hedgehog's.

▲ Tiger, Caspian
RANGE: AROUND THE CASPIAN SEA
HABITAT: GRASSLAND
In 1900 there were eight subspecies of tiger, of which three have already become extinct. The Caspian was the most recent to disappear, in the 1970s.

▼ Tiger, Indo-Chinese
RANGE: MYANMAR TO VIETNAM
HABITAT: MIXED WOODLAND
Tigers are the largest big cats, 10 ft (3 m) from head to tail. They prey at night on large animals, such as deer, stalking their prey then pouncing. The Indo-Chinese tiger lives mostly in mixed forest. It is the second most numerous of the tigers but is disappearing fast; every week at least one is trapped, shot, or poisoned.

▶ Tiger, Siberian or Amur
RANGE: SIBERIA
HABITAT: TAIGA
This is the biggest of the tigers and paler in color. It can survive bitter Siberian winters. There are just 400 or so left.

▼ Tiger, Sumatran
RANGE: SUMATRA
HABITAT: RAIN FOREST
The Sumatran tiger is the last of the three Indonesian subspecies to survive. It is darker colored and smaller than other tigers. About 400 survive in seven nature reserves.

▼ Vaquita
RANGE: GULF OF CALIFORNIA
HABITAT: WARM COASTAL WATERS
The vaquita is one of the smallest porpoises, less than 5 ft (1.5 m) long. It is also one of the rarest, with perhaps fewer than 500 still surviving.

▼ Vicuña
RANGE: CENTRAL ANDES
HABITAT: MOUNTAINS
The vicuña is related to the camel. It lives over 13,000 ft (4,000 m) up in the Andes. The air is thin here but it still manages to run uphill at 30 mph (50 km/h).

▲ Vole, Meadow
RANGE: NORTHERN N. AMERICA
HABITAT: GRASSLAND, FARMLAND
The meadow vole looks so much like a mouse that it is sometimes called a field mouse. It makes tunnels under the grass in meadows, which it keeps neatly trimmed. It is a social animal, though each adult has its own tunnel.

▼ Wallaby, Bridled nail-tailed
RANGE: QUEENSLAND, AUSTRALIA
HABITAT: THICK SCRUB
Wallabies are similar to kangaroos, but half the size and tend to live in more vegetated areas. Some wallabies live in scrub; some in rocks. The nail-tailed wallabies are scrub wallabies that get their name because of the tiny nail at the tip of their tails.

▶ Wallaby, Swamp
RANGE: E., S. E. AUSTRALIA
HABITAT: ROCKY GULLIES, THICKETS
Swamp wallabies live in small herds, but are often difficult to spot because they lie down when danger approaches— then suddenly burst out in different directions if the threat comes too close. They sometimes bound 13 ft (4 m) or more from a standing start.

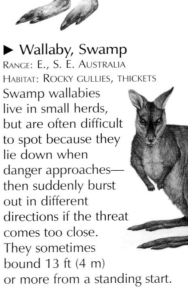

▼ Walrus
RANGE: ARCTIC OCEAN
HABITAT: PACK ICE, ROCKY ISLANDS
The walrus is a huge sea lionlike creature up to 11½ ft (3.5 m) long. The males have huge tusks. It was once thought these were used to help them feed, but it is now believed that they are status symbols that help the male attract a mate.

▼ Warthog
RANGE: AFRICA SOUTH OF THE SAHARA
HABITAT: SAVANNA
The warthog is a very tough creature. It feeds on short grass, fruit, bulbs, and tubers in open savanna and in this almost treeless environment it can be seen very easily by predators. If hunted it may run to take cover in a burrow, but may often stand and fight with its sharp tusks. Warthogs like to wallow in mud to keep cool.

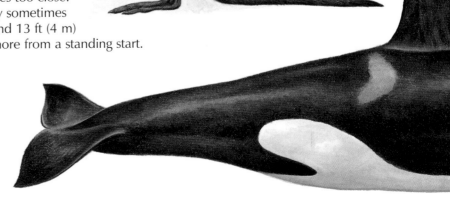

▼ Weasel, Least

RANGE: EURASIA, N. AMERICA, N. AFRICA, INTRODUCED NEW ZEALAND

HABITAT: FARMLAND, WOODLAND

The least weasel is the world's smallest carnivore, less than 6 in (15 cm) long and little thicker than a finger. It is so small that it can pursue the mice it preys on right into their burrows.

▼ Whale, Minke

RANGE: WORLDWIDE

HABITAT: COASTAL WATERS

The minke whale is the smallest of the rorquals—whales, like the humpback and blue—that feed on plankton strained through the baleens in their mouths. The minke whale is typically 26–33 ft (8–10 m) long.

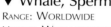

▲ Whale, Blue

RANGE: WORLDWIDE

HABITAT: COLD OCEANS

The blue whale is the biggest animal today, 105 ft (32 m) long and weighing over 140 tons. This giant mammal feeds on tiny shrimplike krill, which it strains out of the water through the baleen plates in its huge mouth. It consumes up to 4 tons of krill a day. In summer it feeds in polar waters, then migrates in winter toward the Equator to mate.

▼ Whale, Northern right

RANGE: NORTHERN HEMISPHERE

HABITAT: COOL SEAS

Right whales got their name because they swim slowly and float when dead, so whalers thought them the "right" whales to hunt—so right, that the Northern right whale has been hunted almost to extinction.

▲ Whale, Humpback

RANGE: WORLDWIDE

HABITAT: OCEANS

The humpback feeds on plankton through baleens like the blue whale, and migrates huge distances. The male is famous for its complex songs.

▼ Whale, Sperm

RANGE: WORLDWIDE

HABITAT: WARM OCEANS

The sperm whale is the largest of the toothed whales, with a fearsome jaw up to 16½ ft (5 m) long. The sperm whale is the world's largest predator. Its huge head is filled with a waxy substance called spermaceti that helps focus sound and control buoyancy.

▼ Whale, Killer

RANGE: WORLDWIDE

HABITAT: COOL OCEANS

The killer whale is the largest dolphin and one of the world's largest predators. It hunts mainly fish and squid but often takes seals. It lives and hunts in family groups, communicating by sound.

▼ Wildebeest, Blue

RANGE: S. AND E. AFRICA

HABITAT: SAVANNA

This large cowlike antelope is Africa's most successful species. In the dry season huge herds migrate 940 miles (1,500 km) or more across the savanna in search of fresh grass and water—there are 1.5 million in Tanzania alone.

▲ Wolf, Gray

RANGE: EURASIA, N. AMERICA

HABITAT: TUNDRA, TAIGA, WOODLAND, GRASSLAND

The gray wolf is the largest member of the dog family. Long persecuted, it now lives only in remote regions, especially dense forests. Gray wolves live in packs and work together when they hunt to bring down much bigger animals, such as caribou and moose.

▲ Wolverine

RANGE: N. EURASIA, NORTHERN N. AMERICA

HABITAT: TAIGA, TUNDRA

This heavily built creature, about the size of a small dog, is the largest of the weasel-like mustelids and is famed for its strength. It is so fierce that it can often drive even bears away from their kills. It is also so famed for its appetite that it is sometimes known as the "glutton." Wolverines often trek over 25 miles (40 km) in a day to find food.

▲ Wombat, Common

RANGE: S. E. AUSTRALIA, TASMANIA

HABITAT: FOREST, SCRUB

Wombats are powerfully built marsupials that look and behave a little like badgers. They dig huge burrows where they rest during the day. At night they emerge to eat grass and other plants. Of the three species of wombat, the common wombat is the largest, weighing up to 77 lb (35 kg).

▶ Woodchuck

RANGE: NORTHERN N. AMERICA

HABITAT: FOREST, FARMLAND

The woodchuck, or groundhog, is a squirrel that can swim and climb trees, but lives in large underground dens where it hibernates all winter. Its emergence in spring is celebrated as Groundhog Day.

▼ Yak, Wild

RANGE: HIMALAYAS

HABITAT: MOUNTAINS

With its thick, shaggy overcoat and warm, woolly undercoat, the yak is well able to cope with icy conditions high in the Himalayas. It is also surprisingly sure-footed and grazes on slopes up to 20,000 ft (6,100 m), higher than any other large mammal.

▼ Zebra, Grevy's

RANGE: N. AFRICA

HABITAT: SAVANNA, SEMI-DESERT

Grevy's zebra is the largest of the zebras and able to live in drier places than the others. It grazes early in the morning and rests in the shade during the heat of the day.

▼ Zorilla

RANGE: AFRICA SOUTH OF THE SAHARA

HABITAT: SAVANNA

The zorilla, or striped polecat, looks a little like a skunk and emits an equally foul smell from its anal glands when threatened. It hunts at night for rodents, reptiles, insects, and birds' eggs.

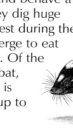

Reptiles

Unlike mammals, reptiles are cold-blooded or, rather, "ectothermic"—that is, their temperature varies with their surroundings. Over 6,800 species of these scaly-skinned creatures are known and live in all the world's warmer regions, both on land and in fresh water. The four main kinds are: the crocodilians (crocodiles and alligators), squamata (lizards and snakes), turtles, and the tuatara (a lizardlike New Zealand reptile).

▼ Adder, Saw-scaled
RANGE: N. AFRICA, S. W. ASIA
HABITAT: DESERT
The saw-scaled adder survives in some of the hottest places in the Sahara, using its potent venom to quickly kill its prey, which includes small rodents, skinks, and geckos. Its bite is fatal to humans.

▼ Agamid, Arabian toad-headed
RANGE: S. W. ASIA
HABITAT: DESERT
This is one of over 300 kinds of agamid lizard, which all have chisel-shaped heads and feed mainly on insects. The toad-headed agamid lives in burrows, but also buries itself in sand.

▼ Alligator, American
RANGE: S. E. U.S.A.
HABITAT: RIVERS, SWAMPS
The American alligator is the biggest reptile in the Americas, growing up to 18 ft (5.5 m) long. It lives in rivers and swamps and eats anything from turtles to deer. In summer it often wallows in deep holes.

▲ Anaconda
RANGE: TROPICAL S. AMERICA
HABITAT: SWAMPS, RIVERS
The anaconda is one of the world's longest snakes, growing to more than 29 ft (9 m) long in the wild. It can climb trees, but spends most of its time lurking in murky water waiting for prey, such as capybaras and turtles. It is a constrictor, killing its victims by squeezing them in its coils.

▲ Anole, Green
RANGE: S. E. U.S.A.
HABITAT: WOODS, OLD BUILDINGS
The green anole changes color like a chameleon, depending on how warm it is, where it is, and its mood. When a rival male approaches it turns from brown to green in seconds. It uses the pink flap under its chin to attract females.

▲ Boa constrictor
RANGE: C. AND S. U.S.A.
HABITAT: RAIN FOREST, SAVANNA
The boa constrictor is one of the world's biggest snakes, growing up to 18 ft (5.5 m) long. The boa catches its prey by lying in wait for victims to pass by, but it can go many weeks without eating. It has no teeth, so it swallows its victims whole.

▼ Boa, Emerald tree
RANGE: S. AMERICA
HABITAT: RAIN FOREST
This boa lives in trees but catches much of its prey on the ground, dangling from a branch by its prehensile tail. It constricts its prey and swallows it while still dangling.

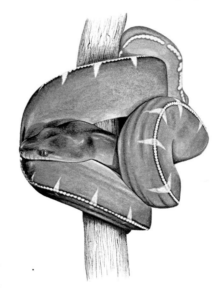

▼ Boomslang
RANGE: AFRICA SOUTH OF THE SAHARA
HABITAT: SAVANNA
The boomslang snake is tree-dwelling and is easily mistaken by its prey—such as chameleons, frogs, and birds—for a branch. It is one of Africa's most poisonous snakes.

▼ Caiman, Spectacled
RANGE: AMAZON
HABITAT: LAKES, SWAMPS
The spectacled caiman is the most common of the five species of caiman, which are small crocodiles—less than 6 ft (1.8 m) long—that live in Amazon waters. Its name comes from the spectacle-like ridges between its eyes.

▼ Chameleon, Jackson's
RANGE: E. AFRICA
HABITAT: SAVANNA TREES
In common with all chameleons, Jackson's can change color to suit its background, and shoots out a sticky tongue as long as its body to catch insects. Unlike other chameleons, Jackson's chameleon has three horns on its head.

▼ Chameleon, Meller's
RANGE: E. AFRICA
HABITAT: SAVANNA TREES
This is the largest chameleon in mainland Africa. Its body is covered in distinctive yellow stripes. Yet, despite its size and bold markings, it is very hard to spot, especially when it sways like a leaf in the breeze.

▼ Chuckwalla
RANGE: S. W. U.S.A.
HABITAT: ROCKY DESERT
The chuckwalla is a plant-eating desert lizard that hides in rocks during the night. When threatened it scurries into a rock crevice and gulps air so that it swells up and becomes wedged in place.

▼ Cobra, Indian
RANGE: INDIA, S. E. ASIA
HABITAT: RAIN FOREST, FARMLAND
The Indian, or spectacled, cobra is one of 11 species of Asian cobras. They are highly venomous snakes that eat rodents, lizards, and frogs and also kill more humans than any other animal.

▼ Cobra, King
RANGE: S. AND S. E. ASIA
HABITAT: FOREST

This is the world's largest venomous snake, growing 16 ft (4.9 m) or more long. It has very toxic venom that it uses to prey on other snakes. It lunges more than 6 ft (1.8 m) when it strikes.

▲ Crocodile, Nile
RANGE: AFRICA (EXCEPT N. W.)
HABITAT: RIVERS, LAKES, MARSHES

Like all crocodiles, the Nile preys on animals, such as zebras, that come to the water's edge to drink. They seize their victim, drag it into the water, stun it with a blow from their powerful tail, then drown it.

▲ Crocodile, Estuarine
RANGE: S. E. ASIA, N. AUSTRALIA
HABITAT: ESTUARIES, MANGROVE SWAMPS

The estuarine, or saltwater, crocodile is the world's biggest reptile, growing up to 19 ft (5.8 m) long. It is also the most dangerous. It is said to kill 1,000 people every year and can kill animals as big as buffaloes. The female lays 25–90 eggs in a mound of sand and leaves on land, and guards the eggs until they hatch.

▼ Fer-de-lance
RANGE: C. AND S. AMERICA
HABITAT: COASTAL LANDS

This is a large, poisonous snake of the pit viper family. Pit vipers have heat-sensitive pits between their eyes and nostrils that they use to track down warm-blooded creatures—mammals.

▲ Crocodile, Mugger
RANGE: INDIAN SUBCONTINENT/MYANMAR
HABITAT: MARSHES, LAKES

The mugger crocodile is the most alligator-like of all crocodiles, with a broad, heavy snout. What makes crocodiles different from alligators is that the fourth tooth of the lower jaw is visible when the mouth is shut.

▼ Gavial
RANGE: N. INDIA
HABITAT: RIVERS

The gavial is a crocodile with a long, thin snout, with 100 sharp teeth—perfect for catching fish and frogs underwater. When it catches a fish it flicks it in the air to turn it around so that it can swallow the fish head first.

▼ Gecko, Giant leaf-tailed
RANGE: MADAGASCAR
HABITAT: RAIN FOREST

This large gecko spends most of the day lying still, head down, on tree trunks where its mottled color and big, leaf-shaped tail make it very difficult to spot. If threatened it gapes its huge, flip-top mouth.

▼ Gecko, Web-footed
RANGE: S. W. AFRICA
HABITAT: DESERT

This rare, desert-living gecko has webbed feet that act like snowshoes to stop it from sinking into soft sand. It digs a burrow in the sand, then sits waiting in the entrance to pounce on insects, such as termites.

▲ Gila monster
RANGE: S. W. U.S.A., N. MEXICO
HABITAT: DESERT

Named after the Gila river in Arizona, the Gila monster is one of only two venomous lizards in the world—the other is the beaded lizard of Mexico and Guatemala. Its tail acts as a food store for times when food is scarce.

▲ Hawksbill
RANGE: ATLANTIC, PACIFIC, AND INDIAN OCEANS
HABITAT: CORAL REEFS, TROPICAL OCEANS

The hawksbill turtle has been hunted almost to extinction for its beautiful shell. Hunting is now widely banned, but the turtle is still in danger. It feeds on sponges.

▼ Iguana, Common
RANGE: C. AND S. AMERICA
HABITAT: FOREST TREES NEAR WATER

Iguanas are 600 or so species of lizards living mainly in the Americas. The common iguana is one of the biggest plant-eating reptiles, growing up to 6 ft (1.8 m) long. It spends most of its time basking in waterside trees, but can also swim.

▼ Iguana, Marine
RANGE: GALAPAGOS ISLANDS
HABITAT: LAVA ROCKS

The marine iguana is the only lizard that lives in the sea. It is a strong swimmer and dives for up to 20 minutes at a time as it searches for seaweed. It comes on land to incubate its eggs in the warm vents of volcanoes.

▼ Iguana, Rhinoceros
RANGE: HAITI, DOMINICAN REPUBLIC
HABITAT: SCRUB

Rhinoceros iguanas are large, heavily built lizards that get their name from the three or five hornlike scales on their noses. They live among thorn manchineel and poisonwood trees.

▼ Jungle runner
RANGE: C. AND S. AMERICA, INTRODUCED FLORIDA
HABITAT: FOREST CLEARINGS

This fast-moving, sun-loving lizard is often seen scooting across the ground as it forages for food, flicking out its long, forked tongue to take in insects.

▼ Kingsnake, Scarlet
RANGE: S. E. U.S.A.
HABITAT: WOODLAND

The scarlet kingsnake is the smallest of the very common American milk snake family. It is actually completely harmless, but looks similar to the deadly coral snake.

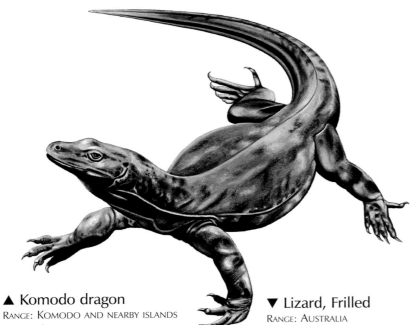

▲ Komodo dragon

RANGE: KOMODO AND NEARBY ISLANDS
EAST OF JAVA
HABITAT: GRASSLAND

The Komodo dragon is the world's biggest lizard, up to 10 ft (3 m) long and strong enough to bring down deer and wild boar. Like all the monitor lizards, the Komodo has strong legs and a long, forked tongue which it uses to test the air for traces of prey. There are about 5,000 left.

▲ Leatherback

RANGE: WORLDWIDE
HABITAT: WARM OCEANS

The leatherback is the world's largest turtle, weighing 770 lbs (350 kg) and growing up to 8 ft (2.4 m) long. It gets its name from its shell, which is made from a thick, leathery material as opposed to the hard plates of other turtles. It is a strong swimmer and can travel vast distances across the ocean, often following jellyfish, its main food.

▲ Lizard, Desert night

RANGE: S. W. U.S.A.
HABITAT: DESERT

The desert night lizard lives in arid lands in rock crevices or under plant debris. It is often found near yucca plants and agaves where it feeds on termites, ants, beetles, and flies. It gets its name because it hunts mostly at night to avoid the worst of the heat.

▼ Lizard, Frilled

RANGE: AUSTRALIA
HABITAT: RAIN FOREST

This lizard has a spectacular rufflike collar of skin around its neck. The lizard is actually harmless, but when threatened, it opens up the ruff and gapes its bright red mouth, then sways and hisses, making it look far bigger and more dangerous than it really is.

▼ Lizard, Transvaal snake

RANGE: SOUTH AFRICA
HABITAT: SAVANNA

Snake lizards look very much like their namesakes and rarely use their tiny legs as they slither quickly like snakes through the grass in search of the insects and spiders that they eat. Some snake lizards have no front legs at all.

▼ Mamba, Eastern green

RANGE: SOUTHERN AFRICA
HABITAT: SAVANNA, FOREST

Green mambas are extremely poisonous snakes, but they are not usually aggressive and tend to flee from danger. They spend much of their lives in trees feeding on birds and lizards. In the breeding season males have ritual fights for females.

▲ Matamata

RANGE: AMAZON
HABITAT: CREEKS AND LAKES

The weird shape of the matamata helps this turtle stay hidden among leaves on the riverbed. When a fish comes close, it opens its mouth wide so that water rushes in, taking the fish along with it.

▲ Pondslider

RANGE: SOUTHERN U.S.A., C. AMERICA, AMAZON
HABITAT: SLOW RIVERS, PONDS

Pondsliders spend most of their lives in water and are often seen basking on floating logs. The young feed on insects, snails, and tadpoles, but adults feed on plants.

▲ Python, Carpet

RANGE: AUSTRALIA, NEW GUINEA
HABITAT: FOREST, SAVANNA

Carpet pythons are the most widespread of Australian pythons. The dark carpet-like pattern on their bodies looks like dead leaves, allowing them to lurk almost invisibly among plant debris.

▲ Python, Indian rock

RANGE: INDIA
HABITAT: RAIN FOREST, MANGROVES

Rock pythons are huge snakes, up to 23 ft (7 m) long, that can easily kill a small deer or a boar. They crush their prey in their coils, then swallow it whole. They are often used by Indian snake charmers.

▼ Racer, Northern black

RANGE: U.S.A.
HABITAT: WOODS, GRASSLAND, FIELDS

Racers are long, fast-moving snakes. They hunt with their heads held high for a better view—then, when they spot prey, such as frogs, lizards, and mice, they make a quick dash and bite their victim repeatedly.

▼ Rattlesnake, Eastern diamondback

RANGE: S. E. U.S.A.
HABITAT: WOODLAND, FARMLAND

This is the largest and most dangerous of the 35 species of rattlesnake, all of which have a rattle at the tips of their tails made from 12 loose, bony rings. Rattlesnakes rattle their tails to warn enemies and to distract prey.

▼ Sidewinder

RANGE: S. W. U.S.A., N. W. MEXICO
HABITAT: DESERT

This poisonous snake has a unique way of moving over sand. Instead of slithering, it throws its body sideways, touching the ground with only two small sections of its body. This keeps the snake out of contact with the hot sand and uses less energy.

▼ Skink, Great Plains

RANGE: U.S.A., MEXICO
HABITAT: PRAIRIE, WOODLAND

Unusually for a lizard, the female Great Plains skink is very maternal. She guards her eggs carefully and turns them to warm them evenly. She rubs her new hatchlings into action and cares for them for 10 days.

▼ Skink, Western blue-tongued
RANGE: S. AUSTRALIA
HABITAT: DESERT

Blue-tongued skinks are large lizards with big heads, short tails, and distinctive blue tongues. If threatened, they stick out their tongues and make a hissing noise. They eat insects, snails, and berries.

▼ Slider, Red-eared
RANGE: S. E. U.S.A.
HABITAT: QUIET WATERS

Red-eared sliders make popular pets and millions are raised each year on turtle farms. They do not actually have red ears, but a large red stripe behind each eye. Some red-eared sliders have lived to over 40 years of age in captivity.

▼ Slow worm
RANGE: EUROPE, E., C., AND S. W. ASIA, N. W. AFRICA
HABITAT: FIELDS, SCRUB

The slow worm is a lizard with no legs that moves like a snake and can shed its tail if seized by an enemy. It feeds mainly on slugs and worms.

▼ Snake, Banded sea
RANGE: INDIAN OCEAN, PACIFIC OCEAN
HABITAT: TROPICAL COASTAL WATERS

Sea snakes are related to cobras and one species has the most powerful poison of any snake, which it uses to kill fish. They have flat tails that work like paddles to help them swim.

▲ Snake, Black rat
RANGE: NORTHEASTERN U.S.A.
HABITAT: FARMLAND, HARDWOOD FOREST

These big snakes are powerful constrictors that prey on rats and squirrels. They are good climbers and are often found in barns and derelict buildings.

▲ Snake, Eastern coral
RANGE: SOUTHEASTERN U.S.A.
HABITAT: PINE WOODS, LAKE EDGES

The eastern coral snake uses its powerful venom to paralyze the snakes it feeds on. Its stripes and coloration are much like the harmless scarlet snake's, but it has a red snout and red and yellow bands side by side.

▲ Snake, Eastern hog-nosed
RANGE: EASTERN U.S.A.
HABITAT: SANDY AREAS, GRASSLAND, WOODLAND

If in danger, the hog-nosed snake hisses, puffs itself up, and flattens its head to scare its enemy. If this does not work, it rolls over, sticks out its tongue, convulses, then plays dead.

▼ Snake, Egg-eating
RANGE: AFRICA SOUTH OF THE SAHARA
HABITAT: SAVANNA

This snake is one of the few snakes to feed entirely on birds' eggs. Its mouth can gape gigantically to swallow an egg whole. Inside its body, special backbones crush the shell, then the egg passes into the stomach and the shell pieces are regurgitated.

▼ Snake, Gopher
RANGE: WESTERN U.S.A.
HABITAT: PINE WOODS, PRAIRIE, SCRUB

Gopher snakes are large constrictor snakes that eat rats and mice. When the gopher is threatened it flattens its head, hisses loudly, and shakes its tail like a rattlesnake—and then launches itself in a sudden attack on its enemy. In winter it often shares dens with rattlesnakes.

▼ Snake, Grass
RANGE: EUROPE, N. ASIA, N. AFRICA
HABITAT: DAMP MEADOWS, MARSHES

The grass snake is a good swimmer and feeds mainly on frogs, toads, and fish, though it occasionally eats small mammals and birds. Its venom paralyzes small mammals but is harmless to humans. It typically swallows its prey alive. If caught in the open it remains completely still and pretends to be dead.

▲ Snake, Northern water
RANGE: EASTERN U.S.A.
HABITAT: PONDS, LAKES, RIVERS

Water snakes feed mainly on small fishes and frogs—though anglers often wrongly blame them for eating all the game fish. They can be seen basking on branches overhanging the water in spring or summer.

▶ Snake, Paradise tree
RANGE: S. E. ASIA
HABITAT: RAIN FOREST

The paradise tree snake is also known as the flying snake because of the way it glides through the air from tree to tree. It stretches out its body and glides down 66 ft (20 m) or more before landing gently.

▲ Snake, Smooth
RANGE: EURASIA
HABITAT: DRY ROCKY AREAS, HEATHLAND

Often mistaken for vipers, smooth snakes are not actually poisonous— they kill their prey by suffocating them in their coils. They like warm, shady areas under rocks.

▲ Snake, Spotted water
RANGE: NORTHERN AUSTRALIA
HABITAT: CREEKS, SWAMPS

Like a number of snakes, the spotted water snake is well adapted to living in water. It has small, upward-pointing eyes and pads of skin to close off its nostrils when diving.

▲ Snake, Western blind

RANGE: S. W. U.S.A.

HABITAT: DESERT

This snake looks a little like an earthworm. It has black spots where its eyes should be, but it is actually totally blind. It tracks ants and termites by following their scent trails.

▲ Soft-shell, Spiny

RANGE: N. AMERICA

HABITAT: RIVERS, CREEKS, PONDS

Unlike other turtles, soft-shells have shells of skin rather than horny plates. Spiny soft-shells are great swimmers that can make a fast getaway if threatened when basking on a sand bar.

▲ Terrapin, River

RANGE: S. E. ASIA

HABITAT: TIDAL RIVERS

Also known as the batagur, this is a plant-eating turtle that nests on sand banks where it lays 50 eggs at a time. People have dug up so many of its eggs for food that it is now quite rare.

▼ Tortoise, African pancake

RANGE: E. AFRICA

HABITAT: ROCKY OUTCROPS

This tortoise gets its name from its shell, which is soft and flat. It does not retreat into its shell when threatened, but wedges itself into a rock crevice by inflating its lungs.

▼ Tortoise, Spur-thighed

RANGE: N. AFRICA, S. EUROPE, S. W. ASIA

HABITAT: MEADOWS

The spur-thighed tortoise has large spurs on its thighs, but otherwise is very similar to the highly domed Hermann's tortoise of southeastern Europe, for which it is often mistaken.

▼ Tortoise, Galapagos giant

RANGE: GALAPAGOS ISLANDS

HABITAT: VARIED

The Galapagos giant tortoise is the biggest of all tortoises, weighing up to 770 lbs (350 kg). It lives on land and feeds on almost any plant, especially cacti. It can live for over 100 years, but in the past many were killed by sailors for food. At least 13 subspecies of giant tortoise have evolved on the islands of the Galapagos group. The subspecies vary in size, length, and shape of the carapace (shell).

▲ Tuatara, Cook-Strait

RANGE: NEW ZEALAND

HABITAT: WOODS

The two species of tuatara are unique reptiles found only in New Zealand—the last survivors of an ancient group called rhynchocephalians (beak heads). Unusually, tuataras do not breed until they are at least 20 years old.

▲ Turtle, Alligator snapping

RANGE: MISSISSIPPI VALLEY, U.S.A.

HABITAT: DEEP RIVERS, LAKES

This is the largest freshwater turtle. It lurks on riverbeds with its mouth gaping to reveal a wiggling, pink appendage, which fish come to investigate. They are then snapped up by the turtle.

▲ Turtle, Green

RANGE: WORLDWIDE

HABITAT: WARM SEAS ABOVE 68°F (20°C)

This is one of the few turtles that spends nearly all its life at sea. At nesting time it swims thousands of miles to lay its eggs on the beach where it was born. It lays its eggs on sandy beaches, hauling itself ashore at night.

▲ Turtle, Loggerhead

RANGE: PACIFIC, INDIAN, ATLANTIC OCEANS

HABITAT: COASTAL WATERS

In the summer breeding season the female loggerhead comes ashore at night and digs her nest at the foot of sand dunes, laying up to five clutches, each of about 100 eggs. Sadly numbers of loggerheads have been reduced by coastal development and fishing nets.

▼ Turtle, Murray River

RANGE: S. E. AUSTRALIA

HABITAT: RIVERS

Unusually, the shape of this turtle's carapace (shell) changes as it grows. When it hatches, the shell is round, then it grows at the back, and finally becomes oval in adult turtles.

▼ Turtle, Wood

RANGE: N. E. U.S.A., GREAT LAKES

HABITAT: WOODS, MEADOWS, MARSHES

The wood turtle spends most of its life on land and is a good climber, feeding on fruit, worms, slugs, and insects. It is a popular pet but has been hunted so much that it is now rare in the wild.

▼ Viper, Common

RANGE: EURASIA

HABITAT: MOORS, HEATHS, SCRUB

Known in Britain as adders, vipers are venomous snakes, but they are very timid and rarely bite humans. They hibernate in winter but emerge only when it gets warmer than 46°F (8°C).

▼ Viper, Gaboon

RANGE: W. C. AND S. E. AFRICA

HABITAT: RAIN FOREST, WOODLAND

The two species of gaboon viper are among the largest vipers, growing up to 6 ft (1.8 m) long. They are slow-moving and often lie in wait for their prey, which include rats, squirrels, and even small antelopes.

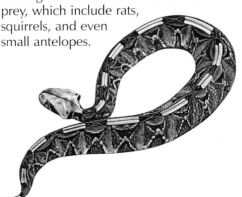

Amphibians

Like reptiles, amphibians are cold-blooded, but have no scales, and their skin is kept moist by secretions from mucus glands. Most amphibians begin life in water, or in a fluid-filled egg sac, and have gills to help them breathe in water. As they develop, they leave the water and spend their adult lives on land. Most of the 4,780 species live in the tropics, and there are three main kinds: frogs and toads (over 4,000 species), salamanders (410), and caecilians (165).

▲ Frog, Glass
RANGE: NORTHERN S. AMERICA
HABITAT: RAIN FOREST
Glass frogs get their name because most have semitransparent skin on the underside, so making their internal organs clearly visible. They spend their lives in trees and are great climbers. They lay their eggs on leaves above pools and streams, so that the tadpoles can drop into the water as they hatch and burrow into the mud on the stream bed.

▼ Axolotl
RANGE: LAKE XOCHIMILCO, MEXICO
HABITAT: MOUNTAIN LAKES
Axolotl is Aztec for "water monster." Uniquely, this salamander never fully grows. Although it grows four legs, it remains a tadpole all its life, even breeding in this state.

▼ Bullfrog
RANGE: N. AMERICA, MEXICO
HABITAT: LAKES, PONDS, SLOW STREAMS
As big as a young rabbit, the bullfrog is an awesome predator, snapping up other frogs, small snakes, fish, and even songbirds. Its call is a grumbling, throaty croak.

▼ Caecilian, South American
RANGE: S. AMERICA
HABITAT: USUALLY FOREST
Caecilians look like earthworms, but they are actually amphibians. Most live in soft soil in rain forests and tunnel through the soil feeding on worms, insects, and centipedes.

▲ Eel, Congo two-toed
RANGE: S. E. U.S.A.
HABITAT: SWAMPS, BAYOUS
Congo eels look like eels but are salamanders and live in the southeast U.S., not the Congo. The two-toed Congo eel has tiny, useless legs with two toes.

▲ Ensatina
RANGE: WESTERN N. AMERICA
HABITAT: FORESTS, UNDER LOGS AND ROCKS
Ensatinas are a varied group of small salamanders. One feature they all share is a narrow base to their tails. If the tail snaps off when escaping a predator, it grows back after two years.

▲ Frog, Common
RANGE: N. EUROPE, W. ASIA
HABITAT: MOIST AREAS NEAR PONDS
The common frog lives mostly on land, but in spring returns to ponds to mate. Each female lays 3–4,000 jelly-coated eggs that float in the ponds in large masses called frogspawn.

▼ Frog, Corroboree
RANGE: NEW SOUTH WALES (AUSTRALIA)
HABITAT: MOUNTAINS, MARSHES
With its striking yellow and black markings, the corroboree frog is instantly recognizable, but there are now fewer than 300 of them left in their habitat in the Snowy Mountains.

▼ Frog, Darwin's
RANGE: SOUTHERN S. AMERICA
HABITAT: COLD STREAMS IN FORESTS
Unusually, the eggs of the Darwin's frog are cared for by the male. After the female lays the eggs, the male gulps in a dozen or so and keeps them safe in the croaking sac in his throat until they hatch.

▼ Frog, European green tree
RANGE: EUROPE, W. ASIA
HABITAT: TREES, BUSHES NEAR LAKES
The European green tree frog is one of the few tree frogs that live outside the tropics. It is a great climber with sticky pads on its toes for clinging on to trees. It feeds mainly on insects.

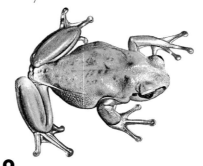

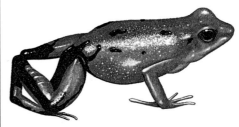

▲ Frog, Golden poison arrow
RANGE: C. AND S. AMERICA
HABITAT: RAIN FOREST
There are about 100 species of poison arrow frogs, most of which are brilliantly colored like the golden poison arrow frog. Glands on their skin contain deadly poisons used by forest peoples to tip their arrows for hunting. The brilliant colors warn predators that they are poisonous, so that they can feed in broad daylight.

▲ Frog, Horned
RANGE: NORTHERN S. AMERICA
HABITAT: RAIN FOREST
The Amazonian horned frog has a plump body that is as wide as it is long. It cannot move very fast, so hides in leaf litter on the forest floor until its prey passes by. Its mouth is so large that it can catch animals that are almost as big as itself, such as small frogs and rodents. The "horns" are projections on its eyelids.

▲ Frog, Marsh
RANGE: S. AND E. EUROPE
HABITAT: FRESHWATER
The marsh frog is bright green and often quite conspicuous, sitting on lily pads and croaking very loudly. Males are particularly loud in the breeding season in spring. It feeds mainly on invertebrates, but also small birds.

▲ Frog, Marsupial
RANGE: ECUADOR, PERU
HABITAT: FOREST
The marsupial frog gets its name because the female has a pouch on her back where the male packs her eggs after she has laid them. When the eggs hatch into tadpoles she uses her toe to release them into the water.

▲ Frog, Northern leopard
RANGE: N. AMERICA
HABITAT: VARIED INCLUDING WET MEADOWS
Leopard frogs get their name from the bold black spots all over their backs. They are very adaptable creatures and will live in almost any kind of place near water.

▲ Frog, South African rain
RANGE: SOUTHERN AFRICA
HABITAT: SAVANNA
This very plump frog gets its name from its habit of hunting for insects during rainstorms. Otherwise the frog spends most of its time in underground burrows, digging with its back feet.

▼ Frog, Termite
RANGE: SOUTHERN AFRICA
HABITAT: SAVANNA
The striking colors of the termite frog indicate to potential predators that it has a foul-tasting skin. As its name implies, it feeds mainly on termites and ants. To get at its prey it may often clamber up tree stumps and rocks, or burrow into the ground. It breeds in shallow pools, attaching its jelly-coated eggs to plants.

▼ Frog, Wallace's flying
RANGE: S. E. ASIA
HABITAT: RAIN FOREST
Flying frogs do not really fly, but glide huge distances from tree to tree. The huge webs between their toes and fingers act like wings to keep them in the air and allow them to glide gently down to another branch. Flying frogs are thought to lay their eggs in nests of foam, high in the trees.

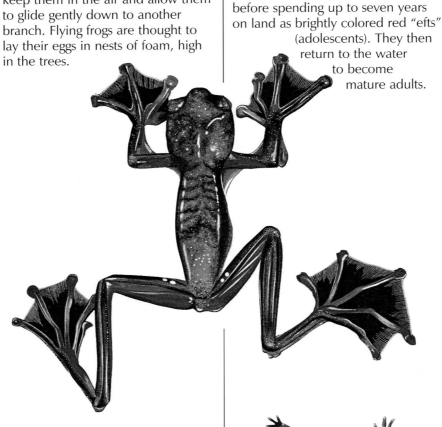

▼ Hellbender
RANGE: EASTERN U.S.A.
HABITAT: ROCKY-BOTTOMED STREAMS
Up to 30 in (80 cm) long, the hellbender is one of the world's largest salamanders and often scares fishermen who see it lurking on stream beds. It is feared poisonous, but is actually completely harmless and feeds on crayfish and snails.

► Mudpuppy
RANGE: CENTRAL N. AMERICA
HABITAT: LAKES, RIVERS, STREAMS
Mudpuppies are nocturnal hunters that crawl through muddy shallows in search of crayfish. They have huge, feathery gills to help them breathe underwater—the muddier the water, the bigger the gills.

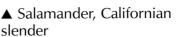

▲ Newt, Eastern
RANGE: EASTERN N. AMERICA
HABITAT: PONDS (ADULTS), MOIST LEAVES (EFTS)
Eastern newts begin life in water before spending up to seven years on land as brightly colored red "efts" (adolescents). They then return to the water to become mature adults.

▲ Newt, Warty
RANGE: EUROPE
HABITAT: STILL WATER
The male warty, or great crested, newt develops a long crest down its back during the breeding season, perhaps to impress the larger female. He usually performs a vigorous mating dance for the female then deposits his sperm for her to walk over.

► Olm
RANGE: SOUTHERN EUROPE
HABITAT: WATER IN CAVES
The olm is one of the few amphibians completely adapted to life in water and retains its feathery gills throughout its life. It lives in total darkness in its cave home and is virtually blind.

▲ Salamander, Californian slender
RANGE: CALIFORNIA, S. W. OREGON
HABITAT: REDWOOD FOREST, GRASSLAND
With its long, slender body, the Californian slender salamander can hide easily in rotting logs and under leaf litter. It moves almost like a snake, curving its body from side to side.

▲ Salamander, Fire
RANGE: W. EURASIA, N. AFRICA
HABITAT: WOODLAND
The striking coloring of the fire salamander is a warning to predators that it is poisonous. It lives in forests and emerges at night, often after rain, to hunt for earthworms.

▲ Salamander, Red
RANGE: E. U.S.A.
HABITAT: SPRINGS AND STREAMS
The red salamander reaches its most brilliant red when about two years old and then fades gradually. Like some other salamanders, it has no lungs but breathes through its skin.

▼ Salamander, Spotted

RANGE: S. CANADA, E. U.S.A.
HABITAT: HARDWOOD FOREST

Spotted salamanders spend most of their life underground, feeding on slugs and worms, but in early spring heavy rains encourage them to gather around breeding ponds where they mate and lay eggs in the water.

▼ Salamander, Texas blind

RANGE: TEXAS, U.S.A.
HABITAT: CAVEWATER

The Texas blind is a rare salamander that lives in water in caves. Its very pale, pink body, tiny eyes, and feathery gills are perfectly adapted for this dark underwater habitat.

▼ Salamander, Tiger

RANGE: N. AMERICA, MEXICO
HABITAT: DRY PLAINS, DAMP MEADOWS

The tiger salamander is the world's biggest land salamander, up to 16 in (41 cm) long, with a stout body, broad head, and small eyes. It lives near water among plant debris.

▼ Salamander, Yonahlossee

RANGE: BLUE RIDGE MOUNTAINS, U.S.A.
HABITAT: WOODED HILLSIDES

The yonahlossee is a striking-looking salamander with a red back. It got its name from the place it was discovered—Yonahlossee Road on Grandfather Mountain, North Carolina.

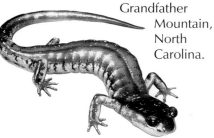

▼ Siren, Greater

RANGE: WEST COAST U.S.A.
HABITAT: SHALLOW FRESHWATER

The siren looks like an eel with its long, thin body and tiny front legs, but it is in fact a kind of salamander, which retains its tadpole gills all its life.

▲ Spring peeper

RANGE: EASTERN N. AMERICA
HABITAT: PONDS AND SWAMPS

Spring peepers get their name from their call, often heard early in spring in New England when they move to ponds where the ice has cleared. They are agile frogs that can jump 17 times their own height.

▲ Toad, African clawed

RANGE: SOUTH AFRICA
HABITAT: PONDS AND LAKES

The African clawed toad spends its entire life in water, with its eyes and nostrils above the surface. It is an extraordinary swimmer, able to dart through the water as fast as any fish and even swim backward. Its fingers are tipped with claws.

▲ Toad, American

RANGE: EASTERN NORTH AMERICA
HABITAT: WOODLAND, GARDENS, PARKS

Easily recognized by the line running down its back, this toad is covered in warts. It rests during the day, but it can often be heard trilling when it is active at night, hunting for insects and other small invertebrates. These toads breed in ponds and streams in spring, with the females laying up to 8,000 eggs.

▼ Toad, Common

RANGE: NORTHERN EURASIA, N. AFRICA
HABITAT: VARIED, USUALLY DRY

The common toad is one of the largest European toads. Like most toads, it has a warty skin and short back legs and hides away during the day. In cold places it hibernates in winter, then congregates to breed in spring.

▼ Toad, Giant

RANGE: C. AND S. AMERICA,
INTRODUCED AUSTRALIA
HABITAT: VARIED, NEAR POOLS

Also called the cane toad, the giant toad is the world's largest, often weighing up to 3 lbs (1.4 kg). Introduced to Australia to control beetles, it has become a serious pest.

▲ Toad, Midwife

RANGE: W. EUROPE
HABITAT: WOODLANDS

The midwife toad gets its name because after the female has laid her eggs in long strings, the male wraps them around his back legs. He then carries the eggs for a month or more, helping to protect them from predators until they hatch.

▲ Toad, Natterjack

RANGE: EUROPE
HABITAT: SANDY PLACES

The natterjack toad has an incredibly loud call that sounds like a machine and carries well over a mile (1.6 km). It usually lives near the sea and may even breed in saltwater.

▶ Toad, Oriental fire-bellied

RANGE: RUSSIA, SIBERIA, CHINA
HABITAT: MOUNTAIN STREAMS, RICE FIELDS

From above, the fire-bellied toad is a dull green, but when frightened it rears up, flashing a startling scarlet and black belly. It lives mostly in ditches and streams and can often be seen floating on the water surface.

▼ Toad, Western spadefoot

RANGE: GREAT PLAINS, U.S.A.
HABITAT: DRY GRASSLAND

The spadefoot toad gets its name from its broad back feet, which it uses like shovels to dig into sandy ground. It likes dry, sandy soil, but, if it rains, it crawls out on to the surface to mate and lay its eggs in rain pools where they hatch two days later.

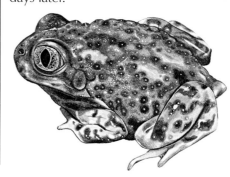

Birds

From soaring condors to swooping swallows, most birds are masters of the air, flying around as easily as fish swim in the sea. Yet it is not flight that makes birds unique, but their coat of feathers. Not all birds can fly, but all have feathers. There are some 9,000 species of bird, from tiny hummingbirds to huge ostriches, and they live in virtually every habitat open to the sky, from Antarctica to the Sahara.

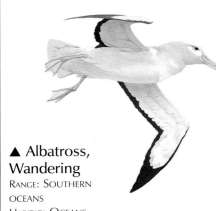

▲ Albatross, Wandering
RANGE: SOUTHERN OCEANS
HABITAT: OCEANS
The wandering albatross has the biggest wings of any bird, with a span of up to 11 ft (3.4 m). On these giant wings it can glide for weeks at a time over the ocean.

▶ Anhinga
RANGE: SOUTHERN U.S.A. TO ARGENTINA
HABITAT: LAKES, RIVERS
The anhinga is a cormorant-like bird that dives deep after fish, paddling with its feet, ready to dart down and impale prey on its sharp beak.

▼ Avocet, Pied
RANGE: BREEDS EURASIA; WINTERS AFRICA
HABITAT: MUDFLATS
Unlike other shorebirds, avocets do not probe for food in the mud. Instead they stride through the shallows, sweeping their bills from side to side to find insects.

▲ Barbet, Double-toothed
RANGE: E. AFRICA
HABITAT: SAVANNA
Barbets are brightly colored birds with big beaks. They are related to woodpeckers and toucans and feed on fruit, especially figs and bananas.

▲ Bee-eater, European
RANGE: BREEDS W. EURASIA; WINTERS AFRICA AND MIDDLE EAST
HABITAT: OPEN WOODLAND
Bee-eaters prey mostly on bees and wasps, which they seize nimbly in the air with their long, downward-curving bills. They then rub the insect on a branch to remove its sting.

▲ Bird of paradise, Blue
RANGE: NEW GUINEA
HABITAT: MOUNTAIN FOREST
The beautiful male blue bird of paradise performs a spectacular display to court the much plainer female, hanging upside down from a branch and flashing open its blue plumes.

▲ Bird of paradise, Raggiana
RANGE: NEW GUINEA
HABITAT: RAIN FOREST
If anything, the male raggiana bird of paradise is even more spectacular than the blue, with its yellow head and crimson tail, which it shows off in the breeding season by posing in treetops to the much drabber female.

◀ Bird of paradise, Ribbon-tailed
RANGE: NEW GUINEA
HABITAT: MOUNTAIN FOREST
The male ribbon-tailed bird of paradise has brilliantly colored green feathers around its head and incredibly long, ribbon-like tail feathers, nearly 3 ft (1 m) long, which it swishes to impress females.

▼ Bird of paradise, Wilson's
RANGE: NEW GUINEA
HABITAT: RAIN FOREST
Birds of paradise got their name because, when Europeans first saw their feathers 500 years ago, they thought they came from paradise. Like all birds of paradise, Wilson's feeds mainly on fruit, but also catches insects.

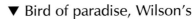

▲ Blackbird, Red-winged
RANGE: N. AND C. AMERICA
HABITAT: MARSHES, FIELDS
In recent years, the red-winged blackbird population has exploded and they are now perhaps the most numerous North American birds. After breeding, males gather into flocks a million or more strong.

▶ Bluebird, Eastern
RANGE: S. AND E. U.S.A.
HABITAT: GRASSLAND, WOODLAND
Eastern bluebirds have lost many of their traditional nest holes to introduced European starlings and sparrows, but the bird has been saved by the building of millions of nest boxes across the U.S.

▲ Bobwhite, Northern
RANGE: S. E. U.S.A.
HABITAT: FIELDS, FARMLAND, SCRUB
The name bobwhite comes from the sound of the male's call during the mating season. For most of the year bobwhites move around in flocks of 30 or so birds, then in spring flocks break up and the birds pair for mating.

▲ Bowerbird, Satin
RANGE: EASTERN AUSTRALIA
HABITAT: FOREST
Male bowerbirds make "bowers" to attract a mate. Some bowerbirds build rings or thatched huts. The satin makes an avenue of sticks which it paints with fruit and saliva.

▲ Budgerigar
RANGE: AUSTRALIA, INTRODUCED U.S.A.
HABITAT: SCRUB
Now very popular as a cage bird in various colors, the budgerigar is a small, green parrot in the wild. It is active early in the morning and late in the afternoon when flocks of the birds scour the ground for grass seeds.

▼ Bulbul, Red-whiskered
RANGE: S. ASIA, INTRODUCED U.S.A., AUSTRALIA
HABITAT: SCRUB

Bulbuls are noisy tropical birds that feed on fruit, berries, and nectar. Red-whiskered bulbuls are considered pests.

▲ Bunting, Snow
RANGE: ARCTIC
HABITAT: TUNDRA
The snow bunting is the most northerly breeding bird. In its white breeding plumage the male perfectly matches his snowy habitat. To escape the cold, these plump little birds sometimes burrow beneath the snow.

▼ Bustard, Great
RANGE: N. EURASIA
HABITAT: STEPPE
This is the world's heaviest flying bird. Outside the breeding season, bustards move around in large flocks searching for seasonally available food.

▲ Buzzard, Rough-legged
RANGE: N. AMERICA, NORTHERN EURASIA
HABITAT: TUNDRA, STEPPE
The rough-legged buzzard is one of the most northerly hunting birds of prey. In summer it hovers over the tundra scanning for prey, such as lemmings and voles.

▲ Capercaillie, Western
RANGE: N. EUROPE
HABITAT: PINE AND OAK FOREST
This turkeylike bird is the biggest of all grouse and is renowned for its leks (courtship displays), when the male's calls echo through the forest. It feeds on pine seeds in winter and leaves and fruit in summer.

▶ Cardinal, Northern
RANGE: E. U.S.A.
HABITAT: WOODLAND, GARDENS, SHRUBBERY
Cardinals get their names from the red robes worn by Roman Catholic cardinals. Their range is extending farther north, perhaps due to global warming, and they now winter as far north as Maine.

▲ Cassowary
RANGE: NEW GUINEA, N. AUSTRALIA
HABITAT: RAIN FOREST
Cassowaries are large, flightless birds with a big, bony shield, or casque, on their heads—thought to help them break through the undergrowth as they search for fallen fruit.

▼ Chickadee, Black-capped
RANGE: N. AMERICA
HABITAT: FOREST, GARDENS
The black-capped chickadee is a small bird with thick, fluffy feathers that help it cope with the winter cold as far north as Alaska. In winter it feeds mainly on seeds and berries.

▼ Chicken, Greater prairie
RANGE: GREAT PLAINS, U.S.A.
HABITAT: GRASSLAND
As its habitat has shrunk, the once abundant prairie chicken—famous for the male's spring courtship—has become increasingly rare.

▼ Cock-of-the-rock, Andean
RANGE: ANDES
HABITAT: FOREST GORGES
Cock-of-the-rocks are brilliantly colored birds that move in swift, weaving flights through rain forest gorges. Females build the nest alone on sheer cliff faces.

▶ Cockatoo, Sulfur-crested
RANGE: NEW GUINEA, AUSTRALIA
HABITAT: RAIN FOREST
These noisy parrots gather in huge flocks for most of the year to feed on seeds, fruits, and insects. Sulfur-crested cockatoos make popular pets because they mimic human speech remarkably well.

▶ Cormorant, Great
RANGE: WORLDWIDE EXCEPT S. AMERICA
HABITAT: COASTS
These fish-eating birds are extraordinary divers that chase prey underwater. They propel themselves through the water with their webbed feet, using their long tail as a rudder, often diving for more than a minute. Prey is brought to the surface then swallowed.

▶ Crane, Common
RANGE: BREEDS N. EURASIA; WINTERS S. EURASIA AND N. AFRICA
HABITAT: BREEDS FOREST SWAMPS; WINTERS WETLANDS
Cranes are long-legged birds, famous for their dancing displays, when they walk in circles, bowing, bobbing, and tossing things over their heads.

▶ Crane, Whooping
RANGE: BREEDS CANADA; WINTERS TEXAS
HABITAT: BREEDS PRAIRIE POOLS; WINTERS COASTAL MARSHES
One of the world's rarest birds, with fewer than 400 remaining in the wild, whooping cranes are opportunist feeders that feed on a wide range of plant and animal food in shallow water and on land.

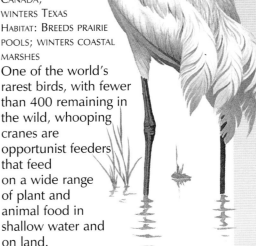

▲ Crow, American
RANGE: N. AMERICA
HABITAT: VARIED
The adaptable American crow lives almost anywhere and feeds on almost anything. To confuse predators, males often build decoy nests.

▲ Cuckoo, Common
RANGE: BREEDS EURASIA; WINTERS AFRICA
HABITAT: FARMLAND, HEATH
The cuckoo returns to the north in late March and the loud breeding call of the male is traditionally taken as the first sign that summer is on its way. Cuckoos are renowned for laying their eggs in the nests of other birds, such as pipits and warblers. The cuckoo chick pushes the other eggs out of the nest and is then fed by its foster parents.

▲ Curassow, Great
RANGE: C. AMERICA
HABITAT: FOREST, SCRUB
Curassows are the only game birds to nest in trees. Although they feed on the ground on leaves and fruit, they quickly fly up into the branches if disturbed.

▲ Curlew, Eskimo
RANGE: BREEDS
CANADA; WINTERS S. AMERICA
HABITAT: BREEDS TUNDRA, WINTERS PAMPAS
Huge flocks of these birds were once seen on their migrations, but so many millions have been shot that they are now very rare.

▼ Dipper, North American
RANGE: N. AMERICA
HABITAT: UPLAND STREAMS
This little bird can often be seen dipping its head into mountain streams to snatch insects and other small creatures from the stream bed. A special membrane shields its eyes from the water. This flashes white as the bird blinks to signal alarm.

▼ Diver, Red-throated
RANGE: N. AMERICA, N. EURASIA
HABITAT: TUNDRA, TAIGA, ARCTIC WATERS
Divers are superb swimmers with streamlined bodies and strong webbed feet that can propel them down to 250 ft (75 m). Dense plumage keeps them warm in icy arctic waters.

▼ Dove, Collared
RANGE: EURASIA
HABITAT: FARMLAND
The collared dove is a very common bird that lives close to human habitation. It often feeds on scraps put out by humans as well as its natural diet of seeds and berries.

▼ Dove, Mourning
RANGE: N. AND C. AMERICA
HABITAT: DRY GRASSLAND, DESERT
The mourning dove gets its name from its mournful call; and its wings make a distinctive whistling when the bird takes to the air. Adults feed their young by coughing up partially digested food, which is called pigeon milk.

▲ Dovekie
RANGE: ARCTIC, N. ATLANTIC
HABITAT: COLD OCEANS
Also known as the little auk, this seabird breeds in vast colonies among the rocks on Arctic shores, where the chicks are constantly preyed upon by glaucous gulls. The dovekie can fly and swim well and feeds on fish.

▼ Duck, Mallard
RANGE: N. AMERICA, N. EURASIA
HABITAT: WIDE RANGE OF WATERS
Mallards are dabbling ducks that feed by upending in ponds, lakes, and rivers to sift plant matter and invertebrates from the water. The colorful males are called drakes.

▼ Duck, Mandarin
RANGE: E. EURASIA, INTRODUCED EUROPE
HABITAT: FOREST RIVERS, LAKES
Long celebrated in Oriental art, male mandarin ducks have orange wing feathers that they display like a pair of sails in the breeding season. Mandarins are most active at dawn and dusk, feeding on plant food and on insects, snails, and small fish.

▶ Eagle, Bald
RANGE: N. AMERICA
HABITAT: LAKES, RIVERS, COASTS
The U.S.A.'s national symbol, the bald eagle is one of the world's largest birds of prey, up to 3 ft (1 m) long. Hunting and poisoning from DDT pesticide reduced numbers to below 2,000, but the bird is now protected and there are approximately 300,000 remaining today.

▶ Eagle, Crested serpent
RANGE: INDIA, S. E. ASIA
HABITAT: FOREST, SAVANNA
This eagle can be hard to spot in the rain forest, except when it is soaring high above the trees. Like other serpent or snake eagles it preys mostly on snakes and watches for its quarry by perching in a tree, then dropping down suddenly and gripping the snake with its talons.

▲ Eagle, Golden
RANGE: EURASIA, N. AMERICA, N. AFRICA
HABITAT: MOUNTAINS, PLAINS, COASTS
One of the most magnificent birds of prey, the golden eagle is a superb flier. It preys on rabbits, marmots, and other mammals, making a fast, low-level attack, then pouncing. Golden eagles nest on crags or in trees where they make a large platform, or aerie, from sticks. They are now rare in most places.

▶ Egret, Great

RANGE: WORLDWIDE

HABITAT: FRESHWATER WETLAND

Also known as the American egret, the great egret belongs to the heron family and, like all herons, has a long neck and a powerful bill, which it uses for stabbing fish. It hunts by standing in wait in the water or by slowly stalking its prey. In the 19 century millions were killed for hat feathers, but they remain widespread.

▼ Eider, Common

RANGE: N. AMERICA, N. EURASIA, ARCTIC

HABITAT: COASTAL WATERS

Eider ducks have very warm plumage to keep out the Arctic chill and people have long valued the down feathers for quilts. The female plucks these feathers from her breast to line the nest.

▼ Emu

RANGE: AUSTRALIA

HABITAT: BUSH

The emu is the world's second largest bird after the ostrich. It is completely flightless and walks far through the bush searching for food, often up to 600 miles (1,000 km) a year.

▲ Falcon, Peregrine

RANGE: WORLDWIDE EXCEPT FOR SAHARA, C. ASIA, S. AMERICA

HABITAT: MOUNTAINS, SEA CLIFFS

To catch birds in flight, falcons climb up high then dive, or stoop, on their target at speeds of up to 125 mph (200 km/h).

▶ Finch, Blue-faced parrot

RANGE: AUSTRALASIA

HABITAT: RAIN FOREST

Parrot finches are grass finches unrelated to the finches of the northern hemisphere. They feed alone or in pairs on seeds in bushes.

◀ Finch, Purple

RANGE: N. AMERICA

HABITAT: WOODLAND

Outside the breeding season purple finches feed together on seeds in large flocks. In the breeding season the male dances around the female, beating his wings and singing a warbling song.

▶ Finch, Zebra

RANGE: AUSTRALIA AND ISLANDS

HABITAT: WOODLAND, SCRUB

The zebra finch is largely sedentary, moving only to find seeds on the ground. Like most grass finches, it builds a domed nest of grass and twigs.

▶ Flamingo

RANGE: S. EURASIA, AFRICA, C. AMERICA, CARIBBEAN

HABITAT: LAGOONS, LAKES

The flamingo is a tall, startlingly pink bird that swims and flies well. Huge colonies are often seen as a pink mass on lagoons and lakes. It feeds on mollusks which, uniquely for a bird, it filters from the water in the same way as a baleen whale.

▲ Flycatcher, Royal

RANGE: C. AND S. AMERICA

HABITAT: RAIN FOREST, CLOUD FOREST

The royal flycatcher has a dull brown body, but the male has a brilliant crimson crest of feathers that it flashes up like a fan when courting. Like all flycatchers, it snaps up flies in the air.

▲ Frigate bird, Great

RANGE: INDIAN AND PACIFIC OCEANS

HABITAT: WARM OCEANS

Frigate birds are wonderful fliers, with a wingspan of almost 6½ ft (2 m). But they are also the criminals of the seabird world, often attacking other birds and stealing their catch.

▶ Gannet

RANGE: NORTH ATLANTIC

HABITAT: OCEANS

Gannets are superb divers. When they spot a fish in the water they dive from at least 100 ft (30 m), folding back their wings just as they plunge into the water. Their strong skulls protect them from the impact.

▼ Goldeneye, Common

RANGE: N. AMERICA

HABITAT: LAKES IN SUMMER; COASTAL BAYS IN WINTER

The goldeneye duck is also known as the whistler because of the whistling sound made by its wings as it flies.

▼ Goldfinch, American

RANGE: N. AMERICA

HABITAT: WOODLAND, FIELDS

These little finches can often be seen feeding in flocks on roadside thistles, taking off and swirling around every time a vehicle passes by. Their nests are lined with milkweed fluff and thistledown.

▼ Goose, Canada

RANGE: ARCTIC, N. AMERICA, INTRODUCED EUROPE

HABITAT: WETLAND

Canada geese breed in the north and migrate south in fall, following the same route year after year. They graze on water and land plants.

▲ Goshawk, Northern
RANGE: N. AMERICA, N. EURASIA
HABITAT: TEMPERATE WOODLAND AND TAIGA
These are swift, agile fliers that ambush prey. They swoop out of the trees to take prey by surprise, killing them instantly with their talons.

▲ Grebe, Pied-billed
RANGE: N. AND S. AMERICA
HABITAT: MARSHES AND PONDS
The pied-billed grebe is a waterbird that can dive so fast it is nicknamed "hell diver." To escape predators it can sink into the water so that only its bill—and its nostrils—are above water.

▼ Grebe, Great crested
RANGE: EUROPE, S. EURASIA, S. AFRICA, AUSTRALIA
HABITAT: STILL FRESHWATER
Few birds have more elaborate courtships than this grebe. Both male and female have dark head plumes that they fan out during their "weed dance." In the dance, pairs shake, dive, and rise from the water breast to breast to present each other with weeds.

▼ Grosbeak, Pine
RANGE: N. AMERICA, N. EURASIA
HABITAT: CONIFEROUS FOREST
The pine grosbeak is a large finch that feeds mainly on berries and buds. The most northerly grosbeaks migrate south and west for winter, often in large numbers; more southerly birds stay put.

▲ Grouse, Black
RANGE: N. EURASIA
HABITAT: MOOR, FOREST
Black grouse are famous for their courting displays during which the males jump about looking threatening, while the females strut nonchalantly between them.

◀ Gull, Great black-backed
RANGE: NORTH ATLANTIC COASTS
HABITAT: COASTS, LOCALLY INLAND
The great black-backed gull is a strongly built aggressive bird with a hook-tipped bill. It feeds on anything from crabs and fish to small birds, such as puffins, and mammals, such as mice and voles.

▼ Gull, Herring
RANGE: N. HEMISPHERE BEYOND TROPICS
HABITAT: COASTAL, INLAND
The herring gull's natural food is rarely herrings—more often shrimps, prawns, and crabs. It has also learned to scavenge rubbish dumps and is now well established in many towns.

▼ Hawk, Red-tailed
RANGE: N. AND C. AMERICA, CARIBBEAN
HABITAT: VARIED, TYPICALLY NEAR TREES
The red-tailed hawk is able to live anywhere from deserts to alpine meadows. It is a versatile hunter, catching a wide range of prey, including rabbits, snakes, and lizards. It sometimes swoops down from a high perch, but it can also chase prey at low levels, or hover in the air.

▼ Heron, Great blue
RANGE: N. AND S. AMERICA
HABITAT: RIVERS, MARSHES, SWAMPS
The largest of the American herons, the great blue is a fearsome hunter. It stands still as a statue in shallow water, watching for fish or frogs. When it sees a target it makes a lightning strike with its sharp bill. Occasionally it hunts actively, running through the water and flicking its wings. It nests in colonies high up in trees.

▼ Hoatzin
RANGE: AMAZON AND ORINOCO
HABITAT: RAIN FOREST
With its long neck and spiky crest, the hoatzin is an odd-looking bird, which clambers clumsily through the trees, occasionally flapping its wings. Nestlings have claws on their wings which they use to cling on to twigs as they explore. These claws are reminiscent of the earliest known bird, *Archaeopteryx*. If threatened, hoatzin chicks drop into water and climb out when danger has past. Adults loaf in trees and feed on leaves.

▼ Honeycreeper, Purple
RANGE: TRINIDAD, TROPICAL S. AMERICA
HABITAT: RAIN FOREST
Honeycreepers feed on fruit, especially bananas, but they also suck nectar from rain forest flowers through their long, curved bills. The male purple honeycreeper is a brilliant violet color, while the female is a deep green. The female builds a neat cup-shaped nest in a tree.

▲ Honeyeater, Cardinal
RANGE: PACIFIC ISLANDS
HABITAT: FOREST, SCRUB
Among the smallest of the honeyeaters, which feed on nectar, this striking bird normally feeds in the treetops, but occasionally it ventures down to sip at flowers at the forest edge.

▶ Hoopoe
RANGE: EURASIA, AFRICA
HABITAT: WOODLAND, GRASSLAND
The hoopoe is notorious for the horrible smell of its nest in holes in trees and walls. The smell is thought to deter predators, but it remains a favorite prey of falcons.

▼ Hornbill, Great Indian
RANGE: S. ASIA
HABITAT: TROPICAL RAIN FOREST
The great Indian is a large hornbill and the casque, or ridge, on its bill amplifies its loud, honking calls. In flight, its wing beats swish so loudly they can be heard more than half a mile (800 m) away. It lives in the rain forest canopy, feeding mainly on fruit.

▼ Hornbill, Southern ground
RANGE: SOUTHERN AFRICA
HABITAT: SAVANNA
Unlike other hornbills, the large southern ground hornbill lives mostly on the ground and feeds on small animals rather than fruit. It typically catches small animals while walking around its territory.

136

▲ Hornero, Rufous
RANGE: S. AMERICA
HABITAT: TREES

The rufous hornero gets its name from its extraordinary nests, built out of wet mud and straw. Hornero is Spanish for baker and the nest looks like an old-fashioned baker's oven.

▲ Hummingbird, Bee
RANGE: CUBA
HABITAT: FOREST

Hummingbirds are tiny, jewel-like birds that feed on nectar, hovering in front of flowers as they feed. The bee hummingbird is the tiniest bird in the world, no bigger than a thumb.

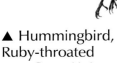

▲ Hummingbird, Ruby-throated
RANGE: BREEDS N. AMERICA; WINTERS C. AMERICA
HABITAT: WOODLAND

This tiny, dazzlingly colored hummingbird can fly more than 500 miles (800 km) over the Gulf of Mexico when it migrates.

▼ Hummingbird, Sword-billed
RANGE: ANDES MOUNTAIN RANGE
HABITAT: SHRUBBY SLOPES

This hummingbird has the longest bill of any bird relative to its body, enabling it to probe into the deepest flowers. When it perches it holds its bill vertically.

▼ Ibis, Glossy
RANGE: S. EURASIA, AFRICA, AUSTRALIA, CARIBBEAN
HABITAT: MARSHES, LAKES

The beautiful glossy ibis is the most widespread of the ibises, living on lakes right around the world, often in large colonies. It eats insects and water creatures which it picks from the mud with its long bill.

▼ Ibis, Hermit
RANGE: MOROCCO, TURKEY
HABITAT: MOUNTAINS, DESERTS

The hermit ibis, also known as the northern bald ibis or waldrapp, was once widespread through southern Europe and the Middle East. Now, perhaps because of changes in the climate, it has become very rare and breeds only in Morocco and Turkey.

◄ Jacamar, Rufous-tailed
RANGE: C. AND S. AMERICA
HABITAT: RAIN FOREST

Jacamars are 17 species of brilliantly colored birds that perch on twigs waiting for insects. The rufous-tailed jacamar typically lives in pairs or family groups and its mournful call can often be heard echoing through the rain forest. The female jacamar digs a breeding tunnel where it lays and hatches its eggs.

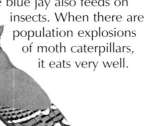

▲ Jacana
RANGE: SOUTHERN U.S.A., C. AMERICA
HABITAT: VEGETATED FRESHWATER

The eight species of jacana have toes so long that they spread their weight as they walk, so that they can seemingly walk on water, treading on the leaves of water lilies. This is why they are also called "lily trotters."

▼ Jay, Blue
RANGE: EASTERN N. AMERICA
HABITAT: WOODS, PARKS

The blue jay is often seen in gardens gathering seeds and nuts. It sometimes buries hoards to tide it over the winter. Even so, many blue jays from the north fly south for the winter. The blue jay also feeds on insects. When there are population explosions of moth caterpillars, it eats very well.

▼ Jungle fowl
RANGE: S. E. ASIA
HABITAT: FOREST

The ancestor of the domestic chicken, the jungle fowl lives on the edge of forests where it finds seeds and insects by scratching with its feet. Like cockerels, male jungle fowl make a noisy, crowing sound. They usually breed in the dry season from March to May.

▲ Kestrel, Common
RANGE: EURASIA, AFRICA
HABITAT: OPEN COUNTRY, FIELDS

Kestrels are small falcons that hunt rodents and insects. They have very acute eyesight and hover over open ground, watching with their wings beating. When prey is targeted they drop down gently on it. They need a head wind to hover, but they are among the biggest of all hovering birds. Typically, they lay their eggs on a ledge or in a hole abandoned by other birds.

▲ King of Saxony's bird of paradise
RANGE: NEW GUINEA
HABITAT: RAIN FOREST

The king of Saxony's bird of paradise was named by European naturalists exploring the forest of New Guinea in honor of their monarch. It looks fairly ordinary except for two amazing plumes that extend from its head. When displaying, the male sits on a high branch with its plumes up, bouncing up and down, swelling its back feathers and hissing. When a female approaches he sweeps his plumes down in front of her then follows her to mate.

▲ Kingbird, Eastern
RANGE: BREEDS N. AMERICA;
WINTERS S. AMERICA
HABITAT: OPEN COUNTRY
WITH TREES
The eastern kingbird will defend
its territory dauntlessly, attacking
much larger birds like hawks and
raining them with blows. It even
attacks aircraft.

▲ Kingfisher, Belted
RANGE: BREEDS N. AMERICA; WINTERS
CARIBBEAN
HABITAT: STREAMS, RIVERS, PONDS
This kingfisher likes to perch on
branches overhanging the water
where it can see fish and dive
after them. Often, though, it
hovers over the water.
It also eats frogs
and crabs.

▲ Kite, Red
RANGE: EUROPE,
MIDDLE EAST, N. AFRICA
HABITAT: WOODLAND, OPEN COUNTRY
Kites are all agile fliers with forked
tails. The red kite is the biggest of
them and feeds on small mammals,
carrion, and young birds.

▼ Kiwi
RANGE: NEW ZEALAND
HABITAT: FOREST
The unusual kiwi is covered in soft,
hairlike plumage, has no tail or
wings, and cannot fly. It has poor
eyesight and hunts by smell. It is
now rare, thanks to introduced dogs,
cats, and stoats.

▼ Lapwing, Northern
RANGE: EUROPE, AFRICA, ASIA
HABITAT: GRASSLAND, FARMLAND, MARSHES
Lapwings are also known as peewits,
after the cry they make when on the
wing. Unlike other lapwings, the
northern lapwing lives in damp,
grassy fields rather than close to
water. In the breeding
season the males often
soar up into the sky in a
spectacular aerial display,
then tumble down.

▼ Lark, Shore
RANGE: N. AMERICA, EURASIA, N. AFRICA
HABITAT: GRASSLAND, TUNDRA
Also known as horned larks, shore
larks are the only larks native to
America as well as Eurasia. In winter
northern groups migrate
south to lowland fields
where they often
flock with
buntings.

▼ Limpkin
RANGE: SOUTHERN U.S.A.,
C. AND S. AMERICA, CARIBBEAN
HABITAT: SWAMPS
The limpkin is a marsh wading bird
similar to cranes, which probes the
mud for water snails with its beak.
It was hunted almost to extinction in
the last century
but is now
protected
by law.

▲ Lorikeet, Rainbow
RANGE: E. AUSTRALIA WEST TO BALI
HABITAT: FOREST, GARDENS
Unlike other parrots, the lorikeet
does not feed on fruit and seeds.
Instead, it licks up nectar and flower
pollen with its tongue. Typically, the
rainbow lorikeet will fly off to search
for food in the trees shortly after
dawn, screeching loudly.

▼ Longclaw, Yellow-throated
RANGE: AFRICA SOUTH OF
THE SAHARA
HABITAT: DAMP GRASSLAND
Longclaws are related to pipits and
wagtails and, like them, forage on
the ground for insects. Longclaws get
their name from their 2 in- (5 cm-)
long hind claw.
They live in
pairs. When
flying, they
occasionally
dive into the
grass for
insects.

▼ Loon, Common
RANGE: FAR NORTH AMERICA AND EURASIA
HABITAT: LAKES, COASTS
Loons, also known as divers, are the
grebes of the polar regions—
perfectly adapted for underwater
swimming. They are very clumsy
when it comes to walking on land
because their feet are set so far back
that they constantly tip forward.

▶ Lyrebird, Superb
RANGE: S. E. AUSTRALIA
HABITAT: MOUNTAIN FOREST
Lyrebirds get their name
from their lyre-like
tails. They are
ground-
living
birds, but hop
up into trees to
roost. Just before
mating the male
builds several mounds of
earth, then dances on them, spreading
out his tail before the female.

▶ Macaw, Scarlet
RANGE: C. AND
S. AMERICA
HABITAT: FOREST,
SAVANNA
Macaws are the
largest of all parrots.
The scarlet macaw is
a brilliantly colored
parrot that feeds high up
in the trees on seeds and
fruits. Although the most
common of the macaws, it
is declining in numbers
because of the destruction of
the rain forest and the
trapping of young birds for
sale as pets.

▶ Magpie, Black-billed
RANGE: EURASIA,
N. AMERICA, N. AFRICA
HABITAT: OPEN COUNTRY WITH TREES
Magpies are lively birds that
feed on insects, snails, slugs,
and spiders, although they
will sometimes steal eggs and
nestlings. In recent years they
have moved into suburban areas.

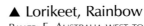

◀ **Manakin, Wire-tailed**
RANGE: TROPICAL S. AMERICA
HABITAT: RAIN FOREST, PLANTATIONS
Manakins are small, colorful birds that typically forage alone for insects and fruit. They prefer humid areas in the forest canopy or just below, but are often seen in clearings and cocoa plantations.

▲ **Martin, Sand**
RANGE: BREEDS EURASIA, N. AMERICA; WINTERS S. AMERICA, AFRICA, S. E. ASIA
HABITAT: STEEP SAND OR GRAVEL BANKS
Like swallows, sand martins feed on insects on the wing, gaping their beaks wide to take the insect in. But their flight is slightly less graceful than the swallow's.

▼ **Meadowlark, Eastern**
RANGE: BREEDS N. AMERICA; WINTERS S. AMERICA
HABITAT: PRAIRIES, FARMLAND
The eastern meadowlark's whistle-like song is one of the first heard on the prairies in spring. It nests on the ground and probes the grass for grasshoppers, ants, and worms with its sharp beak.

▼ **Merganser, Red-breasted**
RANGE: BREEDS NORTHERN N. AMERICA, EURASIA; WINTERS SOUTHERN N. AMERICA, EURASIA
HABITAT: COASTAL, INLAND WATERS
Mergansers are saw-billed ducks, which means the beaks have serrated edges to help them grasp slippery fish. They nest in shallow depressions in the ground, lined with grass, leaves, and down.

▲ **Mockingbird, Northern**
RANGE: N. AMERICA
HABITAT: OPEN WOODLAND, GARDENS
Mockingbirds are tireless singers, singing day and night—mimicking anything from a ringing telephone to a croaking frog. The record for one bird is 39 bird cries and 50 other calls.

▲ **Moorhen**
RANGE: WORLDWIDE EXCEPT AUSTRALIA
HABITAT: SWAMPS, MARSHES
Despite its name, the moorhen is not a moorland bird; the "moor" comes from an Anglo-Saxon word meaning "bog." It is a small, timid bird that swims well and also forages on land.

▶ **Motmot, Blue-crowned**
RANGE: C. AND S. AMERICA, CARIBBEAN
HABITAT: RAIN FOREST, PLANTATIONS
Motmots live in dense vegetation on the forest floor where they ambush insects, spiders, and lizards. They often perch on low branches, swinging their tail from side to side like a pendulum as they wait for prey. They nest in burrows.

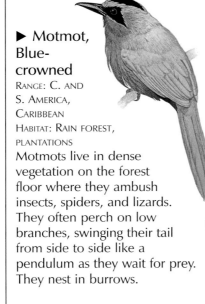

▼ **Nighthawk, Common**
RANGE: BREEDS N. AMERICA; WINTERS S. AMERICA
HABITAT: GRASSLAND, DESERT, OPEN WOODS
Nighthawks are not hawks but are related to nightjars. They are on the wing at dawn and dusk "hawking" for insects with their large mouths.

▲ **Nightingale**
RANGE: BREEDS EURASIA; WINTERS AFRICA
HABITAT: WOODLAND, THICKETS
The nightingale is famed for its beautiful song, which is often heard in woods from dawn to dusk and even at night. It is a secretive, dull brown bird that is hard to see, foraging for food, such as worms and berries, amongst dense vegetation on the woodland floor. It hops around, rather than flying.

▼ **Nightjar, Eurasian**
RANGE: BREEDS EURASIA; WINTERS AFRICA
HABITAT: OPEN COUNTRY, WOODS, SAND DUNES
During the day nightjars lie motionless on the ground, often almost invisible in dead leaves. They take to the air at dusk and catch moths in their wide, gaping beaks.

▲ **Oriole, Golden**
RANGE: BREEDS EURASIA; WINTERS AFRICA, INDIA
HABITAT: FOREST, ORCHARDS
The brilliant yellow golden oriole is surprisingly hard to see as it hides among the leaves in woodland trees. It rarely comes to the ground and its flight is swift and winding. A courting male chases a female at top speed through the branches.

◀ **Osprey**
RANGE: ALMOST WORLDWIDE
HABITAT: LAKES, RIVERS, COASTS
The osprey, or fish hawk, feeds almost exclusively on fish. It flies high over the water, flapping and gliding, then, when it spots a fish, it plummets to the water, entering feet first with a large splash to grab the fish in its talons. After surfacing, it shakes its feathers and carries the fish back to its nest of sticks.

▼ **Ostrich**
RANGE: AFRICA
HABITAT: SAVANNA
The ostrich is the world's largest bird. It cannot fly, but it can run at up to 45 mph (70 km/h) for over 22 miles (35 km). Several females lay in a single nest on the ground, producing a combined clutch of up to 30 eggs.

◀ Owl, Barn

RANGE: ALMOST WORLDWIDE EXCEPT N. ASIA
HABITAT: OPEN COUNTRY, FARMLAND

The barn owl is easily recognized by its heart-shaped face. It roosts by day in places like barns, and hunts for rodents at night, flying low and silently, then swooping.

▶ Owl, Great horned

RANGE: N. AND S. AMERICA
HABITAT: VARIED, WOODS, PARKS

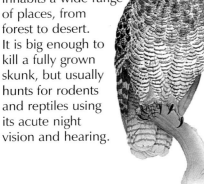

America's largest owl, the great horned owl, inhabits a wide range of places, from forest to desert. It is big enough to kill a fully grown skunk, but usually hunts for rodents and reptiles using its acute night vision and hearing.

◀ Owl, Long-eared

RANGE: N. AMERICA, N. EURASIA, N. AFRICA
HABITAT: CONIFEROUS FOREST

The long-eared owl hunts exclusively at night, using its sharp ears to detect voles and mice—in contrast to the short-eared owl, which often hunts in broad daylight.

▶ Owl, Snowy

RANGE: CANADA, GREENLAND, N. EURASIA
HABITAT: TUNDRA, COASTS

The snowy owl lives in the Arctic, where its white plumage makes it almost invisible against snow. It hunts during the day, preying on lemmings, hares, and small birds. It usually nests in mid-May in a shallow pit scraped into the ground, lined with moss and feathers.

▲ Oystercatcher, Common

RANGE: BREEDS EURASIA; WINTERS AFRICA, S. ASIA
HABITAT: COASTS, ESTUARIES

These handsome shorebirds sometimes use their long beaks to draw worms out of the sand and sometimes to hammer a hole in the shells of cockles, mussels, and limpets. Their courtship display is amongst the noisiest of all shorebirds, as they walk around "piping" agitatedly.

▲ Parrot, Eclectus

RANGE: NEW GUINEA, N. AUSTRALIA
HABITAT: RAIN FOREST

These parrots are called "eclectic" because the males and females are so different in color that for years they were thought to be separate species. The males are bright green but the females are even more vivid red and blue.

▲ Parrot, Gray

RANGE: C. AFRICA
HABITAT: LOWLAND FOREST, SAVANNA

Gray parrots roost together on forest edges or on small islands in rivers, and fly off in pairs at sunrise to find seeds, nuts, and berries, and oil palm fruit. They are great mimics and one has been taught 750 human words.

▲ Parula, Northern

RANGE: BREEDS EASTERN N. AMERICA; WINTERS CARIBBEAN, C. AMERICA
HABITAT: PINE FOREST (SUMMER), MIXED WOODLAND (WINTER)

This blue warbler forages in trees for insects, especially caterpillars, creeping over branches and hopping from perch to perch. Its nest is built in hanging lichen.

▲ Peafowl, Congo

RANGE: CONGO, AFRICA
HABITAT: RAIN FOREST

The Congo peafowl is Africa's largest and most spectacular game bird, only discovered in 1936. It is the only one of 49 pheasant species not native to Asia. Although it looks quite similar to the Asian peafowl and eats the same variety of fruits and insects, it breeds quite differently. Both male and female are equally splendid and form lifelong pairs.

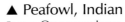

▲ Peafowl, Indian

RANGE: ORIGINALLY INDIA, SRI LANKA
HABITAT: FOREST, FARMLAND

Now kept in parks and gardens all over the world, the male peafowl, or peacock, is one of the most spectacular of all birds, with its huge tail of 150 or more long iridescent feathers which it raises in a huge fan.

▲ Pelican, Brown

RANGE: N., C., AND S. AMERICA
HABITAT: COASTS

Unlike its cousin the great white, the brown pelican hunts in the sea, but it has the same big pouch under its beak for scooping up fish. It typically catches fish by diving down sharply with its wings back from about 50 ft (15 m) up. Cushioning air sacs in its chest soften the impact as it plunges into the water.

▲ Penguin, Adelie

RANGE: ANTARCTICA
HABITAT: OCEANS, ROCKY COASTS

Apart from the emperor penguin, the Adelie penguin lives nearer to the South Pole than any bird, nesting in large colonies along shores that are free of ice only in summer. The Antarctic summer is so short that all the females in each colony lay their eggs within two days in November.

▲ Penguin, King
RANGE: SUBANTARCTIC, FALKLAND ISLANDS
HABITAT: OCEAN, BREEDS COASTS
The king penguin is one of the biggest penguins, almost 40 in (1 m) tall—exceeded only by the huge emperor penguin. It is also one of the deepest diving of the penguins, plunging 150 ft (45 m) or more in pursuit of fish and squid.

▶ Penguin, Little
RANGE: NEW ZEALAND, AUSTRALIA
HABITAT: COASTS
Also known as the fairy penguin, the little penguin is the smallest of the penguins— less than 16 in (41 cm) tall. It is also one of the few to remain active after sunset.

▶ Petrel, European storm
RANGE: ATLANTIC, MEDITERRANEAN
HABITAT: OCEANS
The smallest of European seabirds, the storm petrel was believed to warn of a storm when it followed a ship. In fact, it probably follows to feed on fish brought to the surface by the disturbance.

▲ Pheasant
RANGE: ORIGINALLY C. AND S. E. ASIA; INTRODUCED WORLDWIDE
HABITAT: WOODLAND, FOREST EDGE, HEATH
Called the pheasant in Europe and North America, the common pheasant is one of 49 species of pheasant, many of which, like the common pheasant, came originally from S. E. Asia.

▼ Pigeon, Victoria crowned
RANGE: NEW GUINEA AND ISLANDS
HABITAT: RAIN FOREST
This is the biggest of the pigeons— about the size of a chicken. It has an amazing fan of feathers on its head. It lives in rain forests and feeds on fallen fruit on the forest floor.

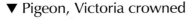

▼ Pipit, Water
RANGE & HABITAT: BREEDS EURASIAN MOUNTAINS; WINTERS LOWLANDS AND S. E. ASIA AND JAPAN
Pipits are small birds that nest on the ground. The water pipit breeds well above the tree line on mountains, usually close to rushing streams and occasionally next to glaciers in the snow.

▼ Pitta, Garnet
RANGE: BURMA, SUMATRA, BORNEO
HABITAT: SWAMPY FOREST
Pittas are stout, thrushlike birds of the tropics. The garnet pitta is a colorful bird of swamp forests that runs about the forest floor foraging for ants, beetles, and other insects as well as snails and fruit.

▶ Plover, American golden
RANGE: BREEDS FAR NORTH AMERICA AND ASIA; WINTERS S. AMERICA AND ASIA
HABITAT: TUNDRA, GRASSLAND
Every year this plover, also known as the lesser plover, flies one of the longest migrations of any land bird, almost 8,000 miles (13,000 km) each way.

▼ Poorwill, Common
RANGE: BREEDS NORTHERN N. AMERICA; WINTERS IN THE SOUTH
HABITAT: BREEDS OPEN WOODS; WINTERS DESERT
The common poorwill, almost uniquely amongst birds, spends the winter in a state like hibernation, when its heart rate slows and its body temperature drops from 106°F (41°C) to 64°F (18°C).

▼ Potoo
RANGE: CARIBBEAN, C. AND S. AMERICA
HABITAT: FOREST EDGE, FARMLAND
Potoos are related to nightjars and look a little like them, but they catch their insects more like flycatchers— that is, by darting out from a perch. But, like nightjars, they hunt mainly at night and by day sit stiffly upright on a broken branch.

▼ Ptarmigan, Rock
RANGE: ARCTIC, FAR NORTH AMERICA AND EURASIA
HABITAT: TUNDRA
The ptarmigans are part of the grouse family but live in the very far north. In winter their plumage turns almost completely white, matching the snow.

▲ Quail, California
RANGE: WESTERN U.S.A.
HABITAT: SCRUB, FARMLAND
The California quail is an elegant bird with a characteristic head plume that feeds on leaves, seeds, and berries. In the breeding season it feeds in small groups, but in winter California quails gather into larger flocks for security from predators.

◀ Quelea, Red-billed
RANGE: AFRICA SOUTH OF THE SAHARA
HABITAT: SAVANNA
The red-billed quelea is probably the world's most abundant bird and often forms huge, cloudlike flocks containing over 100,000 birds. Because of the damage they do to crops, they have been hunted on a huge scale.

▲ Quetzal, Resplendent
RANGE: C. AMERICA
HABITAT: HIGH ALTITUDE RAIN FOREST
The resplendent quetzal is an extraordinary bird which inhabits the lower layers of the tropical forest. Besides its brilliant emerald green and crimson plumage, it also has extraordinary tail feathers, over 2 ft (60 cm) long, which were much prized by the ancient Mayans and Aztecs. Yet surprisingly, the quetzal is hard to spot because it sits motionless for long periods. It feeds on oily fruit and insects.

▲ Redshank, Common
RANGE: BREEDS EUROPE, C. AND E. ASIA; WINTERS S. EUROPE, N. AFRICA, S. ASIA
HABITAT: BREEDS MARSHES, MOORLAND; WINTERS MUDDY AND SANDY SHORES
This "sentinel of the marshes" sends off a harsh, piping alarm to warn of intruders. It adapts to many coasts, feeding mostly on small shrimps, snails, and worms on the surface.

▼ Rhea, Greater
RANGE: S. AMERICA
HABITAT: GRASSLAND
Rheas are the biggest birds in the Americas. Like their African cousin the ostrich, they are completely flightless and, as with ostriches, females often share nests to lay their eggs.

▼ Roadrunner, Greater
RANGE: S. W. U.S.A.
HABITAT: DESERT, SEMIDESERT
Roadrunners are actually a kind of cuckoo, but spend most of their time on the ground. Although they can fly, they usually run, often at speeds of up to 15 mph (25 km/h). They use their tail and wings for balance to help them to swerve around obstructions. They feed mostly on insects, such as crickets and grasshoppers, killing them with a sudden pounce. They nest in cacti or thornbushes.

▲ Robin, American
RANGE: N. AND C. AMERICA
HABITAT: WOODLAND, GARDENS
Originally a woodland species, the American robin has thrived in suburban gardens. It can often be seen on lawns and in flower beds, drawing earthworms from the ground.

▲ Robin, Eurasian
RANGE: EURASIA
HABITAT: WOODLAND, GARDENS
With its striking red breast, the little robin is easily identified. It is very bold, often following gardeners to eat worms turned up during digging. It is also very possessive of its territory, guarding it fiercely from other robins.

▲ Sandgrouse, Pallas's
RANGE: C. ASIA
HABITAT: DESERT STEPPE
Pallas's sandgrouse is a plump ground bird about the size of a pigeon. It is a strong flier, but finds the seeds that it eats on the ground and is able to cope with the grit of the desert.

▶ Screamer, Northern
RANGE: COLOMBIA, VENEZUELA
HABITAT: MARSHES, WET GRASSLAND
Screamers live up to their name with a harsh honking that can be heard 2 miles (3 km) away. They are actually waterfowl, but look a little like turkeys, and feed on land.

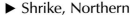

▼ Secretary bird
RANGE: AFRICA SOUTH OF THE SAHARA
HABITAT: SAVANNA
The secretary bird is actually a bird of prey like the hawk, but it has the most extraordinary long legs and strides along the ground, perhaps walking 20 miles (30 km) a day. It catches prey by running after it.

▼ Seriema, Red-legged
RANGE: S. AMERICA
HABITAT: GRASSLAND
This bird rarely flies. Instead, it escapes danger by running along at terrific speed with its head down. It is a predator that preys on snakes. Farmers sometimes use them as watchdogs.

▲ Sheathbill, Snowy
RANGE: SUBANTARCTIC, S. GEORGIA, FALKLAND ISLANDS
HABITAT: COASTS
The snowy sheathbill is a scavenger that makes the most of almost anything edible in its South Atlantic home. It haunts penguin colonies, feeding on carcasses, feces, and offal, or snatching penguin eggs and chicks. It even eats seaweed for the invertebrates on it.

▶ Shrike, Northern
RANGE: BREEDS N. AMERICA, EURASIA
HABITAT: VARIED
Shrikes are songbirds that feed mainly on insects. They are often called "butcher birds" because they sometimes impale their prey on a thorn to save it to eat later.

▼ Sicklebill, White-tipped
RANGE: C. AND S. AMERICA
HABITAT: TROPICAL FOREST
The sicklebill is a tiny hummingbird with a very long, downward-curving bill that allows it to sip nectar from heliconia flowers and also coryanthes orchids. It often clings to the blooms with its feet as it sips.

▼ Skua, Great
RANGE: N. ATLANTIC
HABITAT: OCEANIC
Skuas are big, strong birds that live over the cold waters of the North Atlantic. They not only attack other birds to steal their prey, but also kill and eat birds such as puffins, kittiwakes, and gulls, and take their eggs.

▼ Sparrow, House
RANGE: EURASIA, INTRODUCED WORLDWIDE
HABITAT: FARMLAND, URBAN AREAS
The house sparrow is an amazingly adaptable little bird. A few birds were taken to New York in 1850 and they have now spread all over the Americas.

▲ Sparrow, Song
RANGE: N. AMERICA
HABITAT: THICKETS

This is the most widespread of all American native sparrows. There are various races and each can be identified by its own particular song dialect. The biggest race is the northern song sparrow from the Aleutian Islands.

▲ Starling
RANGE: EURASIA, INTRODUCED WORLDWIDE
HABITAT: FARMLAND, SUBURBS

Starlings are one of the most familiar birds in cities, often massing in huge, swooping flocks before settling. In winter, flocks may feed out in the countryside, then pour into the city to roost as the sun goes down.

▶ Sunbird, Malachite
RANGE: C. AFRICA
HABITAT: MOUNTAINS

Sunbirds are the hummingbirds of Africa and Asia. They feed in the same way on nectar from flowers and have the same brilliant coloring. But they cannot hover like hummingbirds and have to perch on flowers to sip. The malachite sunbird feeds on giant lobelias and protea bushes and also insects.

▼ Sunbird, Yellow-backed
RANGE: INDIA, S. E. ASIA
HABITAT: FOREST, FARMLAND

The yellow-backed, or crimson, sunbird eats insects but usually clings to stems and twigs to suck nectar from flowers. Its pear-shaped nest hangs from a branch.

▲ Swallow, Barn
RANGE: BREEDS N. HEMISPHERE; WINTERS S. HEMISPHERE
HABITAT: BREEDS FARMLAND WITH BUILDINGS

The barn swallow makes its nest from mud and grass in buildings and under bridges, but it spends much of its time in the air, catching insects on the wing.

▲ Swan, Tundra
RANGE: BREEDS ARCTIC; WINTERS N. AMERICA, EURASIA
HABITAT: BREEDS MARSHY TUNDRA; WINTERS MARSHES

The tundra swan is the most northerly breeding of all the swans. Most breeding pairs return each winter to the same spot on the tundra.

▼ Swift, Crested tree
RANGE: MALAYSIA, INDONESIA
HABITAT: FOREST EDGE, WOODLAND

Unlike true swifts, crested swifts can perch and typically they sit on branches and telephone wires from where they can swoop down on insects.

▶ Swift, White-throated
RANGE: N. AMERICA
HABITAT: MOUNTAINS, CLIFFS

Swifts spend almost all their life on the wing, even mating in flight. The white-throated swift is the fastest flying bird in North America, flying up to 186 mph (300 km/h).

▼ Tanager, Scarlet
RANGE: BREEDS EASTERN N. AMERICA; WINTERS S. AMERICA
HABITAT: FOREST

Tanagers are tropical birds that feed on bees, other insects and their larvae. The scarlet tanager is one of the few that migrates north to breed. The male is brilliant scarlet before breeding, then molts to the same olive green as the female.

▼ Tern, Common
RANGE: BREEDS EASTERN N. AMERICA, N. EURASIA; WINTERS TO THE SOUTH
HABITAT: COASTS, ESTUARIES

Terns nest in huge colonies on isolated beaches, islands, and cliffs, where pairs scrape a hollow in the ground. Noisy terneries sometimes fall silent when all the birds rise and sweep out over the sea for a minute or two.

▼ Tinamou, Great
RANGE: C. AND S. AMERICA
HABITAT: TROPICAL FOREST

Tinamous are large birds a little like pheasants, but can barely fly at all. When in danger they lie still and rely on their plumage to hide them. This is why the great tinamou prefers areas of rain forest where there is dense undergrowth. If frightened it may burst from the floor with a roar of wings and fly, but for only a short way. Usually, though, it pecks on the ground for insects and berries.

▲ Toucan, Plate-billed mountain
RANGE: ANDES IN COLUMBIA, ECUADOR
HABITAT: MOUNTAIN FOREST

Also known as the laminated toucan, the plate-billed mountain toucan is the highest living of the toucans, living up to 10,000 ft (3,000 m) in the Andes. Like other toucans it feeds on fruits and berries.

▶ Toucan, Toco
RANGE: S. AMERICA
HABITAT: TROPICAL FOREST

Toucans are tropical birds related to woodpeckers. They have huge, colorful beaks which are full of air spaces to keep them light. Toucans use them to nip fruit and berries from the trees.

▼ Tragopan, Temminck's
RANGE: CHINA, MYANMAR, TIBET
HABITAT: MOUNTAIN FOREST

Tragopans are colorful birds related to pheasants that feed on the ground on seeds, buds, and leaves in the damp forests of Southeastern Asia and China.

▶ Tropic bird, Red-tailed
RANGE: INDIAN AND PACIFIC OCEANS
HABITAT: OCEANS
With its long, dark red tail feathers, the red-tailed tropic bird is an unusual-looking seabird. In the breeding season it goes slightly pink.

▲ Turaco, Red-crested
RANGE: AFRICA
HABITAT: FOREST, SAVANNA
Turacos are colorful African relatives of cuckoos. They live in tropical forests and feed on fruit. The red-crested turaco is a poor flier, but runs, hops, and climbs very nimbly and swiftly through the branches of rain forest trees.

▲ Turkey, Wild
RANGE: U.S.A., MEXICO
HABITAT: WOODED COUNTRY, SCRUB
Wild turkeys are big fowl that strut around woodlands in groups of 20 or so for most of the year, foraging for seeds, nuts, and berries. They are strong fliers over short distances and roost in trees.

▲ Vireo, Red-eyed
RANGE: BREEDS N. AMERICA; WINTERS S. AMERICA
HABITAT: FOREST
The red-eyed vireo is a tireless songster, singing right through the day. It builds a neat cup-shaped nest in a tree fork. Nestlings leave the nest after 12 days.

▼ Vulture, King
RANGE: C. AND S. AMERICA
HABITAT: RAIN FOREST, SAVANNA
Like the giant condors of California and the Andes, the king vulture is one of seven American vulture species. Like African vultures it feeds on carrion and has a bald head for plunging into messy carcasses. But unlike African vultures, king and other American vultures are related to storks, not birds of prey. The king vulture relies on smell to track prey.

▼ Vulture, Lappet-faced
RANGE: AFRICA, MIDDLE EAST
HABITAT: SAVANNA, DESERT
This is the biggest of the African vultures and, though often last to arrive at a carcass, it pushes the other vultures out of the way. With its big, powerful beak it can cut easily through flesh and its bald head saves its plumage from getting soiled with blood.

▲ Warbler, Willow
RANGE: BREEDS EURASIA; WINTERS AFRICA, S. ASIA
HABITAT: WOODLAND, FARMLAND
The willow warbler is one of more than 300 warblers spread widely across Eurasia and Australia. All mainly eat insects and each has a distinctive song.

▲ Warbler, Yellow
RANGE: BREEDS N. AMERICA; WINTERS C. AND S. AMERICA
HABITAT: THICKETS BY STREAMS, SWAMPS
The yellow warbler is one of the most widespread of American wood warblers. Like all warblers it forages in trees for insects.

▲ Wigeon, American
RANGE: BREEDS NORTHERN N. AMERICA; WINTERS IN THE SOUTH
HABITAT: MARSHES
Wigeons are called dabbling ducks, but they find very little food by dabbling. Usually they graze on grass in marshes in huge, tightly packed flocks. They may even snatch the food of other diving birds.

▲ Woodcock, American
RANGE: BREEDS N. AMERICA; WINTERS TO THE SOUTH
HABITAT: WOODLAND
Woodcocks are actually waders but they have left the shore to live in woods where they probe soft soil for worms with their long bills.

▼ Woodcreeper, Long-billed
RANGE: S. AMERICA
HABITAT: RAIN FOREST
This bird is one of 49 species of woodcreepers in the Americas. They are the equivalent of the treecreepers of Africa and, like them, climb trees, picking insects from crevices in the bark.

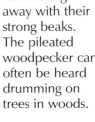

▶ Woodpecker, Pileated
RANGE: N. AMERICA
HABITAT: FOREST
Woodpeckers feed mainly on ants and termites and find their food by clinging to tree trunks with their sharp claws and hammering away with their strong beaks. The pileated woodpecker can often be heard drumming on trees in woods.

▼ Wren
RANGE: EURASIA, N. AFRICA
HABITAT: WOODLAND, FARMLAND
Wrens are tiny songbirds with short, upright tails that hop about the ground searching for insects and spiders. They nest in hollow tree stumps or among tree roots.

▼ Zitting cisticola
RANGE: SOUTHERN EURASIA, N. AFRICA, AUSTRALIA
HABITAT: DAMP GRASSLAND, RICE FIELDS
This little warbler is well known for the male's song flight, during which it spirals up to 100 ft (30 m) above the ground while singing.

Invertebrates

Creatures without backbones, such as insects, snails, and worms are called invertebrates. Most invertebrates are small, but there are more of them than all other animals put together. Of the world's million and a half known animal species, a million are insects, and there are huge numbers of other invertebrates living on land—including centipedes, arachnids such as spiders, and crustaceans such as woodlice.

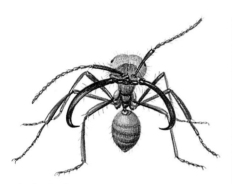

▲ Ant, Army
RANGE: C. AND S. AMERICA
HABITAT: RAIN FOREST
Unlike other ants, army ants do not make a permanent nest. Instead they crawl across the forest floor, devouring any small creature in their path and then spend the night in a temporary nest called a bivouac, with walls made by ants clinging to each other.

▲ Ant, Carpenter
RANGE: WORLDWIDE
HABITAT: WOOD
Colonies of carpenter ants make their nests in wooden buildings or in rotting tree trunks. The nests can destroy the timber in roofs or walls.

▶ Ant, Fire
RANGE: S. AMERICA, INTRODUCED N. AMERICA
HABITAT: WOODS, FIELDS
Fire ants get their name because they inflict a very painful bite, which they use to attack other insects. They were introduced into Alabama from South America and are now major pests because they build huge nests, damage grain, and attack poultry.

▼ Ant, Harvester
RANGE: WORLDWIDE
HABITAT: FIELDS
These ants get their name from their habit of gathering seeds and storing them in special granary areas in the nest, ready to eat in times of need.

▼ Ant, Leafcutter
RANGE: C. AND S. AMERICA
HABITAT: RAIN FOREST
Leafcutter ants spend the night in nests under the rain forest floor, then at dawn workers crawl out and climb trees to cut pieces of leaves to bring back to the nest. Instead of eating the leaves, they use them to make a compost on which a fungus grows. They eat the fungus.

▼ Ant, Red wood
RANGE: EURASIA
HABITAT: WOODLAND
By preying on plant-eating insects, wood ants play a key role in reducing the damage done to forest trees. Wood ants also feed on the sticky honeydew secreted by aphids.

▼ Ant, Velvet
RANGE: WORLDWIDE, ESPECIALLY TROPICS
HABITAT: VARIED
These are not ants but wasps, covered with velvety hair. They get their name because the females are wingless and antlike.

▲ Ant lion
RANGE: WORLDWIDE, ESPECIALLY TROPICS
HABITAT: SCRUB AND DRY, SANDY AREAS
Ant lions get their name from their larvae, which dig a pit in sandy soil to trap ants. When an ant comes near, the larvae tosses soil at it so that it falls into the trap.

▼ Aphid
RANGE: WORLDWIDE
HABITAT: GREEN PLANTS
Aphids are tiny insects that feed on the sap of leaves and plants and can do great damage. They multiply rapidly, but may be eaten by ladybugs and wasps.

▼ Bedbug
RANGE: WORLDWIDE
HABITAT: HUMAN AND ANIMAL HOSTS, CREVICES
Bedbugs stay hidden during the day, but come out at night to feed on the blood of birds and animals, including humans.

▶ Bee, Carpenter
RANGE: WORLDWIDE
HABITAT: NEAR FLOWERS
Female carpenter bees chew into wood, making a tunnel-like nest for their brood cell. They line the nest with sticky pollen, lay a single egg, then seal the cell.

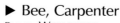

▶ Bee, Cuckoo
RANGE: WORLDWIDE
HABITAT: NEAR FLOWERS
Cuckoo bees cannot carry pollen so, like cuckoo birds, they lay their eggs in the nests of others—in this case, bees. The cuckoo bees' eggs hatch first and the larvae eat up their host's food store.

▲ Bee, Leafcutter
RANGE: WORLDWIDE
HABITAT: VARIED
Leafcutter bees live alone rather than in swarms. They cut out pieces of leaf with their jaws and use them to line their nests—usually a tunnel in rotting wood.

▲ Bee, Mining
RANGE: WORLDWIDE EXCEPT AUSTRALIA
HABITAT: NEAR SPRING FLOWERS
The mines of mining bees are long, branching tunnels they dig into the ground. They stock them with nectar and pollen for their larvae to eat when they hatch.

▲ Bee, Orchid
RANGE: TROPICS WORLDWIDE
HABITAT: NEAR ORCHIDS
Orchid bees feed on the nectar from orchids, such as the gongora. They play a crucial role in spreading the pollen of these flowers. Some orchids mimic the bees' shape to attract them.

▲ Bee, Plasterer
RANGE: WORLDWIDE, ESPECIALLY
S. HEMISPHERE
HABITAT: SOIL
Plasterer bees nest in tunnels in the ground, which they line with a secretion from glands in their abdomen. The secretion dries to form a clear, waterproof "plaster."

▲ Bee, Stingless
RANGE: TROPICS WORLDWIDE
HABITAT: WOODLAND
Stingless bees cannot sting, but they can protect their nests by biting the skin of intruders, coating them with resin, and getting up their nose. Often the bees simply retreat into their underground nests.

▲ Beetle, Carrion
RANGE: WORLDWIDE,
MAINLY N. HEMISPHERE
HABITAT: CARCASSES, DUNG, FUNGI
These beetles bury the corpses of small animals, such as mice. They lay their eggs in the carcass so that their young will have plenty of food.

▼ Beetle, Click
RANGE: WORLDWIDE, ESPECIALLY TROPICS
HABITAT: LEAF LITTER, ROTTEN WOOD
If a click beetle finds itself upside down, it arches its body and snaps itself straight with a loud click, launching its body into the air. If threatened, it can feign death.

▼ Beetle, Darkling
RANGE: WORLDWIDE, ESPECIALLY DESERTS
HABITAT: ON THE GROUND
Darkling beetles are especially common in deserts. They come out in the cool of the night to forage for food, such as rotting wood and insect larvae.

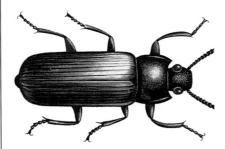

▼ Beetle, Diving
RANGE: WORLDWIDE
HABITAT: BOGS AND LAKES
Diving beetles live in ponds and lakes. Their hind legs are covered with hairs, which flatten out like paddles to drive them through the water. When they dive they can stay under the water for some time, breathing air trapped under their wing cases.

▶ Beetle, Goliath
RANGE: C. AFRICA
HABITAT: RAIN FOREST
The goliath beetle is among the largest of all beetles— 5 in (13 cm) long. Unusually, Goliath larvae prey on other insects. They also help to break down rotting wood and so enrich the soil.

▲ Beetle, Jewel
RANGE: WORLDWIDE, ESPECIALLY TROPICS
HABITAT: FOREST
Jewel beetles come in brilliant metallic colors, often with stripes, bands, and spots. They like to lay their eggs in wood in freshly burned forests and the larvae chew oval tunnels in the wood. Adults feed on flower nectar.

▼ Beetle, Longhorn
RANGE: WORLDWIDE, MAINLY TROPICAL
HABITAT: FOREST
Longhorn beetles have antennae up to four times as long as their bodies. Their larvae are serious pests as they eat into timber and trees.

▲ Beetle, Rove
RANGE: WORLDWIDE
HABITAT: SOIL, FUNGI, LEAF LITTER
Rove beetles are long beetles with short wings and, like the Devil's coach horse beetle, have an abdomen that they curve up like a scorpion if threatened.

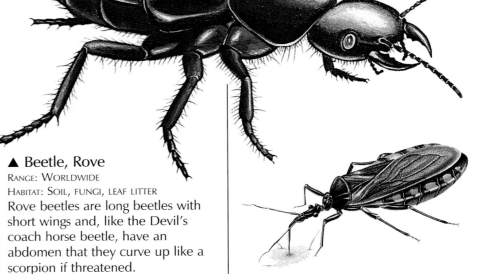

▶ Beetle, Stag
RANGE: WORLDWIDE, ESPECIALLY TROPICS
HABITAT: BROAD-LEAVED FOREST
With large heads and massive jaws, stag beetles are fearsome-looking beetles, but they are actually quite harmless, feeding mostly on tree sap. However, males often lock antlers to fight over females.

▲ Beetle, Whirligig
RANGE: WORLDWIDE
HABITAT: POND AND STREAM SURFACES
These shiny, black beetles are the only beetles that can swim on a film of water. They gather together and swim rapidly in whirling circles.

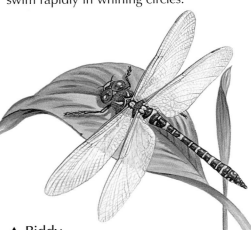

▲ Biddy
RANGE: WORLDWIDE
HABITAT: WOODLAND STREAMS
Biddies, or spiketails, are large black-and-yellow dragonflies, often seen hovering above woodland streams. Unlike some other dragonflies, the adults have eyes that meet at the top of their head.

▲ Bug, Assassin
RANGE: WORLDWIDE, ESPECIALLY TROPICS
HABITAT: VARIED
Assassin bugs are killers that attack other insects, such as caterpillars. They stab their prey with their proboscis and inject a toxin that dissolves tissue. The bugs then suck out their victim's body juices.

▲ Bug, June
RANGE: WORLDWIDE
HABITAT: FARMLAND
June bugs are one of more than 100 kinds of scarab beetle, once held sacred by the ancient Egyptians. June bugs feed on overripe fruit, but their white grubs or larvae feed on the roots of plants and can cause tremendous damage to crops, such as corn and sugar cane.

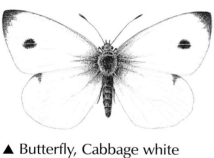

▲ Bumblebee
RANGE: WORLDWIDE, EXCEPT SOUTHERN AFRICA
HABITAT: NEAR FLOWERS
Bumblebees are large, hairy honeybees, typically black and yellow. Like all honeybees, they sip nectar from flowers to turn into honey, and also play a crucial role in pollinating flowers.

▲ Butterfly, Cabbage white
RANGE: ORIGINALLY EURASIA, NOW ALSO N. AMERICA, AUSTRALIA
HABITAT: FARMLAND
Known also as the large white, the caterpillar of this butterfly feeds on cabbage, stripping the leaves. It is regarded as a pest in some places.

▲ Butterfly, Cairns birdwing
RANGE: S. E. ASIA, N. AUSTRALIA
HABITAT: RAIN FOREST
The largest Australian butterflies, Cairns birdwings can measure over 6 in (15 cm) across. They typically live on pipevines in forest clearings.

▲ Butterfly, Copper
RANGE: EURASIA, N. AMERICA
HABITAT: HEDGES, SCRUB, GARDENS
Coppers are a large family of butterflies, including small coppers, which are one of the most common butterflies in the northern hemisphere. The caterpillars feed on dock and sorrel.

▲ Butterfly, Fluminense swallowtail
RANGE: AMAZON
HABITAT: SWAMPS, SCRUB
The fluminense is one of the world's most endangered butterflies because its habitat has been cleared and drained to make way for factories, houses, and banana plantations.

▼ Butterfly, Monarch
RANGE: AMERICAS, SPREADING ELSEWHERE
HABITAT: MILKWEED (CATERPILLAR)
Every fall millions of monarchs fly thousands of miles from Canada to Mexico. They lay their eggs the following spring, on their way back north. Young adults continue the journey north for the summer.

▲ Butterfly, Morpho
RANGE: S. AMERICA
HABITAT: TROPICAL RAIN FOREST
With their shimmering blue coloring, morphos are among the most beautiful of all butterflies. They are fast flying and flit through the forest, with males often chasing each other through patches of sunlight. They feed on the juices of fallen fruit.

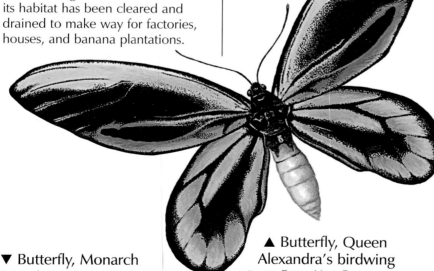

▲ Butterfly, Queen Alexandra's birdwing
RANGE: PAPUA NEW GUINEA
HABITAT: RAIN FOREST
The female Queen Alexandra's birdwing is the world's biggest butterfly, 11 in (28 cm) across. The male has a bright yellow abdomen indicating to predators that it is poisonous. This butterfly is so highly prized by collectors that it has been hunted almost to extinction.

▼ Butterfly, Swallowtail
RANGE: N. AMERICA
HABITAT: FOREST, ORCHARDS
The giant swallowtail is one of the largest butterflies in North America, growing up to 5½ in (14 cm) across. The caterpillar feeds on orange trees in southern North America. Adults eat plants, such as lantana and azalea.

▼ Centipede
RANGE: WORLDWIDE
HABITAT: VARIED, ESPECIALLY LEAF LITTER
Centipedes are tiny predators, typically with 15 pairs of legs. They are not insects but belong to their own class. They use poison claws to kill prey, such as insects and spiders.

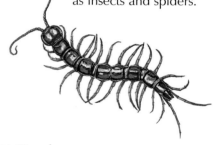

▼ Cicada
RANGE: WORLDWIDE, MOSTLY WARMER PLACES
HABITAT: SHRUBS AND TREES
Cicadas are famous for the loud mating song of the males. The song is made by a pair of structures called tymbals on the abdomen, which are vibrated by special muscles.

▼ Cockroach, American
RANGE: ORIGINALLY AFRICA, NOW WORLDWIDE
HABITAT: MOIST, DARK CREVICES
Cockroaches have flat bodies, which allow them to squeeze into crevices in order to find food or escape from predators. Certain pest species thrive in warm, dirty places, especially where there is food.

▲ Cockroach, German
RANGE: WORLDWIDE

HABITAT: LEAF LITTER, GARBAGE, BUILDINGS

The German cockroach is a common pest in kitchens and food stores. It multiplies rapidly. Unlike common cockroaches, such as the American, it has proper wings.

▶ Cockroach, Madagascan hissing
RANGE: MADAGASCAR

HABITAT: RAIN FOREST

Males of this species fight each other. When they win they often hiss by squeezing air out of the breathing holes on their bodies called spiracles. Males also hiss to court females.

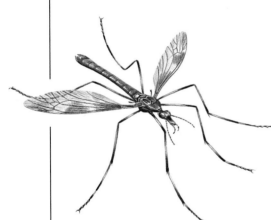

▲ Crane fly
RANGE: WORLDWIDE

HABITAT: TYPICALLY NEAR WATER

Crane flies look like large, long-legged mosquitoes, but they do not bite. In fact, they do not eat anything at all because they do all their eating when they are larvae.

▲ Cricket, Mole
RANGE: WORLDWIDE

HABITAT: DAMP SAND OR SOIL NEAR STREAMS

Looking remarkably like tiny moles, mole crickets are covered in velvety hairs and burrow through the ground with their large, spadelike legs.

▼ Cricket, True
RANGE: WORLDWIDE

HABITAT: WOODLAND, ON THE GROUND IN MEADOWS

True crickets "sing" to attract mates by rubbing together special ridges at the base of their forewings. The sound is a high-pitched chirrup.

▼ Damselfly
RANGE: WORLDWIDE

HABITAT: SWAMPS, BOGS, POOLS

Damselflies, such as stalk- or spread-winged damselflies, are related to dragonflies but they are smaller and thinner. When they rest, they cling vertically to stalks with their wings out.

◀ Damselfly, Narrow-winged
RANGE: N. HEMISPHERE

HABITAT: PONDS, BOGS, STREAMS

Damselflies feed on small insects on plants. The narrow-winged damselfly folds its wings together when at rest on stalks.

▼ Darter
RANGE: WORLDWIDE

HABITAT: VARIED, INCLUDING MOUNTAIN FOREST NEAR STREAMS

Darter, or skimmer, dragonflies get their name from their fast, darting flight, often skimming just over the surface of the water as they pursue their prey.

▶ Dragonfly, Club-tailed
RANGE: WORLDWIDE

HABITAT: PONDS, LAKES, RIVERS

Unlike other dragonflies, the club-tailed dragonfly spots its prey by watching from a perch. Once it sights its prey, it darts out to seize it, then returns to the perch.

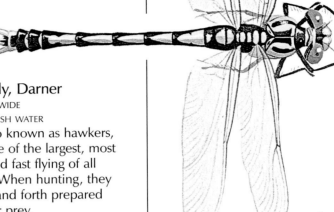

▼ Dragonfly, Darner
RANGE: WORLDWIDE

HABITAT: SLUGGISH WATER

Darners, also known as hawkers, include some of the largest, most powerful, and fast flying of all dragonflies. When hunting, they zoom back and forth prepared to seize their prey.

▼ Dysedera crocata
RANGE: WORLDWIDE

HABITAT: CREVICES IN WOOD

Most spiders have eight eyes; dysderid spiders like crocata have only six, set in a circle. The crocata spends the day hiding under stones, then comes out at night to hunt woodlice. This spider can pierce a woodlouse's tough body armor with its huge fangs.

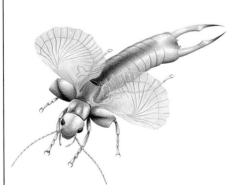

▼ Earthworm
RANGE: WORLDWIDE

HABITAT: MOSTLY DAMP SOIL

Earthworms are the most common of the segmented worm group. As they tunnel into the ground, they swallow soil and digest dead leaves and rotting plant matter, then excrete the rest. This mixes up the soil and helps to keep it fertile.

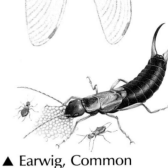

▲ Earwig, Common
RANGE: ORIGINALLY EUROPE, NOW WORLDWIDE

HABITAT: VARIED

Earwigs eat plants and other insects. They have pincers at the end of their body to catch prey. They often live in flowers and are considered garden pests.

▲ Earwig, Long-horned
RANGE: WORLDWIDE, MAINLY TROPICS

HABITAT: SHORES, LEAF LITTER, DEBRIS

Also known as striped earwigs, long-horned earwigs are nocturnal, coming out at night to prey on other insects. If attacked, they squirt out a foul-smelling liquid.

▲ Firebrat
RANGE: WORLDWIDE

HABITAT: HOT, DAMP PLACES

Firebrats are a kind of silverfish. They live in hot places in buildings, such as near ovens and hot pipes. They run quickly and scurry around finding crumbs of food to eat.

▲ Firefly
RANGE: WORLDWIDE
HABITAT: WOODLAND, MOIST GRASSLAND

Fireflies, or lightning bugs, emit flashes of cold, green light when mating. The males fly, flashing, just above the ground and females flash back from the ground or trees to guide the males toward them.

▲ Flea, Cat
RANGE: WORLDWIDE
HABITAT: ON CATS

Fleas are tiny insects that live on mammals and feed on their blood. They have no wings, but they are amazing jumpers, able to jump 200 times their own length to get from host to host. Cat fleas are the most common in homes, biting people and dogs, as well as cats.

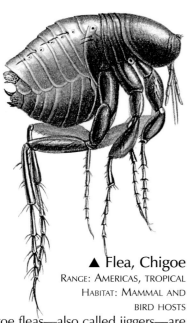

▲ Flea, Chigoe
RANGE: AMERICAS, TROPICAL
HABITAT: MAMMAL AND BIRD HOSTS

Chigoe fleas—also called jiggers—are parasites that attack various animals, including humans. Typically, pregnant females burrow into people's feet where the flea causes a reaction that makes the skin of the foot grow to engulf the insect. When the fleas hatch, they drop off their host and spend the rest of their life on the ground.

▼ Fly, Fruit
RANGE: WORLDWIDE
HABITAT: TYPICALLY FRUIT

Fruit flies feed on nectar from flowers and the juice of overripe fruit. Some species lay their eggs on the skin of fruit, such as oranges, and the larvae eat away the fruit.

▼ Fly, House
RANGE: WORLDWIDE
HABITAT: FLOWERS, DUNG, GARBAGE

House flies are among the most numerous animals on Earth. They suck liquid from anything sweet or rotting. Typically their larvae grow up in dung or garbage.

▼ Fly, Hover
RANGE: WORLDWIDE
HABITAT: TYPICALLY FLAT-TOPPED FLOWERS

Hover flies are amazing fliers, able to dart this way and that, backward and forward as they search for flowers to sip for nectar. Some hover flies deter predators by mimicking wasps.

▼ Fly, Large caddis
RANGE: MAINLY N. HEMISPHERE
HABITAT: NEAR PONDS, LAKES, RIVERS

Caddis flies look a little like moths, but their bodies are covered in hair, not scales. Females typically lay strings of eggs encased in jelly on plants just below the water surface. The larvae transform to adults and then emerge from the water.

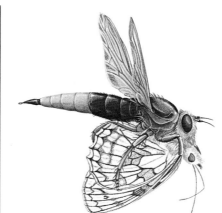

▲ Fly, Robber
RANGE: WORLDWIDE
HABITAT: VARIED, ESPECIALLY DRY GRASSLAND

These are fast-flying, powerful insects that catch and kill other insects in midair, or pounce on them on the ground. They stab their victims through the neck and suck them dry.

▲ Froghopper
RANGE: WORLDWIDE, ESPECIALLY TROPICS
HABITAT: SHRUBS, TREES

These little insects can jump like tiny frogs. They lay their eggs on plant stems. When the nymphs hatch they cover themselves in a foam a little like saliva.

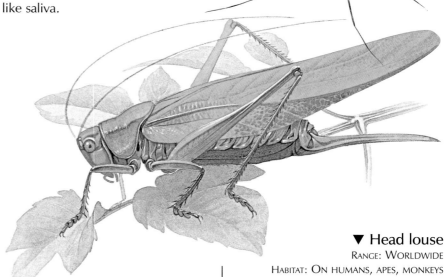

▲ Grasshopper, Long-horned
RANGE: WARM AREAS WORLDWIDE
HABITAT: TYPICALLY IN GRASS

Grasshoppers are part of a large order called Orthoptera, along with crickets, katydids, and locusts. Grasshoppers and locusts are vegetarians, feeding mainly on plants.

▼ Grasshopper, Short-horned
RANGE: WARM AREAS WORLDWIDE
HABITAT: TYPICALLY IN GRASS

Short-horned grasshoppers have short antennae. Like all grasshoppers, they have powerful back legs, which they use to jump huge distances, aided by their small wings.

▼ Harvestman
RANGE: WORLDWIDE, MAINLY TEMPERATE
HABITAT: UNDER STONES, IN LEAF LITTER

Harvestmen look like spiders, but their bodies are more oval and have no waist. They feed on small insects, such as springtails, but do not spin a web.

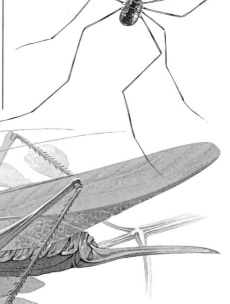

▼ Head louse
RANGE: WORLDWIDE
HABITAT: ON HUMANS, APES, MONKEYS

The head louse is a small, flat insect. It clings on to its host's hairs with its strongly clawed legs and then sucks on their blood.

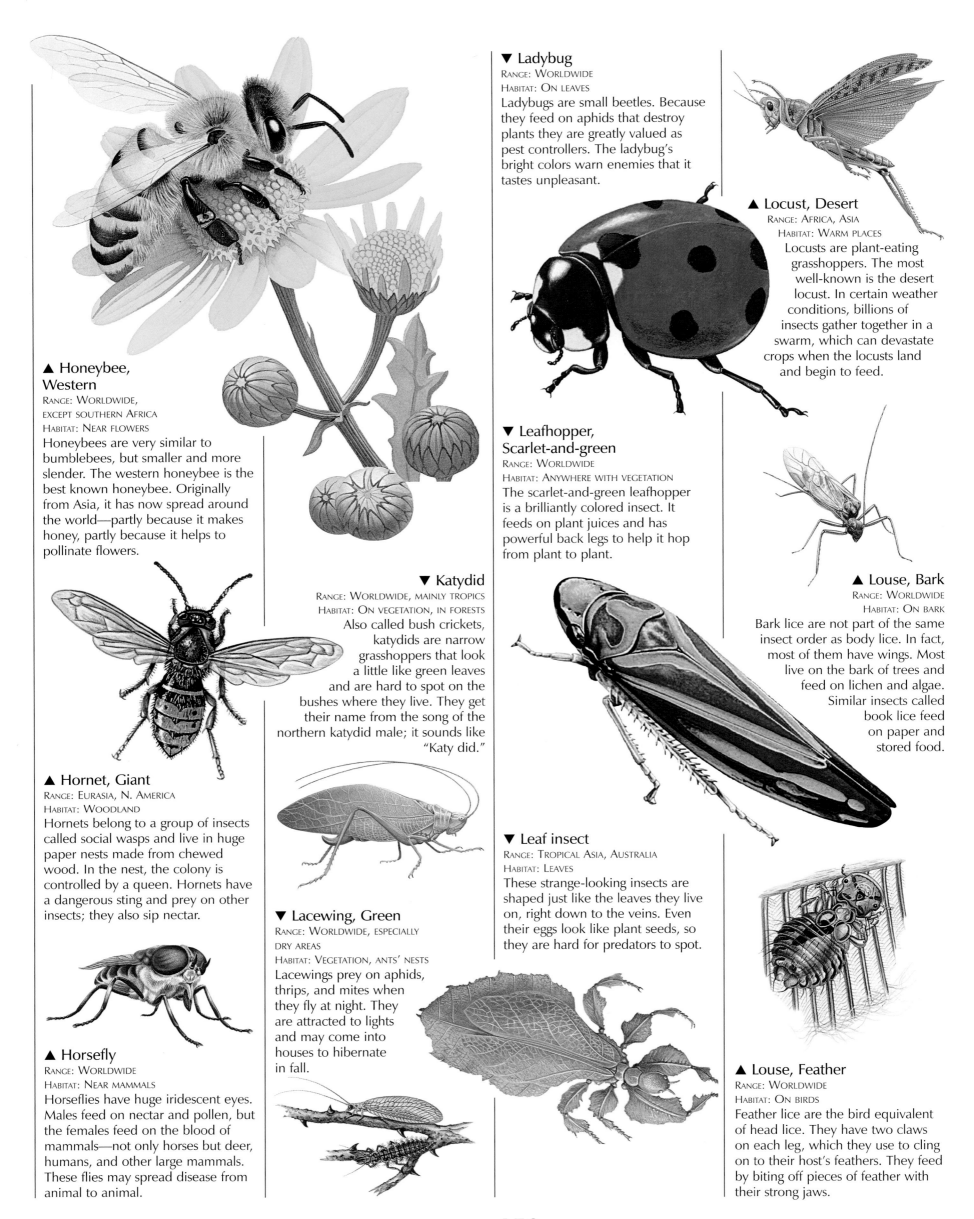

▲ Honeybee, Western

RANGE: WORLDWIDE, EXCEPT SOUTHERN AFRICA
HABITAT: NEAR FLOWERS

Honeybees are very similar to bumblebees, but smaller and more slender. The western honeybee is the best known honeybee. Originally from Asia, it has now spread around the world—partly because it makes honey, partly because it helps to pollinate flowers.

▲ Hornet, Giant

RANGE: EURASIA, N. AMERICA
HABITAT: WOODLAND

Hornets belong to a group of insects called social wasps and live in huge paper nests made from chewed wood. In the nest, the colony is controlled by a queen. Hornets have a dangerous sting and prey on other insects; they also sip nectar.

▲ Horsefly

RANGE: WORLDWIDE
HABITAT: NEAR MAMMALS

Horseflies have huge iridescent eyes. Males feed on nectar and pollen, but the females feed on the blood of mammals—not only horses but deer, humans, and other large mammals. These flies may spread disease from animal to animal.

▼ Katydid

RANGE: WORLDWIDE, MAINLY TROPICS
HABITAT: ON VEGETATION, IN FORESTS

Also called bush crickets, katydids are narrow grasshoppers that look a little like green leaves and are hard to spot on the bushes where they live. They get their name from the song of the northern katydid male; it sounds like "Katy did."

▼ Lacewing, Green

RANGE: WORLDWIDE, ESPECIALLY DRY AREAS
HABITAT: VEGETATION, ANTS' NESTS

Lacewings prey on aphids, thrips, and mites when they fly at night. They are attracted to lights and may come into houses to hibernate in fall.

▼ Ladybug

RANGE: WORLDWIDE
HABITAT: ON LEAVES

Ladybugs are small beetles. Because they feed on aphids that destroy plants they are greatly valued as pest controllers. The ladybug's bright colors warn enemies that it tastes unpleasant.

▼ Leafhopper, Scarlet-and-green

RANGE: WORLDWIDE
HABITAT: ANYWHERE WITH VEGETATION

The scarlet-and-green leafhopper is a brilliantly colored insect. It feeds on plant juices and has powerful back legs to help it hop from plant to plant.

▼ Leaf insect

RANGE: TROPICAL ASIA, AUSTRALIA
HABITAT: LEAVES

These strange-looking insects are shaped just like the leaves they live on, right down to the veins. Even their eggs look like plant seeds, so they are hard for predators to spot.

▲ Locust, Desert

RANGE: AFRICA, ASIA
HABITAT: WARM PLACES

Locusts are plant-eating grasshoppers. The most well-known is the desert locust. In certain weather conditions, billions of insects gather together in a swarm, which can devastate crops when the locusts land and begin to feed.

▲ Louse, Bark

RANGE: WORLDWIDE
HABITAT: ON BARK

Bark lice are not part of the same insect order as body lice. In fact, most of them have wings. Most live on the bark of trees and feed on lichen and algae. Similar insects called book lice feed on paper and stored food.

▲ Louse, Feather

RANGE: WORLDWIDE
HABITAT: ON BIRDS

Feather lice are the bird equivalent of head lice. They have two claws on each leg, which they use to cling on to their host's feathers. They feed by biting off pieces of feather with their strong jaws.

▲ Mantis, Angola
RANGE: ANGOLA
HABITAT: TROPICAL RAIN FOREST
The Angola mantis is almost impossible to see on a lichen-covered branch. It waits motionless for prey, then strikes in an instant.

▲ Mantis, Flower
RANGE: TROPICS WORLDWIDE EXCEPT AUSTRALIA
HABITAT: VEGETATION
Flower mantises prey on the insects that live on flowers. They are often colored to help them hide on the flower.

▲ Mantis, Praying
RANGE: WORLDWIDE, MAINLY WARMER PLACES
HABITAT: VEGETATION
Praying mantises are deadly hunters that catch their prey by remaining perfectly still, then striking suddenly. While they wait they hold their powerful front legs together as if they are praying.

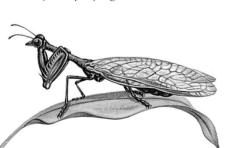

▲ Mantisfly
RANGE: WORLDWIDE, MAINLY WARM REGIONS
HABITAT: LUSH VEGETATION
Mantisflies are relatives of lacewings, but they look exactly like small praying mantises and use their front legs to seize prey in just the same way.

▲ Mayfly
RANGE: WORLDWIDE
HABITAT: STREAMS, RIVERS, PONDS
Mayflies live for several years as nymphs underwater, feeding on algae, but once they leave the water as adults they cannot eat, and they die in a few hours—just enough time to mate and lay eggs.

▲ Midge, Non-biting
RANGE: WORLDWIDE
HABITAT: NEAR PONDS, STREAMS
Midges are tiny flies that are either biting or nonbiting. Both are seen in swarms at dusk. Biting midges suck blood and have a very irritating bite.

▲ Millipede, Armored
RANGE: N. HEMISPHERE
HABITAT: LEAF LITTER
Armored, or flat-backed, millipedes have an unusually flat shape for a millipede. If attacked when crawling through the leaf litter, they can spray poisonous chemicals.

▲ Millipede, Cylinder
RANGE: MAINLY N. HEMISPHERE
HABITAT: LEAF LITTER, ROTTING WOOD
Millipedes are not insects, but long creatures in a class of their own. They move through leaf litter and eat plants.

▼ Mite, House dust
RANGE: WORLDWIDE
HABITAT: HOUSES
Mites are a huge group of tiny arachnids (like spiders). House dust mites feed on scales of skin found in house dust and their droppings can often cause allergic reactions.

▼ Mite, Velvet
RANGE: WORLDWIDE, ESPECIALLY TROPICS
HABITAT: MOSTLY IN OR ON SOIL
Velvet mites have red or orange velvety bodies. They live in the soil and feed mostly on insect eggs. At certain times of year, usually after rain, adults emerge to mate.

▼ Moth, Atlas
RANGE: SOUTHERN ASIA
HABITAT: TROPICAL FOREST
With wings measuring 12 in (30.5 cm) across, this is one of the world's largest moths. Its wings are richly colored and each has two triangular windows that are almost transparent.

► Moth, Bee sphinx
RANGE: AUSTRALIA
HABITAT: GRASSLAND
The bee sphinx, or hawk, moth flies by day and looks remarkably like a bee as it hovers, sipping nectar from flowers. Bee sphinx caterpillars feed on the leaves of canthium.

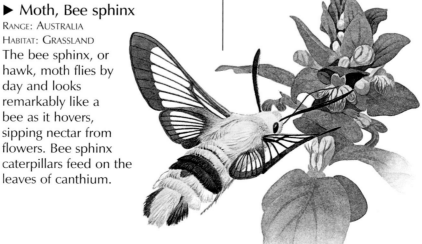

▲ Moth, Clothes
RANGE: WORLDWIDE
HABITAT: CLOTHES STORES, ANIMAL NESTS
Clothes moths are small moths that often spend their whole lives in houses. They lay their eggs on woolen clothes and the caterpillars live inside tents of silk, making holes in the wool as they feed.

▲ Moth, Cottonball
RANGE: WARM REGIONS IN THE AMERICAS
HABITAT: COTTON
Cottonball moths are night-flying moths with two eye flashes on their wings. Their yellow-green caterpillars feed on cotton plants and can do tremendous damage to cotton crops.

▲ Moth, Geometrid
RANGE: SOUTHERN EURASIA, AFRICA
HABITAT: BROAD-LEAVED WOODS
Geometrid moths are unusual among moths in that they spread their wings flat when at rest. Their caterpillars, known as inchworms, form geometrical loops on leaves that can be damaging to the tree.

▼ Moth, Gypsy
RANGE: ORIGINALLY EURASIA,
NOW ALSO N. AMERICA
HABITAT: TEMPERATE FORESTS
Gypsy moths were brought to North America in 1869 to provide silk. The project failed, the moths escaped, and in the wild their caterpillars do a great deal of damage, eating their way through both evergreen and broad-leaved forests. They can sometimes strip a whole forest in a single season.

▼ Moth, Hummingbird
RANGE: EURASIA EXCEPT SOUTH
HABITAT: SCRUB
Hummingbird moths can look remarkably like hummingbirds when they hover in front of flowers, sipping on nectar through their long feeding tube.

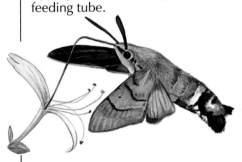

▼ Moth, Moon
RANGE: N. AMERICA
HABITAT: BROAD-LEAVED FORESTS
Like its African and Indian counterparts, the American moon moth is a large, beautiful, pale-colored moth with long, trailing tails on its wings. Its caterpillar feeds on trees, such as hickory, walnut, and birch.

▼ Moth, Oleander sphinx
RANGE: AFRICA, S. ASIA; SUMMER EUROPE
HABITAT: SUBTROPICAL FORESTS
The oleander sphinx or hawk moth is strikingly colored in green and purplish pink, but the patterns camouflage it very well against leaves. Its caterpillar feeds on oleander, periwinkle, and grapevine.

▲ Moth, Poplar sphinx
RANGE: EUROPE, W. ASIA
HABITAT: CATERPILLAR ON POPLAR TREES
Like other sphinx or hawk moths, the poplar feeds at night. During the day it rests on tree trunks, where its patterning keeps it remarkably well camouflaged against the bark.

▲ Moth, Tiger
RANGE: EURASIA, SOMETIMES N. AMERICA
HABITAT: WOODLAND, GARDENS
Tiger moths are so brightly colored that they look almost like butterflies. The colors warn predators that they taste nasty or mimic other nasty tasting species.

▲ Moth, White-lined sphinx
RANGE: N. AMERICA, EURASIA, AFRICA
HABITAT: WARM OPEN PLACES, INCLUDING DESERTS AND GARDENS
Like all sphinx or hawk moths, the white-lined is one of the fastest-flying insects and can reach speeds of over 30 mph (50 km/h). It also flies long distances to breed.

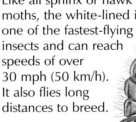

▲ Plant bug
RANGE: WORLDWIDE
HABITAT: VEGETATED AREAS
Bugs are tiny insects that have needle-like mouth parts for piercing food and sucking out juices. Most plant bugs feed on leaves, including crops, but others feed on aphids.

▼ Pseudoscorpion
RANGE: WORLDWIDE, ESPECIALLY WARMER REGIONS
HABITAT: LEAF LITTER, TREE BARK
Pseudoscorpions are tiny relatives of the scorpion that live in leaf litter, but instead of stings in their tails they have venom glands in their pincers.

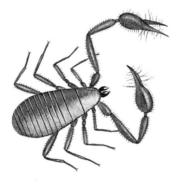

▼ Sawfly, Common
RANGE: WORLDWIDE, ESPECIALLY COOL N. HEMISPHERE
HABITAT: GARDENS, PASTURES, WOODS
Sawflies look a little like wasps, but do not have a sting. The female lays eggs on leaves, forming scars or galls.

▼ Scorpion
RANGE: WORLDWIDE, MOSTLY WARM PLACES
HABITAT: TYPICALLY DESERTS
Many scorpions have a dangerous sting in their tails, which can be fatal to humans. However, they usually catch their prey with their pincers.

▲ Scorpion, Whip
RANGE: TROPICAL N. AMERICA, S. AMERICA, S. ASIA
HABITAT: SOIL, CAVES, DESERTS
Whip scorpions have a long, thin tail and no sting. They are sometimes called vinegaroons because they can spray a vinegary liquid from the base of their tail when threatened.

▲ Scorpion, Wind
RANGE: C. AMERICA AND SOUTHERN N. AMERICA
HABITAT: WARM, DRY AREAS SUCH AS DESERTS
Wind scorpions, also known as sun spiders, are fast-running hunters that prey at night on insects and even small lizards.

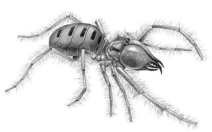

▲ Scorpionfly, Common
RANGE: WORLDWIDE, MOSTLY N. HEMISPHERE
HABITAT: SHADY AREAS IN VEGETATION
Scorpionflies get their name because the male has swollen, upturned genitals in its tail that look just like a scorpion's sting.

▲ Silverfish
RANGE: WORLDWIDE, ESPECIALLY WARMER PLACES
HABITAT: DARK, WARM PLACES
Silverfish are tiny wingless insects. Some species live in dark, warm places indoors, eating flour, damp cloth, paper, and wallpaper paste.

▼ Skimmer

RANGE: WORLDWIDE

HABITAT: TYPICALLY NEAR SLOW-FLOWING STREAMS, PONDS

Skimmers are dragonflies with stout, flat bodies but often quite long wings, with a span up to 4 in (10 cm). They are usually seen flying near still or slow-moving water.

▼ Slug, Great black

RANGE: EUROPE, N. AMERICA

HABITAT: WOODLAND, FARMLAND, GARDENS

Slugs are mollusks, like snails, but have no shell and, as they move, lay down a trail of shiny mucus or slime to ease their passage. Slugs find the plants they eat by smell.

▼ Snail, Garden

RANGE: ORIGINALLY EUROPE, INTRODUCED ELSEWHERE

HABITAT: WOODLAND, FARMLAND, GARDENS

Snails are a kind of mollusk called gastropods, which feed on plants and animals using a special mouth part called a radula, filled with rows of teeth.

▼ Snakefly

RANGE: N. HEMISPHERE

HABITAT: WOODS, VEGETATION

Snakeflies get their name from their long necks, which they raise like a cobra to catch their prey, seizing it with a sudden lunge. They prey on beetle larvae and aphids.

▼ Spider, Black widow

RANGE: SOUTHERN U.S.A.

HABITAT: WOOD PILES OR GARBAGE

Female American black widows have a bite with venom more deadly than a rattlesnake. Although the amount of venom is small, it can kill a person unless anti-venom is given quickly.

▼ Spider, Common house

RANGE: EURASIA, N. AMERICA, AUSTRALIA

HABITAT: BUILDINGS

The house spider has long, hairy legs and builds large, flat webs in dark corners. It lurks in a silken tube under the web waiting for prey, then rushes out to catch any victim tangled in the sticky strands.

▲ Spider, Funnel web

RANGE: TROPICS WORLDWIDE EXCEPT S. AMERICA

HABITAT: ON THE GROUND, TREE TRUNKS

These spiders live in burrows and make funnel-shaped webs to trap their prey. The Sydney funnel-web is very poisonous.

▲ Spider, Crab

RANGE: WORLDWIDE

HABITAT: MEADOWS, GARDENS

Crab spiders get their name because they scuttle sideways like a crab. They do not make webs, although the smaller males use silk to tie the female down for mating. They usually lurk in wait for prey on flowers.

▲ Spider, Garden

RANGE: WORLDWIDE

HABITAT: GRASSLAND, FOREST, GARDENS

This spider weaves a web at night and waits during the day for prey to get caught in it. If the web is damaged, the spider eats it and makes a new one rather than repairing it.

▲ Spider, Golden-silk

RANGE: SUBTROPICAL, TROPICAL AMERICAS

HABITAT: DAMP OPEN FORESTS

These are spiders that build a strong web to protect them from predators and to capture prey. The drag line of their web is actually stronger than Kevlar, the fiber used in bullet-proof vests. Females weigh 100 times as much as males.

▲ Spider, Green lynx

RANGE: WORLDWIDE IN WARMER PLACES

HABITAT: SHRUBS, TALL GRASS

Lynx spiders are fast-moving hunters that rarely spin webs. Instead they chase their prey over plants, jumping from leaf to leaf. They have good eyesight and pounce on plant bugs, fire ants, and other insects, using their green color to hide them.

▲ Spider, Jumping

RANGE: WORLDWIDE, ESPECIALLY WARM REGIONS

HABITAT: WOODS, GRASS, GARDEN WALLS

Jumping spiders have unusually good eyesight for spiders and rely on jumping on victims to catch them rather than building a web. Before jumping, they attach a silk safety line to help them get back to their hideout.

153

Spider, Lichen
RANGE: WARM REGIONS WORLDWIDE
HABITAT: ON THE GROUND, TREE TRUNKS
Spiders, such as the lichen, rely on their drab colors and soft outline to keep them hidden as they hunt at night. They can move sideways with enormous speed to catch prey.

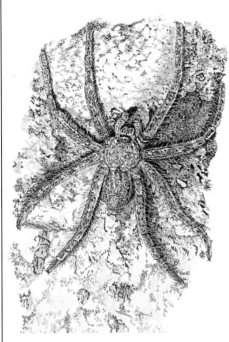

Spider, Nursery-web
RANGE: WORLDWIDE
HABITAT: ON THE GROUND, WATER PLANTS
Nursery-web spiders weave webs not to catch prey but to protect their young. The female carries her egg sac with her until the eggs are almost ready to hatch, then spins a web around them. She then stands guard until they hatch.

Spider, Ogre-faced
RANGE: WORLDWIDE
HABITAT: WOODLAND, GARDENS
The ogre-faced spider gets its name from its large-eyed face. It is a net-casting spider, which means it carries its web with it, and throws it like a net over its prey.

Spider, Orchard
RANGE: WORLDWIDE
HABITAT: WOODLAND, GARDENS
The orchard spider is an orb-web spider, but does not spin a web. Instead, it sits on tree branches and waits to grab passing moths with its strong front legs, perhaps relying on its scent to attract them.

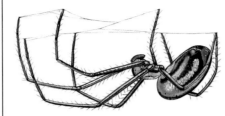

Spider, Purse-web
RANGE: WORLDWIDE
HABITAT: IN THE GROUND
This spider weaves a long silk tube inside a sloping burrow. The top of the tube projects above the ground but is camouflaged with leaves. When an insect lands on the tube, the spider grabs it and drags it inside.

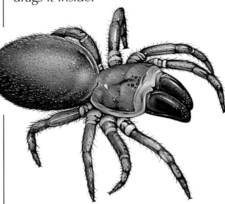

Spider, Sheet web
RANGE: WORLDWIDE
HABITAT: GRASSLAND, FORESTS, GARDENS
This family of over 3,500 tiny spiders weaves sheetlike webs that hang from threads. Insects flying into these threads fall on to the web and are caught. Among many species are the money spiders and bowl-and-doilies.

Spider, Spitting
RANGE: WARM REGIONS WORLDWIDE EXCEPT AUSTRALIA, NEW ZEALAND
HABITAT: UNDER ROCKS, IN BUILDINGS
This spider traps its prey by spitting out two zigzag lines of a sticky substance to literally stick the victim down.

▲ Spider, Trapdoor
RANGE: WORLDWIDE
HABITAT: IN THE GROUND
Trapdoor spiders live in burrows with hinged lids at the top. The spider waits in its burrow until it senses prey moving overhead, then jumps out of the door and grabs the prey.

▲ Spider, Water
RANGE: EURASIA
HABITAT: SLOW FLOWING OR STILL WATER
This is the only spider to spend its life underwater. It can swim and dive and is able to live in the water by spinning itself a bell-shaped air bubble from which it can launch its attacks on prey.

▲ Spider, Wolf
RANGE: WORLDWIDE
HABITAT: VARIED
Wolf spiders are roving hunters with sharp eyesight that creep up on prey and seize it after a final dash. Females weave silk cocoons for their eggs.

▲ Stick insect
RANGE: WORLDWIDE, ESPECIALLY AUSTRALASIA
HABITAT: ON SHRUBS AND TREES
Stick insects look so much like twigs that, when they are motionless during the day, predatory birds can hardly see them. They move to feed on leaves at night.

▼ Stinkbug
RANGE: WORLDWIDE
HABITAT: SHRUBS AND TREES
Stinkbugs get their name from the foul-smelling liquid that they squirt at any attacker. Like all bugs they suck nourishment from plants or insects.

▼ Stonefly, Common
RANGE: WORLDWIDE EXCEPT AUSTRALIA
HABITAT: PLANTS NEAR STREAMS
Stoneflies look a little like dragonflies, but they are not strong fliers and spend much of the day resting on stones with their wings folded. They also feed mostly on plants, though some hunt insects.

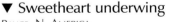

▼ Sweetheart underwing
RANGE: N. AMERICA
HABITAT: FOREST, GARDENS
This moth is usually very hard to see because its mottled colors blend so well into the bark of the tree where it rests during the day, but if alarmed it flashes the bright pink underwings that give it its name to startle the attacker.

▲ Tarantula, Red-kneed
RANGE: WARM REGIONS WORLDWIDE, ESPECIALLY S. AMERICA
HABITAT: DESERT, FOREST
Tarantulas are big spiders. The largest are called bird-eating spiders because they sometimes prey on small birds. These can measure up to 11 in (28 cm) across.

▲ Termite, Drywood
RANGE: TROPICS
HABITAT: DRY WOOD, INCLUDING TIMBER
These termites attack dry wood, including furniture, beams, and planks in houses. Microorganisms in their gut help them to digest the wood. Special soldier termites with large heads and horns defend the colony.

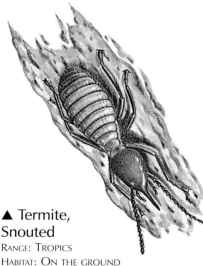

▲ Termite, Snouted
RANGE: TROPICS
HABITAT: ON THE GROUND
Most termite colonies have special soldiers to defend them against enemies, such as ants. The snouted termite soldiers have especially long snouts, which they use to spray a sticky, foul-smelling fluid at any unfortunate intruder.

▼ Termite, Subterranean
RANGE: TROPICS
HABITAT: IN SOIL AND WOOD
These termites live in underground nests in warm, wooded areas. They feed on the wood of rotting trees and their roots, but some species are also serious timber pests.

▼ Tick, Hard
RANGE: WORLDWIDE
HABITAT: ON BIRD, MAMMAL, REPTILE HOSTS
Ticks are parasites that feed on the blood of birds, mammals, and reptiles. Young ticks stick on their host for several days while feeding, then drop off to turn into an adult.

▼ Treehopper
RANGE: WARMER REGIONS WORLDWIDE
HABITAT: ON TREES
These little bugs are sometimes known as thorn bugs because they have an extraordinary thorn-shaped extension on their thorax called a pronotun. This acts as a disguise and also makes them difficult to eat.

▼ Wasp, Blue-black spider
RANGE: WORLDWIDE, ESPECIALLY WARMER REGIONS
HABITAT: VARIED, NEAR SPIDERS
Adult spider wasps feed on nectar, but when they are about to lay their eggs, the female will catch spiders by paralyzing them with her sting. She then drags the spider to her nest, lays an egg, and seals it. The spider will provide food for the hatchling.

▲ Wasp, Common
RANGE: EURASIA
HABITAT: ATTICS OR BURROWS
These wasps build paper nests in attics or in the ground. They feed on nectar and ripe fruit, but also catch insects to feed their young. Such wasps are well known for the sting at the end of their tail.

▲ Wasp, Gall
RANGE: WORLDWIDE, MOSTLY N. HEMISPHERE
HABITAT: HOST TREES, PLANTS
Gall wasps are tiny wasps that lay their eggs on plants. The plant then produces a scar called a gall, which protects and nourishes the larvae as they hatch.

▲ Wasp, Ichneumon
RANGE: WORLDWIDE, ESPECIALLY TEMPERATE REGIONS
HABITAT: HOST INSECTS SUCH AS BEETLES
These wasps lay their eggs on or inside other insects or their larvae. When the eggs hatch the larvae feed on the host.

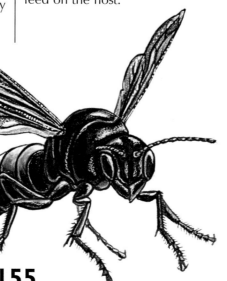

▼ Wasp, Paper
RANGE: WORLDWIDE
HABITAT: VARIED
Paper wasps belong to the family of social wasps that live in colonies organized around a queen. They build nests of papery material made from chewed wood and saliva.

▼ Weevil, Boll
RANGE: SOUTHERN U.S.A.
HABITAT: COTTONFIELDS
Weevils are beetle-like insects that eat plants. The boll weevil attacks the bolls (seed pods) of cotton plants and can devastate a cotton crop. The female can lay an egg in up to 300 bolls.

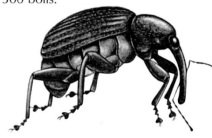

▼ Woodlouse
RANGE: EURASIA
HABITAT: LEAF LITTER, WOOD DEBRIS
Woodlice are crustaceans like crabs, but live on land. They hide in moist, dark places in the day and come out at night to feed on decaying plant matter and insect corpses.

▼ Yellow jacket
RANGE: N. AMERICA
HABITAT: FOREST, FIELDS, TOWNS
Yellow jackets are the American equivalents of European wasps. Like them, they feed on nectar and other sweet things, but prey on insects to feed their young. The female stings aggressively if her nest is threatened.

Glossary

algae Plantlike organisms that usually live in water.

amphibian A four-legged vertebrate animal that can live on land and in water.

arboreal Dwelling mainly in (forest) trees.

arthropods The largest group of invertebrate animals, including insects, spiders, and crustaceans.

biome A large, characteristic grouping of plants and animals adapted to survive in a particular geographic zone.

camouflage Colors or patterns on an animal that make it difficult to see against its background. *See also* mimicry.

carnivore A meat-eating animal.

carrion The remains of recently dead animals.

cells Microscopically small packages from which all living things are made up.

class Level in the system of animal classification below a phylum. Amphibians are one class; reptiles are another.

cold-blooded *See* ectothermic.

colony Large group of animals of the same species living together.

deciduous Tree that loses its leaves in fall to save water during the winter.

diurnal Active during the day, or occurring daily.

dormancy A sleeplike state in which a plant or animal ceases to be active. *See also* estivation, hibernation.

echolocation A way in which animals navigate, or find prey by sending out bursts of sounds and detecting the reflections.

ectothermic Animal with a body temperature that depends mainly on its surroundings, like reptiles. Also known as cold-blooded.

endemic Species native to an area.

endothermic Animal that is able to maintain its own constant body temperature, like mammals. Also known as warm-blooded.

epiphyte Plant that grows in trees, high off the ground.

estivation A time of dormancy in hot or dry weather. Many animals in the subtropics estivate during the long dry season.

evolution Gradual changing of animal species through time.

exoskeleton A skeleton forming a hard shell around the outside of its body, like an insect's.

extinction The final disappearance of a species.

family A level in the system of animal classification below an order. Families, such as big cats and eagles, are divided into genera.

food chain A series of organisms, each of which depends on the next as a source of food.

food web An interlinking network of food chains from a particular environment. Typically, each species in the web is involved in more than one food chain.

genus (plural **genera**) A level in the system of animal classification below a family. Genera are divided into species.

grub Young insect larva with a thick, soft body which may or may not have legs.

habitat The natural surroundings an animal needs to survive.

herbivore Animal that feeds mainly on plants.

hibernation Deep, sleeplike period of dormancy in winter during which an animal's body cools and its body processes slow down.

host Animal used by a parasite for its food and home.

incubation The process whereby an embryo develops inside an egg before hatching.

insectivore Animal that eats mainly insects.

invertebrate An animal without a backbone, such as an insect.

kingdom One of the five basic divisions of the living world, such as animals or plants.

larva (plural **larvae**) A young animal, such as an insect, that looks completely different from its adult form. *See also* pupa.

lepidoptera The order of insects made up by the 150,000 species of butterfly and moth.

life cycle All the stages in the life of an animal, from its beginning through reproduction to its death.

marsupial A mammal whose young are born before they are fully developed and are carried in a pouch on the mother's belly.

metamorphosis The dramatic change in body shape as a young animal becomes an adult, such as when a tadpole becomes a frog or a caterpillar becomes a butterfly.

migration Long journey made, often yearly, by animals to breed or find food. Most animals that migrate leave at particular times and follow particular routes, guided by instinct.

mimicry A kind of camouflage in which an animal looks like another animal, plant, or object. Many insects are mimics.

niche The place or role in a habitat which an animal can fill.

nocturnal Active at night.

nymph Young insect resembling its parents, but without fully formed reproductive organs.

order Level in the system of animal classification below class. Orders, such as all the primates, are divided into families.

Orthoptera Order of 18,000 insect species, mostly with long back legs for jumping, including grasshoppers and crickets.

parasite An animal that lives or feeds on or inside another living animal.

photosynthesis The processes that allow plants to capture energy from the sun and store it as sugars.

phylum (plural **phyla**). Level in the system of animal classification below kingdom. Phyla are divided into classes.

plankton Microscopic organisms that float in lakes and oceans. Plankton include algae.

prairie Grassland found in North America, or any area of tall grass in temperate regions.

predator Animal that kills other animals and eats them.

prehensile Able to curl around things and grip them.

proboscis A nose or long noselike set of mouthparts. An elephant's trunk is a proboscis; so is a butterfly's nectar-sipping tongue.

pupa (plural **pupae**) Stage in the life cycle of an insect in which the larva's body breaks down and is rebuilt as an adult. Pupae usually have a hard outer case, often inside a cocoon.

savanna Dry, tropical grassland, especially in Africa.

scavenger Animal that lives on leftovers, including human refuse and remains of predator's kills.

species A single kind of living thing. Members of a species can breed with each other, producing offspring like themselves.

steppe Grassland in Eastern Europe and Asia, or any area of short grass in temperate regions.

temperate Zone with moderate temperatures—basically the areas of the world between the tropics and the polar regions.

terrestrial Living mainly on the ground.

territory Area claimed by an animal, either for feeding or breeding.

understory Layer of vegetation on the ground in forests.

vertebrate Animal with a backbone—basically fish, mammals, reptiles, amphibians, and birds.

warm-blooded *See* endothermic.

Index

Note: Figures in italics refer to illustrations or maps, generally in addition to text entries. Figures in bold refer to major entries.

Acknowledgments

PHOTOGRAPHIC CREDITS
t = top; b = bottom; c = center; l = left; r = right

2t Getty Images/Stone/Manoj Shah; **2c** Corbis/Chase Swift; **2b** Shutterstock/Jakob Metzger; **3tl** Oxford Scientific Films/Terry Heathcote; **3tr** BBC Natural History Unit/David Tipling; **3cl** Oxford Scientific Films/Tom Ulrich; **3cr** Corbis/Galen Rowell; **3b** Corbis/Kennan Ward; **4–5** Digital Vision; **6–7** Getty Images/Stone/Manoj Shah; **7t** BBC Natural History Unit/Richard Du Toit; **7b** Oxford Scientific Films/Paul Franklin; **11t** BBC Natural History Unit/Ross Couper-Johnston; **11c** BBC Natural History Unit/Martha Holmes; **11bl** Oxford Scientific Films/Wendy Shatti & Bob Rozinski; **11br** BBC Natural History Unit/Torsten Brehm; **15t** Oxford Scientific Films/Michael Powles; **15c** BBC Natural History Unit/Keith Scholey; **15bl** Corbis/Frank Lane Picture Agency/Fritz Polking; **15br** Shutterstock/Jiri Haureljuk; **19t** Oxford Scientific Films/Hans & Judy Beste; **19c** Oxford Scientific Films/A.G. (Bert) Wells; **19bl** BBC Natural History Unit/John Cancalosi; **19br** Oxford Scientific Films/Robin Bush; **20–21** Corbis/Chase Swift; **21t** Oxford Scientific Films/J.A.L. Cooke; **21b** Shutterstock/M Reel; **25t** BBC Natural History Unit/Anup Shah; **25c** Oxford Scientific Films/Dieter Plage; **25bl** Shutterstock/Helen E. Grose; **25br** Ardea/Kenneth W. Fink; **29t** BBC Natural History Unit/Neil P. Lucas; **29c** BBC Natural History Unit/Ingo Arndt; **29bl** Shutterstock/Nicola Gavin; **29br** Shutterstock/Jose AS Reyes; **32** BBC Natural History Unit/Anup Shah; **33t** Corbis/Tom Brakefield; **33c** BBC Natural History Unit/Anup Shah; **33b** Corbis/Edward Van Altena; **34–35** Shutterstock/Jakob Metzger; **35t** Corbis/Sharna Balfour/Gallo Images; **35b** Oxford Scientific Films/Michael Fogden; **39t** Shutterstock/Tomasz Pado; **39c** Corbis/Joe MacDonald; **39bl** BBC Natural History Unit/Tony Heald; **39br** Frank Lane Picture Agency/Francois Merlet; **43tl** BBC Natural History Unit/Christoph Becker; **43tr** Shutterstock/Dennis Donohue; **43c** BBC Natural History Unit/Paul N. Johnson **43b** Corbis/Galen Rowell; **47t** Oxford Scientific Films/J.A.L. Cooke; **47c** Marty Stouffer/Animals Animals/Oxford Scientific Films; **47b** Andrew Watson/Travel Ink; **48–49** Shutterstock/David Gallaher; **49t** Shutterstock/Sally Wallis; **49b** Shutterstock/Paul Aniszewski; **52** Jim Hallett/BBC Natural History Unit; **53t** Shutterstock/Dean Bertoncelj; **53c** Shutterstock/Colette3; **53b** Shutterstock/Sally Wallis; **57t** Shutterstock/Dennis Donohue; **57c** Shutterstock/Dirk Brink; **57b** Shutterstock/K R Crowley; **60** Oxford Scientific Films/Stanley Breeden; **61t** BBC Natural History Unit/Lynn Stone; **61c** Oxford Scientific Films/Michael Powles; **61b** Save China's Tigers; **65t** Oxford Scientific Films/Robin Bush; **65c** Corbis/Frank Lane Picture Agency; **65bl** Oxford Scientific Films/Steve Turner; **66–67** Shutterstock/Jim Parkin; **67t** Shutterstock/Eugeny Perepelov; **67b** Shutterstock/Photography Perspectives-Jeff Smith; **71t** Corbis/Jeff Vanuga; **71b** Oxford Scientific Films/Animals Animals/Jack Wilburn; **74** Shutterstock/Ivan Cholakov Gostock-dot-net; **75t** Shutterstock/S. Cooper Digital; **75c** Shutterstock/Dennis Donohue; **75b** Shutterstock/Konstantin Kikvidze; **76–77** Shutterstock/Tyler Olson; **77t** Shutterstock/36clicks; **77b** Shutterstock/George Spade; **80** Shutterstock/Florian Andronache; **81t** Shutterstock/2009fotofriends; **81c** Shutterstock/Wesley Aston; **81b** Shutterstock/Nik Niklz; **85t** Oxford Scientific Films/David M. Dennis; **85b** BBC Natural History Unit/Tom Vezo; **86–87** Shutterstock/Richard Fitzer; **87c** Shutterstock/Calin Tatu; **87b** Shutterstock/Mika Heittola; **91t** Shutterstock/Wayne Johnson; **91b** Shutterstock/LindyCro; **95t** Nature/Chris Gomersall; **95b** Shutterstock/Jiri Cvrk; **99t** Shutterstock/Stephen Meese; **99b** Shutterstock/aimvotalphotos; **100–101** Corbis/Galen Rowell; **101t** Shutterstock/Kshishtof; **101c** Shutterstock/Daniel Prudek; **101b** Shutterstock/Sebastian Wahsner.

ARTWORK CREDITS
10–11, 76–77, 86–87 Gill Tomblin
14–15, 32–33 Richard Bonson
18–19, 28–29, 60–61, 64–65, 70–71, 74–75 Michael Woods
24–25, 46–47, 56–57 Chris Orr Associates
38–39 Christian Webb/Temple Rogers
42–43, 94–95, 98–99 Peter David Scott/Wildlife Art Agency
52–53, 80–81 Brian Delf
84–85, 90–91, 100–101 Ian Jackson/Wildlife Art Agency

Maps
Alan Collinson Design

Mammals
Graham Allen, Sandra Doyle/Wildlife Art Agency, John Francis, Tudor Humphries, Eric Robson, Dick Twinney, Michael Woods

Birds
Norman Arlott, Dianne Breeze, Chris Christoforou, Barry Croucher/Wildlife Art Agency, Malcolm Ellis, Robert Gilmour, Peter Hayman, Denys Ovenden, David Quinn, Chris Rose, Andrew Robinson, Owen Williams, Ken Wood, Michael Woods

Reptiles
Steve Kirk, Alan Male, Eric Robson, Peter David Scott/Wildlife Art Agency

Amphibians
Robin Boutell/Wildlife Art Agency, Alan Male

Insects and Invertebrates
Joanne Cowne, Sandra Doyle/Wildlife Art Agency, Ian Jackson/Wildlife Art Agency, Bridget James, Steve Kirk, Adrian Lascom, Alan Male, Colin Newman, Steve Roberts, Michael Woods

Fish
Colin Newman

Every effort has been made to credit all photographs and illustrations correctly. Marshall Editions apologizes for any unintentional omissions or errors and, if informed of any such cases, would be pleased to update any future editions.

GREYSCALE

BIN TRAVELER FORM

Cut By	Kim Williamson	Qty 37	Date 8/6/24
Scanned By		Qty	Date

Scanned Batch IDs

Notes / Exception

_____

_____

_____

_____

_____